Rev. Donald C. Swope   I 56

A NEW INTRODUCTION TO GREEK

A NEW INTRODUCTION TO GREEK

THIRD EDITION
REVISED AND ENLARGED

BY

ALSTON HURD CHASE
PHILLIPS ACADEMY
Andover, Massachusetts

HENRY PHILLIPS, JR.
PHILLIPS EXETER ACADEMY
Exeter, New Hampshire

HARVARD UNIVERSITY PRESS
CAMBRIDGE, MASSACHUSETTS

LONDON, ENGLAND

Typography by Burton L. Stratton

Library of Congress Catalog Card Number 61—13748

ISBN 0–674–61600–6

Printed in the United States of America

20   19   18   17   16   15   14   13   12

PREFACE

This book is designed primarily for college students and for seniors in secondary schools, a class of beginners in Greek which is increasing in numbers. No introduction to Greek exists which attempts in brief compass to introduce to such students reading of wide variety.

Real Greek has, in large measure, been selected for the reading material; continuous narrative has been introduced early. It is hoped that those studying this book may acquire, in addition to knowledge of the forms of the Greek language, some conception of the importance of Greek civilization. The authors assume that the majority of those studying Greek today will not be able to continue for so long a time in the language as was possible twenty-five years ago. Beginners today must early meet Democritus, Plato, Thucydides, and Herodotus if they are ever to be encouraged to go farther.

The vocabularies contain words which are of great enough frequency in the Greek literature commonly read in schools and colleges (excluding poetry) to justify recommending that these words be learned permanently as soon as met. Guidance in the choice of words has been furnished by the booklet, *Basic Greek Vocabulary*, by J. R. Cheadle (New York: Macmillan, 1939).

For securing as large a vocabulary as possible, it is strongly recommended that many of the sentences be learned by heart. The brevity of the book and the character of the reading do not provide for repetition of vocabulary on any systematic scale. The instructor can easily provide material for reviews; or, better still, provide for memorizing the sentences.

In Lessons 15 and following are given, and designated by letters (A, B, C, D), passages of merit and interest which should elicit discussion of the basic ideas they contain. These should not be assigned, but worked out in class by students and instructor. They are particularly worth memorizing.

There is ample reading material in the lessons. Not all need be prepared in advance. Extra passages, annotated in the text for more rapid reading, occur in many of the later lessons.

The order in which the lessons are presented in this book is different from that of other such books. For example, the μι– and contract verbs have been placed early. This has made easier the choice of real Greek to be read in the early stages.

The book is designed to be completed in one semester of a college course, where classes normally meet three times a week. In the schools there is usually more time available.

The authors are grateful for the many helpful suggestions offered by users of this book in previous editions. They wish in particular to record their gratitude to the late Professor Carl Newell Jackson of Harvard University, who inspired them to undertake the present work. Dr. Cedric Whitman has offered much valuable assistance. Professor O. J. Todd of the University of British Columbia has contributed advice of the most valuable and painstaking nature.

The illustrations were selected and the captions written by Sterling Dow, Hudson Professor of Archaeology in Harvard University, who has helped the book in numerous ways. He and we wish to thank Mrs. J. J. Whitehead, Jr., of New York for advice and encouragement; and not less the Bollingen Foundation, for a subsidy to the Archaeological Institute of America which made the illustrations possible.

A. H. C.
H. P., Jr.

PREFACE TO THE THIRD EDITION

Twenty years and two wars have gone by since this book was first published. The authors hope that they, like Solon, have learned much as they have grown older. The changes in the present edition reflect their own experience and that of many friends who have used the book.

The paradigms have been set in larger type. Sentences in Greek and in English have been composed to provide review of vocabulary and syntax. Lists of prepositions and of the commonest irregular verbs have been added. Both the Greek-English and English-Greek vocabularies have been rewritten.

The illustrations and their captions have proved to be a notable feature of the book.* For the present edition, Professor Dow has revised the text of the captions, and has added two new illustrations. Professor Homer A. Thompson, Director of the Agora Excavations, has supplied an up-to-date photograph for Figure 5. All classical studies are a unity, and archaeology ought to play a part from the very beginning.

We wish to acknowledge the generous assistance of Professor Zeph Stewart of Harvard University, Dr. W. Ernest Gillespie of the Phillips Exeter Academy, and of many others who have used the book.

A. H. C.

H. P., JR.

---

* Reproduced in full, these served as the basis for an article by Sterling Dow, "Illustrations in Textbooks," *Journal of General Education*, 5 (1951), 101–115.

CONTENTS

x

xi

ILLUSTRATIONS

The order of the illustrations is chronological. Read consecutively, the captions give a brief history of Greece. The vase-painting below is reproduced from *Monumenti Inediti: Pubblicati dall'Instituto di Corrispondenza archeologica*, I (1829–1833), Plate LI.

Scene from a Chalcidian vase painted about 560 B.C. At this early date the Greeks sometimes wrote backwards (like the Phoenicians) as well as forwards; and there are odd, non-Attic, forms of letters. The main subject is the death of the greatest of the Homeric heroes. Achilles has been shot in his one vulnerable spot (although, for credibility, he has been hit in the side also). Glaucus, having roped the ankle, is about to drag the body away, so as to get the armor; but the mighty Ajax runs him through. Meanwhile the archer Paris skulks off, shooting as he goes, while Aeneas (one of his earliest appearances in art, some 500 years before Vergil) and another Trojan charge into the fray. Beyond them Echippus and Laodocus are

engaged in mortal combat, and at the far right, in contrast, Diomedes is having his finger bandaged by Sthenelus. One person who does not need to be labeled is Athena, goddess of war; she is adequately identified by her unique snake-bordered garment, the aegis.

Homer's epics told about people and events which even for his time were in the remote past, back in the Bronze Age. For centuries epic poets had handed down the tales of Troy, until, only a few generations before the present vase was painted, Homer himself gave these tales such form that the *Iliad* and *Odyssey* became the supreme books of Greece, known to everyone for a thousand years.

A NEW INTRODUCTION TO GREEK

Greek Written in "Linear B": Clay Tablet, ca. 1400 B.C.

From the Minoans of Crete, the Greeks first learned to write in the Bronze Age. The Minoans used elaborate signs, each of which stood, not for a single letter, but for a whole syllable. In 1952 a young English architect, Michael Ventris, deciphered this syllabary, and thus gave us Greek 500 years earlier than Homer. On the tablet above, there is a name in 7 syllables, then "rams, 202; ewes, 750;/billy-goats, 125; nanny-goats, 240; boars, 21; sows, 60 [note the pigs' heads]; bulls, 2; cows, 10."

Greek Inscribed in Marble, ca. 334 B.C.

After the Trojan War, savage Dorians invaded Greece and destroyed the Bronze Age civilization, including literacy. The Greeks were illiterate for centuries (ca. 1200– ca. 750 or later) and then learned to write all over again. Their new teachers were Phoenicians, who taught not syllable-signs but letters: first *aleph*, the simplified picture of an ox, *alpha* to Greek ears; then *beth*, a house (all writing begins as pictures), and so on through the *alphabet*. The early Greeks used only capitals; no gaps; no accents; little or (as here) no punctuation. Βασιλεὺς Ἀλέξανδρος ἀνέθηκε τὸν ναὸν Ἀθηναίηι Πολιάδι. "King Alexander dedicated the temple to Athena Polias."

Greek Written with Pen on Papyrus, ca. 330–300 B.C.

As developed and passed on to the Romans, and so to us, the Greek alphabet, in its simplicity and clarity (contrast Linear B), became one of the foundations of our civilization. The letters could be inscribed by hammer and chisel on marble, or written with a pen point on papyrus. Great numbers of inscriptions and papyri have survived, and the study of them, along with Linear B, is an exciting challenge — the growing point of our knowledge of the classics. The oldest Greek literary papyrus is a play, the *Persians* by Timotheus, previously lost. Above, its opening lines.

THE GREEK ALPHABET. PUNCTUATION

1. The Greek alphabet has twenty-four letters:

A α alpha, pronounced when short like the first *a* in *aha*; when long, like the *a* in *archon*.

B β beta, pronounced like the *b* in *biology*.

Γ γ gamma, pronounced like the *g* in *graph*.

Δ δ delta, pronounced like the *d* in *democracy*.

E ϵ epsilon, pronounced like the *e* in *epigram*.

Z ζ zeta, pronounced like the *z* in *glaz'd* (zd) or *adze* (dz).

H η eta, pronounced like the *e* in *fête*, or the *a* in *paper*.

Θ θ theta, pronounced like the *th* in *theater*.

I ι iota, pronounced like the *i* in *geranium*, when short; when long, like the *i* in *police*.

K κ kappa, pronounced like the *k* in *kinetic*.

Λ λ lambda, pronounced like the *l* in *labyrinth*.

M μ mu, pronounced like the *m* in *metaphor*.

N ν nu, pronounced like the *n* in *naphtha*.

Ξ ξ xi, pronounced like the *x* in *axiom*.

O o omicron, pronounced like the *o* in *optics*, or the *o* in *polemic* (not a diphthong).

Π π pi, pronounced like the *p* in *perimeter*.

P ρ rho, pronounced like the *r* in *rhinoceros* (ρ is trilled).

Σ σ sigma, pronounced like the *s* in *semaphore*. The form *s* is used at the end of a word, σ elsewhere.

T τ tau, pronounced like the *t* in *tactics*.

Y υ upsilon, pronounced like the *u* in French *tu*, when short;

when long, like the *u* in French *sur*, German *ü* in *hübsch*.

Φ φ phi, pronounced like the *ph* in *Philip*.

X χ chi, pronounced like the *ch* in German *machen*, or, less correctly, like the *ch* in *chorus*.

Ψ ψ psi, pronounced like the *ps* in *eclipse*.

Ω ω omega, pronounced like the *o* in *ode*, or else between *o* of *ocean* and *o* of *orgy*.

2. The capital letters are used at the beginning of names. They are not used at the beginning of sentences unless the sentences begin a paragraph or quotation.

3. There is no letter *h* in Greek. When a word begins with a vowel, if *h* should be pronounced before it, the sign ', called a rough breathing, is written over the initial vowel or over the second vowel of a proper diphthong. If *h* is not to be pronounced, the sign ', called a smooth breathing, is written in similar fashion. Initial ρ and υ always have the rough breathing.

4. The letter γ is pronounced like *ng* in *angle* when it comes before κ, γ, χ, or ξ, e.g., ἄγγελος, ἄγκυρα, λάρυγξ, ἄγχουσα.

5. The letters ζ, ξ, and ψ are known as double consonants, θ, φ, and χ as aspirated consonants.

6. The vowels ε and ο are always short; η and ω are always long; α, ι, υ are sometimes long and sometimes short.

7. The diphthongs are:

αι pronounced like *ai* in *aisle*.
αυ pronounced like *ou* in *house*, *now*.
ει pronounced like *ei* in *feign*.
ευ pronounced like the *e* in *met* plus the *oo* in *moon*.
ηυ pronounced like the *e* in *fête* plus the *oo* in *moon*.
οι pronounced like the *oi* in *foil*, *boy* with close *o*.
ου pronounced like the *oo* in *moon*.
υι pronounced like the English *we*.

8. The letter iota (ι) is often written beneath α, η, and ω. It is then known as iota subscript and is not pronounced. When such an

2

iota accompanies a capital it is written on the line, but it is still not pronounced.

9. The Greek question mark is like the English semicolon. For the semicolon Greek uses a single point set above the line. The period and comma are like the English.

10. The following words may be used for practice:

δρᾶμα, ἄσβεστος   νάφθα, νέκταρ
βιογραφία, βιβλίον   ἀξίωμα, ἔξοδος
γραφή, γυμνάσιον, γένεσις   ὄρνις, ὄψις
δημοκρατία, διάγνωσις   ποιητής, περίμετρον
ἐπίγραμμα   ῥινόκερως, ῥεῦμα
ζῷον, ζώνη, σχίζω   συνώνυμος, νέμεσις
ἀστήρ, ὑπερβολή   τακτικός, τονή
θέατρον, πάνθηρ   ὕβρις, ὕμνος
γεράνιον, πολίτης, βίος   Φίλιππος, φύλαξ, φίλος
κρίσις   χορός, χαρακτήρ
λόγος, λαβύρινθος   ψυχή, ἔκλειψις
μεταφορά, μέτρον   ᾠδή, ὠκεανός

DIPHTHONGS (δίφθογγοι)

φαινόμενον, δαίμων   εὐγενής, ἰχνεύμων
παύω, ναῦς   ὅμοιος
σπονδεῖος   πλοῦτος

ACCENTS

1. It is customary to write most Greek words with accents, which occur only on the last three syllables. These originally denoted a quality of pitch, not of stress, but they are now usually given a stress value.

A Greek word has as many syllables as it has vowels and diphthongs.

The last syllable of a word is called the ultima, the next to the last the penult, the one before the penult the antepenult.

There are three accents:

(a) The acute accent, ´, may stand upon any one of the last three syllables, but stands upon the antepenult only when the ultima is short.

(b) The grave accent, `, is written instead of the acute when the latter would naturally stand upon the last syllable of a word followed by another word in the sentence without any intervening mark of punctuation. Enclitics (Lesson 11) involve exceptions to this rule. Thus the grave accent is found only upon the ultima.

(c) The circumflex accent, ˆ, stands only upon a long vowel or diphthong and only upon the penult or ultima. It stands on the long penult only when the ultima is short.

A word bearing the acute upon the ultima is known as an oxytone, one with the acute upon the penult as a paroxytone, one with the acute upon the antepenult as a proparoxytone. One which bears the circumflex upon the ultima is called a perispomenon, one with the circumflex upon the penult is a properispomenon. These terms, though formidable, will save much laborious periphrasis.

4

2. The following rules of accent are of great importance:

(a) The position of accent in Greek is conditioned by the quantity of the ultima, in Latin by that of the penult: e.g., Κικέρων but Cícero.

(b) The accent of a noun, adjective, and participle is *persistent*, that is, it tends to remain upon the syllable receiving the accent in the nominative case, so far as the quantity of the ultima allows. Its position in the nominative must be learned by observation.

(c) The accent of the finite forms of a verb is *recessive*, that is, it goes as far back from the ultima as the quantity of the ultima allows, e.g., λαμβάνουσι.

(d) When the ultima includes a long vowel or a diphthong, the antepenult cannot be accented, e.g., λαμβάνειν.

(e) When the ultima includes a long vowel or a diphthong, the circumflex cannot stand upon the penult, e.g., πλοῖα, but πλοίων.

(f) A long penult before a short ultima, if accented, must bear the circumflex, e.g., πλοῖα.

Accent may be graphically represented by the following table (s = syllable):

	ś s š			
Acute	s ś̆ š	Circumflex	s̊ š	Grave s̀ (before another word).
	s ś s̄		s s̊	
	s s ś			

The Greeks considered a syllable long if it contained a long vowel or a diphthong. αι and οι, when they are the last two letters of a word, are counted short in determining accent, except in the optative mood and the adverb οἴκοι.

When breathing and accent must be written over the same initial vowel, the breathing is written before the acute or grave accent and beneath the circumflex. Both are written before capitals, with the same arrangement. Breathing and accent are written over the second vowel of an initial diphthong. E.g., ἄ, ἂ, οὗ, οἴ, Ἄ, Ἅ, Ὧ.

A few words called proclitics and some of those called enclitics have no accent.[1]

---

[1] The proclitics are the forms ὁ, ἡ, οἱ and αἱ from the definite article, the prepositions ἐν (in), ἐκ (out of), and εἰς (into), and the words εἰ (if), ὡς (as, so that), and οὐ (not). For enclitics see Lesson 11.

5

FIRST AND SECOND DECLENSIONS.
THE DECLENSION OF ἀγαθός.
THE DEFINITE ARTICLE

---

1. Besides the singular and plural, the Greek has another number, the dual, used to refer to two persons or things. The dual is obsolescent in classical Greek, though frequent in Homer. It is limited in Attic for the most part to natural pairs (hands, a pair of oxen, etc.), and even so, other words in agreement with it are sometimes found in the plural.

Throughout the text of this book dual forms will be omitted from paradigms but will appear in the complete inflectional appendices on pages 158–186. For a description of the forms see page 158, note 1.

2. Greek has three grammatical genders—masculine, feminine, and neuter.

3. Greek has the following five cases:
   Nominative, the case of the subject of a finite verb.
   Genitive, the case of possession, origin, and separation.
   Dative, the case of the indirect object and of locative and instrumental relationships.
   Accusative, the case of the direct object.
   Vocative, the case of direct address.

4. Learn the declension of ἀγαθός, good.

	SINGULAR			PLURAL		
	M	F	N	M	F	N
N	ἀγαθός	ἀγαθή	ἀγαθόν	ἀγαθοί	ἀγαθαί	ἀγαθά
G	ἀγαθοῦ	ἀγαθῆς	ἀγαθοῦ	ἀγαθῶν	ἀγαθῶν	ἀγαθῶν
D	ἀγαθῷ	ἀγαθῇ	ἀγαθῷ	ἀγαθοῖς	ἀγαθαῖς	ἀγαθοῖς
A	ἀγαθόν	ἀγαθήν	ἀγαθόν	ἀγαθούς	ἀγαθάς	ἀγαθά
V	ἀγαθέ	ἀγαθή	ἀγαθόν	ἀγαθοί	ἀγαθαί	ἀγαθά

5. This adjective exemplifies the endings of the nouns of the second, or *o*, declension, and of a large number of nouns in the first, or *α*, declension. Masculine nouns of the second declension are declined like ἀγαθός, neuters like ἀγαθόν. The second declension consists almost entirely of masculine and neuter nouns, with a few rare feminines like ὁδός, road, which follow the masculine nouns in their declension. Many nouns of the first declension are declined like ἀγαθή.

6. Learn the declension of the definite article: Note that only in the forms ὁ and τό does it differ from the endings of ἀγαθός.

	SINGULAR			PLURAL		
	M	F	N	M	F	N
N	ὁ	ἡ	τό	οἱ	αἱ	τά
G	τοῦ	τῆς	τοῦ	τῶν	τῶν	τῶν
D	τῷ	τῇ	τῷ	τοῖς	ταῖς	τοῖς
A	τόν	τήν	τό	τούς	τάς	τά

7. In general, the definite article is used in Greek as it is in English. Thus, ὁ ἀγαθὸς ἄνθρωπος, the good man.

8. The adjective is most commonly placed in what is known as the attributive position. In this position the article appears directly before the adjective or other modifier, as in ὁ ἀγαθὸς ἄνθρωπος above. A more formal arrangement, bearing the same meaning, is the following: ὁ ἄνθρωπος ὁ ἀγαθός. Sometimes there occurs a third arrangement ἄνθρωπος ὁ ἀγαθός. In place of the adjective may be used a possessive genitive, as ὁ Κύρου φίλος, Cyrus's friend; an adverb, as οἱ τότε ἄνθρωποι (or simply οἱ τότε), the men of that time; or a prepositional phrase, as οἱ ἐν τῷ πεδίῳ ἵπποι, the horses in the plain. The article is sometimes used to denote a class, e.g. ὁ ἄνθρωπος, man. This is called the generic article.

9. A complete sentence may be formed of a noun or a pronoun as subject and an adjective as predicate, the verb *to be* being omitted. In this case, the adjective is outside the article noun group, that is, it does not directly follow the article, and it is said to be in the predicate position.

ὁ ἄνθρωπος ἀγαθός. The man is good.
ἀγαθὸς ὁ ἄνθρωπος. The man is good.
τὰ τοῦ ἀνθρώπου παιδία καλά. The man's children are beautiful.

7

10. The article is commonly used in place of a possessive where ownership is clearly implied, as ἔλαβε τὸ βιβλίον, he took his book.

11. With μέν and δέ the article means the one . . . the other, as ὁ μέν . . . ὁ δέ; or, in the plural, οἱ μέν . . . οἱ δέ, some . . . others.

12. There is no indefinite article (a, an) in Greek. Sometimes the indefinite pronoun, used as adjective, is so employed.

13. Learn the declension of the following nouns. Note that oxytones of the first and second declensions circumflex the genitive and dative of both numbers, and that the ultima of the genitive plural of the first declension is always circumflexed. See also Rules (d) and (f) on p. 5.

	M speech	M man	F road	F opinion	N gift
			SINGULAR		
N	λόγος	ἄνθρωπος	ὁδός	γνώμη	δῶρον
G	λόγου	ἀνθρώπου	ὁδοῦ	γνώμης	δώρου
D	λόγῳ	ἀνθρώπῳ	ὁδῷ	γνώμῃ	δώρῳ
A	λόγον	ἄνθρωπον	ὁδόν	γνώμην	δῶρον
V	λόγε	ἄνθρωπε	ὁδέ	γνώμη	δῶρον
			PLURAL		
N	λόγοι	ἄνθρωποι	ὁδοί	γνῶμαι	δῶρα
G	λόγων	ἀνθρώπων	ὁδῶν	γνωμῶν	δώρων
D	λόγοις	ἀνθρώποις	ὁδοῖς	γνώμαις	δώροις
A	λόγους	ἀνθρώπους	ὁδούς	γνώμας	δῶρα
V	λόγοι	ἄνθρωποι	ὁδοί	γνῶμαι	δῶρα

READING

1. ἀθάνατος ἡ ψυχή. 2. χαλεπὰ τὰ καλά. 3. μέτρον ἄριστον. 4. τῷ σοφῷ ξένον οὐδέν.—ANTISTHENES. 5. κοινὰ τὰ τῶν φίλων.—ARISTOTLE. 6. ὁ χρόνος ἰατρὸς τῶν πόνων ἐστίν. 7. λόγος γὰρ ἔργου σκιά. 8. λύπης ἰατρός ἐστιν ἀνθρώποις χρόνος. 9. εἴδωλον ἔργων ἐστὶν ἀνθρώπου λόγος. 10. μέτρον γὰρ τοῦ βίου τὸ καλόν, οὐ τὸ τοῦ χρόνου μῆκος.—PLUTARCH.

Notes: 1. ἀθάνατος: compound adjectives, and some others, have the same endings for the feminine as masculine. 2. τὰ καλά, beautiful things, beauty. The neuter singular or plural of an adjective, preceded by an article, often forms a substantive. Cf. Sentence 10, τὸ καλόν. 3. μέτρον, "the golden mean." 4. ξένον (adjective), strange [xenophobia]; οὐδέν, nothing. 5. τά, the neuter plural of the article is used here as a substantive: the things = the property. 6. ἰατρός, physician [psychiatry]; πόνων, of pain (lit., of pains); ἐστιν, is (Lesson 12). 7. σκιά (nominative), shadow [sciagraph]. 8. λύπης, of pain. For the accent of ἰατρός, see Lesson 12. 9. εἴδωλον, likeness [idol]. 10. μῆκος (neuter noun, 3rd declension), length.

(Words in square brackets are derivatives, not necessarily translations.)

VOCABULARY

ἄνθρωπος, -ου, ὁ, man, human being [anthropology]
βίος, -ου, ὁ, life [biography]
γνώμη, -ης, ἡ, opinion
δῶρον, -ου, τό, gift
ἔργον, -ου, τό, work, deed, act [erg]
λόγος, -ου, ὁ, word, speech, reason, account [logic]
μέτρον, -ου, τό, measure, "mean"
ὁδός, -οῦ, ἡ, road
παιδίον, -ου, τό, child
φίλος, -ου, ὁ, friend
χρόνος, -ου, ὁ, time [chronometer]
ψυχή, -ῆς, ἡ, soul

ἀγαθός, -ή, -όν, noble, good
ἀθάνατος, -ον, deathless (ἀ- privative + θάνατος, death) [Athanasius]
ἄριστος, -η, -ον, best [aristocrat]
καλός, -ή, -όν, good, beautiful.
κοινός, -ή, -όν, common [epicene]
σοφός, -ή, -όν, wise [Sophomore]
χαλεπός, -ή, -όν, difficult, harsh

ἐστί[ν], he, she, it is (from the verb εἰμί, to be; see Lesson 12)

ἀεί, always (adverb)
γάρ, for (conjunction, postpositive)
ὁ, ἡ, τό, the (definite article)
οὐ, not (adverb, proclitic). This word is written οὐκ before a word beginning with a smooth breathing, οὐχ before a rough breathing.

ENGLISH SENTENCES

1. Men's souls (are) immortal. 2. For the words of friends (are) best. 3. Good men (are) not always deathless. 4. The property of the best (men) is (in) common. 5. The opinion of noble men is wise. 6. The best road (is) difficult for (dative) a child.

REVIEW EXERCISES

Write out, with correct accents and breathings:

Genitive plural of τὸ δῶρον
Dative singular of ὁ βίος
Nominative plural of ὁ ἄνθρωπος
Masculine genitive singular of ἀθάνατος
Feminine dative singular of κοινός

Genitive plural of ἡ γνώμη
Feminine accusative singular of σοφός
Accusative plural of ὁ ἄνθρωπος
Nominative plural of τὸ παιδίον
Neuter dative singular of ἄριστος

9

2 DELPHI, ON THE SLOPE OF MOUNT PARNASSUS

Above all others, Olympia and Delphi were the national shrines of Greece. The view shows Delphi, the modern village, on the left; and to the right of the central ridge, the ancient precinct. The stadium is clearly visible as a horizontal light gray band at the top of the precinct just to the right of this same central ridge. Lower and farther to the right, near the mouth of the chasm, is a bowl-like white patch, the theater. The oracle and Apollo's temple were slightly below the theater.

From the olive plain far beneath and out of sight, the road zigzags up to the town. Above, a trail to the high summer pastures on Parnassus has been trodden out by shepherds for centuries, perhaps from earlier even than the time when Apollo ('Απόλλων) took over the sanctuary. Before Apollo, it belonged to Γῆ, the old Mother-Earth goddess of the pre-Greek inhabitants, and Γῆ retained a minor cult. Later, when a new and wild worship arrived, that of Dionysus (Διόνυσος), Apollo's priests applied their motto μηδὲν ἄγαν ("nothing overmuch," i.e., no excess), and Dionysus became civilized. In fact, it was Delphi which taught all Greece the sane, wise, essentially humane doctrine of moderation, the Golden Mean.

The houses of the citizens of the city-state (which managed the oracle) may have looked from a distance much as the town does today in the picture. Then as now the citizens lived mostly on olive-culture and grazing. The economic basis of ancient Greece was largely agrarian, alike under the early kings and in all later periods. Excavations have revealed much of Delphi's history, from the early formative Homeric years all the way down into the Roman time when Plutarch, himself a priest of Delphi, gathered up in his writings a thousand years of tradition.

FIRST DECLENSION NOUNS (continued).
THE RELATIVE PRONOUN

1. Nouns of the first declension fall into four classes:
    (a) Feminines declined like the feminine of ἀγαθός, as γνώμη.
    (b) Feminines with bases ending in ε, ι, or ρ, which have α (long) or α (short) instead of η in the singular, as πεῖρα and θεά.
    (c) A few other feminines ending in α (short), as θάλαττα.
    (d) A few masculine nouns that have -της or -ης (or, after ε, ι, ρ, -ας) in the nominative singular, -ου in the genitive singular, as στρατιώτης, νεανίας.

2. All first declension nouns are declined alike in the plural.

3. Review the principles of declension governing nouns of the first declension as given in paragraph 13, Lesson 3. The α in the genitive and dative singular of all first declension nouns and adjectives is long.

4. Learn the declension of the following nouns; and of the adjective ἄξιος, which has a feminine in ᾱ.

	F goddess	F sea	F attempt	M soldier	worthy (adjective)		
				SINGULAR			
N	θεά	θάλαττα	πεῖρα	στρατιώτης	ἄξιος	ἀξία	ἄξιον
G	θεᾶς	θαλάττης	πείρας	στρατιώτου	ἀξίου	ἀξίας	ἀξίου
D	θεᾷ	θαλάττῃ	πείρᾳ	στρατιώτῃ	ἀξίῳ	ἀξίᾳ	ἀξίῳ
A	θεάν	θάλατταν	πεῖραν	στρατιώτην	ἄξιον	ἀξίαν	ἄξιον
V	θεά	θάλαττα	πεῖρα	στρατιῶτα	ἄξιε	ἀξία	ἄξιον
				PLURAL			
N	θεαί	θάλατται	πεῖραι	στρατιῶται	ἄξιοι	ἄξιαι	ἄξια
G	θεῶν	θαλαττῶν	πειρῶν	στρατιωτῶν	ἀξίων	ἀξίων	ἀξίων
D	θεαῖς	θαλάτταις	πείραις	στρατιώταις	ἀξίοις	ἀξίαις	ἀξίοις
A	θεάς	θαλάττας	πείρας	στρατιώτας	ἀξίους	ἀξίας	ἄξια
V	θεαί	θάλατται	πεῖραι	στρατιῶται	ἄξιοι	ἄξιαι	ἄξια

5. Practice the declension of τιμή, γέφυρα, ἡμέρα, ὑγίεια, ναύτης, χώρᾱ, νίκη, φυγή, μοῖρα, γλῶττα, στοά, βοή, ἀκοή, βασιλείᾱ, τράπεζα, ἀλήθεια, νεανίας (-ου), δεσπότης, ποιητής.

6. Learn the declension of the relative pronoun:

	SINGULAR				PLURAL		
	M	F	N		M	F	N
N	ὅς	ἥ	ὅ	N	οἵ	αἵ	ἅ
G	οὗ	ἧς	οὗ	G	ὧν	ὧν	ὧν
D	ᾧ	ᾗ	ᾧ	D	οἷς	αἷς	οἷς
A	ὅν	ἥν	ὅ	A	οὕς	ἅς	ἅ

7. The relative pronoun agrees with its antecedent in gender and number, but it takes its case from its construction in its own clause.[1]

READING

1. καλὸν ἡσυχία. 2. ἡ τοῦ σοφοῦ ψυχὴ ἥσυχός ἐστιν ἐν ταῖς τοῦ βίου συμφοραῖς. 3. ἄδικος πλοῦτος οὔποτε βέβαιός ἐστιν. 4. φεῦγε τὴν τῶν κακῶν φιλίαν καὶ τὴν τῶν ἀγαθῶν ἔχθραν. 5. οἱ νόμοι ψυχὴ τῆς πολιτείας εἰσίν. 6. σκηνὴ πᾶς ὁ βίος. 7. ὁ τῶν ἀνθρώπων βίος δῶρον τῶν θεῶν ἐστιν. 8. ἀνθρώπῳ σοφῷ ὁ κόσμος πατρίς ἐστιν. 9. ἐν τῇ τῶν πολιτῶν εὐσεβείᾳ καὶ ἐν τῇ τῶν στρατιωτῶν ἀνδρείᾳ καὶ ἐν τῇ τῶν δικαστῶν δικαιοσύνῃ ἡ τῆς πολιτείας ῥώμη ἐστίν. 10. τὰ δίκαια ἀεὶ καλά. 11. βεβαία ἡ πόλις ἧς δίκαιοι οἱ πολῖται.

Notes: 1. καλόν, in predicate ("a fine thing"). 2. ἥσυχος, -ον, calm (for second accent, see Lesson 11). 3. βέβαιος, secure. 4. φεῦγε, flee (imperative, 2nd person singular); ἔχθραν, enmity. 5. πολιτεία, government [polity]; εἰσίν, are (Lesson 12). 6. πᾶς, all (with βίος). 8. κόσμος, world [cosmos]; πατρίς, native land (nominative). 9. εὐσέβεια, reverence; ἀνδρεία, bravery; δικαιοσύνη, justice; ῥώμη, strength. 11. πόλις, city.

VOCABULARY

δικαστής, -οῦ, ὁ, juryman
ἡσυχία, -ας, ἡ, calmness
θάλαττα, -ης, ἡ, sea
θεά, -ᾶς, ἡ, goddess
θεός, -οῦ, ὁ and ἡ, god, goddess [theology]
νόμος, -ου, ὁ, law
πεῖρα, -ας, ἡ, trial, attempt

[1] A relative which has an antecedent in the genitive or dative case, and which would itself normally stand in the accusative, is generally attracted into the case of the antecedent, e.g., from the cities which he has, ἐκ τῶν πόλεων ὧν ἔχει (for ἅς ἔχει).

πλοῦτος, -ου, ὁ, wealth [plutocrat]
πολίτης, -ου, ὁ, citizen [politician]
σκηνή, -ῆς, ἡ, tent, stage building, or stage [scene]
στρατιώτης, -ου, ὁ, soldier
συμφορά, -ᾶς, ἡ, misfortune
φιλία, -ας, ἡ, friendship

ἄδικος, -ον, unjust
ἄξιος, -α, -ον, worthy
δίκαιος, δικαία, δίκαιον, just
κακός, -ή, -όν, bad
μικρός, -ά, -όν, small

ὅς, ἥ, ὅ, who, which (relative)
ἐν, in, among (proclitic preposition with dative)
καί, and (conjunction); also, even, merely (adverb; precedes the word it
   modifies)
οὔποτε, never (adverb)

ENGLISH SENTENCES

1. Wealth (is) never secure in disasters. 2. Good soldiers and just jurymen have (ἔχουσι) the friendship even of the citizens. 3. The children (are) among friends. 4. The laws (are) just and worthy of the citizens. 5. The misfortunes of life (are) also common. 6. The friend of the juryman is fleeing (φεύγει). 7. Unjust (is) the misfortune of the soldiers. 8. The justice of the jurymen (is) secure. 9. The citizens' words (are) unjust.

REVIEW EXERCISES

I. Translate:

1. οἱ γὰρ τῶν ἀρίστων λόγοι σοφοί. 2. κοινὰ τὰ δῶρα τὰ τῶν φίλων. 3. ἀθάνατός ἐστιν ὁ τῶν ἀγαθῶν ἀνθρώπων βίος. 4. ἔργον χαλεπὸν ψυχῆς ἀγαθῆς καλόν ἐστι μέτρον. 5. ἡ τῶν παιδίων γνώμη οὐκ ἀεὶ σοφή ἐστιν.

II. Write in Greek:

1. The time (is) not good for the children. 2. The wise men (are) not always the best. 3. The beautiful road (is) difficult. 4. The child's gift (is) best. 5. The opinion of the good man (is) wise.

REGULAR VERBS: PRESENT AND FUTURE INDICATIVE ACTIVE. INFINITIVE IN INDIRECT DISCOURSE

1. The Greek verb has three voices: the *active* and *passive* are used as in English, and the *middle* represents the subject as acting upon itself or in its own interest. The Greek verb has six moods: indicative, subjunctive, optative, imperative, infinitive, participle.

2. The Greek verb has seven tenses, classified as follows:

Primary		*Secondary*
Present	Perfect	Imperfect
Future	Future Perfect	Aorist [1]
		Pluperfect

3. The same personal endings are used for both the present and future indicative active of regular verbs. As in Latin, pronoun subjects are usually omitted. Learn the following endings:

	SINGULAR	PLURAL
1st person	-ω	-ομεν
2nd person	-εις	-ετε
3rd person	-ει	-ουσι(ν)[2]

4. The future is formed by placing σ before these endings.

5. Learn the present and future indicative of παιδεύω, educate.

PRESENT INDICATIVE

SINGULAR		PLURAL	
παιδεύ-ω[3]	*I educate*	παιδεύ-ομεν	*we educate*
παιδεύ-εις	*you educate*	παιδεύ-ετε	*you educate*
παιδεύ-ει	*he, she, it educates*	παιδεύ-ουσι(ν)	*they educate*

---

[1] The aorist is a past tense denoting a single action. It is similar to the French and Spanish preterite.

[2] ν is added to final -σι and to all third personal endings in -ε, when a word beginning with a vowel follows, or at the end of a sentence. It is called ν-movable.

[3] Note that the accent of verbs is recessive. (Page 5, rule 2.c.)

SINGULAR	PLURAL
παιδεύ-σ-ω *I shall educate*	παιδεύ-σ-ομεν *we shall educate*
παιδεύ-σ-εις *you will educate*	παιδεύ-σ-ετε *you will educate*
παιδεύ-σ-ει *he, she, it will educate*	παιδεύ-σ-ουσι(ν) *they will educate*

6. When the stem of a Greek verb ends in a mute, certain changes are made before σ in the future.

    (a) A labial mute—π, β, φ—combines with the σ to make ψ: πέμπω, πέμψω, send.

    (b) A palatal mute—κ, γ, χ—combines with the σ to make ξ: ἄγω, ἄξω, lead.

    (c) A dental mute—τ, δ, θ—is dropped before the σ: πείθω, πείσω, persuade. (So also the voiced dental ζ.)

7. The present active infinitive is formed by adding -ειν to the stem of the verb, as παιδεύειν, to educate.

8. The future active infinitive is formed by adding both the σ of the future and -ειν to the stem, as παιδεύσειν.

9. Many verbs of saying and thinking, as φημί (to be studied later) and νομίζω, are followed by indirect statement in the infinitive. In such cases the verb of the direct statement is changed in the indirect to the same tense of the infinitive, and the subject is put into the accusative case.

If the subject of the verb of saying or thinking and the subject of the infinitive are the same, and are not emphatic, the subject of the infinitive is not expressed, and its modifiers remain nominative.

    The teacher educates the boy. ὁ διδάσκαλος παιδεύει τὸ παιδίον.

    He thinks that the teacher is educating the boy. νομίζει τὸν διδάσκαλον παιδεύειν τὸ παιδίον.

    He said that the teacher was educating the boy. ἔφη τὸν διδάσκαλον παιδεύειν τὸ παιδίον.

    The teacher will educate the boy. ὁ διδάσκαλος παιδεύσει τὸ παιδίον.

    He thinks that the teacher will educate the boy. νομίζει τὸν διδάσκαλον παιδεύσειν τὸ παιδίον.

    He said that the teacher would educate the boy. ἔφη τὸν διδάσκαλον παιδεύσειν τὸ παιδίον.

    The teacher said that he would educate the boy. ὁ διδάσκαλος ἔφη τὸ παιδίον παιδεύσειν.

15

READING

1. οἱ νόμοι τοὺς ἀνθρώπους παιδεύουσιν. 2. πιστεύομεν τοῖς τῶν φίλων λόγοις. 3. τοὺς φίλους πείθει πιστεύειν τοῖς νόμοις. 4. ἡ ἐπιθυμία ἡδονῶν πολλάκις ἀνθρώπους εἰς ἀδικίαν ἄγει. 5. κακὸν φέρουσι καρπὸν οἱ κακοὶ φίλοι. 6. ἔφη κακοὺς φίλους φέρειν καρπὸν κακόν. 7. νομίζουσιν οἱ Ἀθηναῖοι τὸν θάνατον εἶναι καὶ ὕπνον. 8. τοὺς νόμους οἱ Ἀθηναῖοι εἰς λίθους γράφουσιν. 9. οὐκ ἔφασαν τὸν θάνατον κακὸν εἶναι ἀνθρώποις. 10. νομίζουσιν οἱ ἄνθρωποι καλὸν εἶναι ἀγαθοὺς φίλους ἔχειν.

Notes: 4. ἐπιθυμία, desire; ἡδονῶν, objective genitive; ἀδικίαν, injustice (ἀ privative + root δικ-). 5. καρπόν, fruit [carpology]. 9. οὐκ ἔφασαν, said not (Latin, *nego*).

VOCABULARY

Ἀθηναῖοι, -ων, οἱ, Athenians
ἡδονή, -ῆς, ἡ, pleasure [Hedonism]
θάνατος, -ου, ὁ, death
λίθος, -ου, ὁ, stone [lithography]
ὕπνος, -ου, ὁ, sleep [hypnotism]

ἄγω, ἄξω, lead, drive [pedagogue]
γράφω, γράψω, write [graphite]
εἶναι, to be (infinitive of εἰμί, Lesson 12)
ἔφη, he said, replied; ἔφασαν, they said (followed by the infinitive in indirect statement) [euphemism]
ἔχω, ἔξω or σχήσω, have, hold
νομίζω, think (takes infinitive in indirect statement)
παιδεύω, -σω, educate
πείθω, πείσω, persuade (+ accusative)
πέμπω, πέμψω, send
πιστεύω, πιστεύσω, trust (+ dative)
φέρω, bear, carry

εἰς, into (+ accusative)
πολλάκις, often

ENGLISH SENTENCES

1. I trust the laws of the Athenians. 2. He said that he was persuading his (= the) friends. 3. We are not carrying the stones. 4. They said that death was sleep. 5. He will persuade the soldiers to trust the Athenians. 6. The pleasures of life are often small. 7. He will persuade the Athenians to write their laws on stones. 8. The just citizens said that men often lead their friends into injustice.

REVIEW EXERCISES

I. Translate:

1. μικρὰ ἡ σκηνὴ ἐν ᾗ ἐστιν ὁ στρατιώτης. 2. δικαία ἡ τῶν ἀδίκων συμφορά. 3. ἡ ἐν τῇ θαλάττῃ ἡσυχία καλή ἐστιν. 4. οἱ νόμοι τῶν πολιτῶν ἄξιοι. 5. οἱ θεοὶ καὶ αἱ θεαὶ οὔποτε ἄδικοι τοῖς ἀγαθοῖς.

II. Write in Greek:

1. Wealth is a bad thing for the unjust jurymen. 2. The words of the good citizens (are) fair. 3. The friends of the gods (are) immortal. 4. The difficult road is a disaster for the soldiers. 5. The citizen's friendship for the juryman is not just.

THE THIRD OR CONSONANT DECLENSION. CLAUSES OF RESULT

---

1. The third declension includes a large group of nouns of all three genders. The stems of these nouns end for the most part in a consonant, and the stem is seen in the genitive singular when the ending -ος is dropped. The nominatives singular of these nouns vary greatly, but they often end in -ς, and the remaining forms are usually regular.[1] Learn the declension of the following nouns:

	F *shield*	M *thief*	M *guard*	M *divinity*	M *old man*	F *favor*
			SINGULAR			
N	ἀσπίς	κλώψ	φύλαξ	δαίμων	γέρων	χάρις
G	ἀσπίδος	κλωπός	φύλακος	δαίμονος	γέροντος	χάριτος
D	ἀσπίδι	κλωπί	φύλακι	δαίμονι	γέροντι	χάριτι
A	ἀσπίδα	κλῶπα	φύλακα	δαίμονα	γέροντα	χάριν
V	ἀσπί	κλώψ	φύλαξ	δαῖμον	γέρον	χάρι
			PLURAL			
N	ἀσπίδες	κλῶπες	φύλακες	δαίμονες	γέροντες	χάριτες
G	ἀσπίδων	κλωπῶν	φυλάκων	δαιμόνων	γερόντων	χαρίτων
D	ἀσπίσι	κλωψί	φύλαξι	δαίμοσι	γέρουσι	χάρισι
A	ἀσπίδας	κλῶπας	φύλακας	δαίμονας	γέροντας	χάριτας
V	ἀσπίδες	κλῶπες	φύλακες	δαίμονες	γέροντες	χάριτες

2. It is necessary to learn the nominative and genitive singular and the gender of the nouns of the third declension in order to understand the manner in which a particular noun will be declined.

[1] Masculine and feminine nouns usually form the accusative singular by adding α to stems ending in a consonant; ν to stems ending in ι or υ. The vocative singular of masculine and feminine nouns is usually the pure stem, e.g., ἀσπί, but there are a number of exceptions, e.g., φύλαξ. Nouns which do not accent the ultima usually drop the dental of the stem and add ν to ι or υ; e.g., χάριν. But nouns accented on the ultima in the nominative, and having a dental stem, keep the dental and add α; e.g., ἀσπίδα.

3. The ending of the dative plural is -σι, with ν-movable before a word beginning with a vowel; this ending is often the cause of certain changes in the final consonant of the stem, which must be learned by observation of various nouns.

4. The accent of these nouns is persistent except in the case of monosyllabic stems, and of a few other irregular nouns. Monosyllabic stems of the third declension accent the ultima of the genitive and dative, singular and plural.

5. Result is expressed in Greek in two ways:

   (a) Actual result is expressed by ὥστε plus the indicative. The negative is οὐ. He did not come, so that the Greeks were worried. οὐχ ἧκεν· ὥσθ' οἱ Ἕλληνες ἐφρόντιζον.

   (b) Natural result, which often denotes intention, tendency, or capacity, is expressed by ὥστε and the infinitive. The negative is μή. He was so brave as not to flee. οὕτως ἀγαθὸς ἦν ὥστε μὴ φεύγειν.

READING

1. ἡ σωφροσύνη κόσμος ἐστὶ γέρουσι καὶ νεανίαις. 2. τὸν οὐρανὸν οἱ ποιηταὶ αἰθέρα ὀνομάζουσιν. 3. τὸν ἥλιον λέγουσιν ὀφθαλμὸν τοῦ οὐρανοῦ. 4. ἔχω πλοῦτον ὥστε ἀγοράζειν τὰ δῶρα. 5. καλὸν καὶ γέρουσι μανθάνειν σοφά. 6. ὁ γέρων τοῖς νεανίαις ἔφη τὴν σωφροσύνην εἶναι κόσμον. 7. ὁ πολίτης τοῖς Ἀθηναίοις πιστεύσει οἳ φίλιοί εἰσιν. 8. τοὺς στρατιώτας ἄξει εἰς τὴν σκηνὴν ἐν ᾗ ἐστιν ὁ πλοῦτος. 9. ὥστε οὐ νομίζουσι τὸν θάνατον καὶ ὕπνον εἶναι. 10. ὁ σοφὸς ἡσυχίαν ἄγει ἐν ταῖς συμφοραῖς. 11. οὐκ ἔφη εἶναι ποιητής, ἀλλὰ κριτὴς τῶν ποιητῶν.

Notes: 1. σωφροσύνη, self-control; κόσμος, ornament [cosmetics]. 2. αἰθέρα (accusative), sky [ethereal]; ὀνομάζουσιν, call [synonym]. 3. λέγουσιν, they call; ὀφθαλμόν (accusative), eye [ophthalmia]. 4. ἀγοράζειν, to buy, cf. ἀγορά, market. 5. μανθάνειν, to learn [mathematics]. (An infinitive may be used as a noun as the subject or object of a sentence.) 10. ἡσυχίαν ἄγει, is calm. 11. κριτής, judge, critic (from κρίνω, to judge [crisis]); οὐκ ἔφη, said not; cf. English "I don't think."

VOCABULARY

ἄρχων, -οντος, ὁ, ruler
ἀσπίς, -ίδος, ἡ, shield
γέρων, γέροντος, ὁ, old man [Gerontion]
δαίμων, -ονος, ὁ, divinity
ἥλιος, -ου, ὁ, sun [helium]

κλώψ, κλωπός, ὁ, thief
νεανίας, -ου, ὁ, young man
οὐρανός, -οῦ, ὁ heaven [uranium]
ποιητής, -οῦ, ὁ, poet
φύλαξ, -ακος, ὁ, guard
χάρις, χάριτος, ἡ, favor, grace

ἐσθλός, -ή, -όν, noble
μόνος, -η, -ον, only, sole [monolith]
φίλιος, -ᾱ, -ον, friendly (cf. φίλος, φιλία)

ἦν, he, she, it was; ἦσαν, they were

ἀλλά, and by elision ἀλλ', but
μή, not (negative with conditions and infinitives except infinitives in
    indirect discourse)
οὕτω (before vowels, οὕτως), thus, so
ὥστε, and so, so that, therefore (elided to ὥστ' before a smooth breath-
    ing, ὥσθ' before a rough breathing)

ENGLISH SENTENCES

1. It was a good thing for the young men to learn to be calm.
2. The rulers will send the shields to the old men. 3. The noble poets
will persuade the young men to trust them (αὐτοῖς). 4. The guards
are wise, and so they persuade the citizens. 5. The divinities will send
their favors to poets and rulers so as to educate them (αὐτούς).
6. They lead the thieves into the tent in which the guard was.

REVIEW EXERCISES

I. Translate:

1. ἔφασαν τοὺς Ἀθηναίους πιστεύσειν τοῖς σοφοῖς καὶ δικαίοις πολίταις.
2. τὰ παιδία φέρει τοὺς λίθους εἰς τὴν ὁδόν. 3. ἔφη τοὺς σοφοὺς νομίζειν
τὸν θάνατον ὕπνον εἶναι. 4. οὐ πολλάκις παιδεύει τοὺς ἀνθρώπους ἡ
ἡδονή. 5. πείσει τοὺς σοφοὺς πολίτας νόμους γράφειν καὶ πέμπειν τοῖς
στρατιώταις.

Note: 2. A neuter plural subject regularly takes a singular verb.

II. Write in Greek:

1. He said that the soldiers would lead the horses into the road.
2. They think that pleasure is not a good thing. 3. They said that
they would not have a tent. 4. Sleep will lead the soldiers into death.
5. We do not think it is a pleasure to carry stones for our (the)
friends.

20

IRREGULAR AND NEUTER NOUNS
OF THE THIRD DECLENSION.
EXPRESSIONS OF TIME.
DATIVE OF POSSESSION

1. Learn the declension of the following nouns:

M	F	N	N	M	M
king	*city*	*army*	*race*	*father*	*man*
		SINGULAR			
βασιλεύς	πόλις	στράτευμα	γένος	πατήρ[1]	ἀνήρ
βασιλέως	πόλεως	στρατεύματος	γένους	πατρός	ἀνδρός
βασιλεῖ	πόλει	στρατεύματι	γένει	πατρί	ἀνδρί
βασιλέα	πόλιν	στράτευμα	γένος	πατέρα	ἄνδρα
βασιλεῦ	πόλι	στράτευμα	γένος	πάτερ	ἄνερ
		PLURAL			
βασιλεῖς	πόλεις	στρατεύματα	γένη	πατέρες	ἄνδρες
βασιλέων	πόλεων	στρατευμάτων	γενῶν	πατέρων	ἀνδρῶν
βασιλεῦσι	πόλεσι	στρατεύμασι	γένεσι	πατράσι	ἀνδράσι
βασιλέας	πόλεις	στρατεύματα	γένη	πατέρας	ἄνδρας
βασιλεῖς	πόλεις	στρατεύματα	γένη	πατέρες	ἄνδρες

2. The first four are each typical of a large class of nouns.
Nouns like γένος have a stem -ες which drops the ς and allows the
ε to contract with the following vowel, e.g., γένεσος, γένους; γένεσα,
γένη.

3. Duration of time and extent of space are expressed by the
accusative case without a preposition: He marched five days. ἤλαυνε
πέντε ἡμέρας.

[1] μήτηρ, mother, is declined: μήτηρ, μητρός, μητρί, μητέρα, μῆτερ (singular); μητέρες, μητέρων, μητράσι, μητέρας, μητέρες (plural). The vocative of
nouns in -τηρ has recessive accent and shortens η to ε.

21

Time when is expressed by the dative case, usually without a preposition: He will come on the next day. ἥξει τῇ ὑστεραίᾳ.

Time within which is expressed by the genitive case, usually without a preposition: He will come within ten days. ἥξει δέκα ἡμερῶν.

4. Simple possession is often expressed by the verb *to be* with the dative, the dative denoting the possessor: Cyrus has a general. τῷ Κύρῳ ἐστὶ στρατηγός.

READING

1. Ἕλληνές εἰσιν ἄνδρες οὐκ ἀγνώμονες καὶ μετὰ λογισμοῦ πάντα πράττουσιν. 2. κρίνει φίλους ὁ καιρός, ὡς χρυσὸν τὸ πῦρ. 3. οἱ ἰατροὶ τὰ τῶν πολιτῶν σώματα θεραπεύουσιν. 4. ἀλλ' εἰσὶ μητρὶ παῖδες ἄγκυραι βίου. 5. ἡ ἡμέρα μικρὸν μέρος τοῦ ἔτους ἐστίν. 6. γύναι, γυναικὶ κόσμον ἡ σιγὴ φέρει. 7. χεὶρ χεῖρα νίζει. 8. ὁ ἐσθλὸς βασιλεὺς νομίζει τὴν δικαιοσύνην δῶρον εἶναι τῶν θεῶν. 9. οἱ γὰρ ἀγαθοὶ δαίμονες πέμπουσι τοῖς ἀνθρώποις πάντα (all things) ἃ ἄξει εἰς βίον ἀθάνατον. ὥστε οἱ ἄνθρωποι ἀποδώσουσι (will give back) τοῖς θεοῖς ὃ φίλον ἔσται (will be), ὥστε ἔχειν τὴν φιλίαν αὐτῶν (their). 10. χάρις χάριν φέρει. 11. ὁ χρόνος ἐστὶν ἐν ᾧ καιρός, καιρὸς ἐν ᾧ χρόνος οὐ πολύς (much).—HIPPOCRATES.

Notes: 1. ἀγνώμονες, ignorant; λογισμοῦ, reasoning; πάντα, everything (neuter plural accusative). 2. χρυσόν, gold (accusative) [chrysolite]. 3. ἰατροί, physicians; θεραπεύουσι, treat [therapeutics]. 4. ἄγκυραι, anchors, mainstays. 5. μέρος, τό, part [polymeric]; ἔτους, year (τὸ ἔτος) [Etesian]. 6. σιγή, silence. 7. νίζει, washes. 8. -σύνη, suffix like English-*ness*. 9. ἄξει: singular verb with neuter plural subject; φίλον, pleasing.

VOCABULARY

ἀνήρ, ἀνδρός, ὁ, man, husband
βασιλεύς, -έως, ὁ, king
γένος, ους, τό, race, kind
γυνή, γυναικός[2], ἡ, woman, wife [gynecology]
Ἕλλην, Ἕλληνος, ὁ, a Greek
ἡμέρα, -ας, ἡ, day [ephemeral]
καιρός, -οῦ, ὁ, critical time, occasion
μήτηρ, μητρός, ἡ, mother (for declension see note, p. 21)
παῖς, παιδός, ὁ, child (cf. παιδεύω), vocative παῖ; genitive plural παίδων
πατήρ, πατρός, ὁ, father
πόλις, -εως, ἡ, city

[2] γυνή is declined: γυνή, γυναικός, γυναικί, γυναῖκα, γύναι (singular); γυναῖκες, γυναικῶν, γυναιξί, γυναῖκας, γυναῖκες (plural).

πῦρ, πυρός, τό, fire [pyromaniac]
στράτευμα, -ατος, τό, army
σῶμα, σώματος, τό, body [chromosome]
χείρ, χειρός, ἡ, hand [chiropractor]
χρῆμα, -ατος, τό, thing; plural = money, things

κρίνω, judge, decide
πράττω, πράξω, do [practical]

μετά, preposition with genitive, with; with accusative, after
ὡς, as (proclitic)
δέκα, ten (undeclinable) [decalogue]

ENGLISH SENTENCES

1. The child will write a letter (ἐπιστολή) to (his) father within ten days. 2. The Greek said that he would send fire to the men. 3. The child's mother has (ἔχει) money in her (= the) hand. 4. The wife of the Greek is for ten days carrying fire to (παρά + accusative) her mother. 5. The jurymen think that they judge with calmness and pleasure. 6. The king thinks that silence and justice are ornaments.

REVIEW EXERCISES

I. Translate:

1. ἦν γὰρ οὕτω καλὴ ὥστε τοὺς νεανίας δῶρα πέμπειν. 2. οὐ δίκαιοι ἀλλὰ ἄδικοι ἦσαν οἱ δικασταί, ὥστε τοὺς πολίτας μὴ πιστεύειν τοῖς λόγοις. 3. ἕξει γὰρ ὁ νεανίας ἡδονὴν καὶ τὴν χάριν τὴν τῶν θεῶν. 4. τὰς τῶν ποιητῶν γνώμας οὐ γράψομεν. 5. ἔφη ὁ σοφὸς τὰ τῶν δαιμόνων ἔργα καλὰ εἶναι.

II. Write in Greek:

1. The rulers were so wise as to trust only the wise and noble citizens. 2. The old man is not friendly, so that he will not send the shield to the young man. 3. The poets think that the sun is a divinity in the heavens. 4. The guards will lead the thief into the ruler's tent. 5. The just have the favor of the gods.

THE IMPERFECT.
THE FIRST AND SECOND AORISTS
INDICATIVE AND INFINITIVE

---

1. Past time in Greek verbs is denoted by two means:

   (a) by a different set of personal endings from those previously studied; and

   (b) by augmentation of the verb stem.

2. Augment is of two kinds:

   (a) Syllabic augment. Verbs which begin with a consonant prefix the vowel ε to form the imperfect, aorist, and pluperfect tenses, e.g., πέμπω, ἔπεμπον, ἔπεμψα.

   (b) Temporal augment. Verbs which begin with a vowel lengthen that vowel. The most frequent changes are α to η; ε to η and ο to ω; αι to η. Also ι (short) augments to ι (long); υ (short) to υ (long); αυ to ηυ; οι to ῳ. E.g., ἄγω, ἦγον. In certain verbs ε is augmented to ει, e.g., ἔχω, εἶχον.

3. The terms *first aorist* and *second aorist* denote different forms, not different tenses. Most verbs have a first aorist, but a number of important verbs have a second aorist instead. The second aorist generally occurs in consonant stems, and is similar to the past of strong verbs in English, e.g., λείπω, ἔλιπον; cf. sing, sang.

The stem of the imperfect, and of the first aorist, is that of the present tense, while the stem of the second aorist is that of the root of the verb (it is sometimes called the strong aorist). The personal endings of the second aorist are the same as those of the imperfect; no σ is added to the stem. Whether a verb has a first or second aorist must be learned from the principal parts (given in the general vocabulary).

24

4. Learn the following forms:

IMPERFECT

ἐ-παίδευ-ο-ν   *I was educating,*
ἐ-παίδευ-ε-ς   *etc.*
ἐ-παίδευ-ε(ν)

ἐ-παιδεύ-ο-μεν
ἐ-παιδεύ-ε-τε
ἐ-παίδευ-ο-ν

IMPERFECT

ἔ-λειπ-ο-ν   *I was leaving,*
ἔ-λειπ-ε-ς   *etc.*
ἔ-λειπ-ε(ν)

ἐ-λείπ-ο-μεν
ἐ-λείπ-ε-τε
ἔ-λειπ-ο-ν

FIRST AORIST

ἐ-παίδευ-σα   *I educated,*
ἐ-παίδευ-σα-ς   *etc.*
ἐ-παίδευ-σε(ν)
ἐ-παιδεύ-σα-μεν
ἐ-παιδεύ-σα-τε
ἐ-παίδευ-σα-ν

SECOND AORIST

ἔ-λιπ-ο-ν   *I left,*
ἔ-λιπ-ε-ς   *etc.*
ἔ-λιπ-ε(ν)
ἐ-λίπ-ο-μεν
ἐ-λίπ-ε-τε
ἔ-λιπ-ο-ν

LIQUID FIRST AORIST

ἔ-μειν-α   *I remained,*
ἔ-μειν-α-ς   *etc.*
ἔ-μειν-ε(ν)

ἐ-μείν-α-μεν
ἐ-μείν-α-τε
ἔ-μειν-α-ν

5. The tense sign of the first aorist is σα. When the verb stem ends in a mute or in ζ, the same changes occur as before the σ of the future, e.g., πέμπω, ἔπεμψα.

6. When a verb stem ends in a liquid (λ, μ, ν, or ρ), the first aorist endings are added directly to the stem without the σ. Usually the vowel of the stem is lengthened in this case, α becoming η; ε, ει; ι (short), ι (long); υ (short), υ (long); e.g., μένω, aorist ἔμεινα.

7. The ending of the first aorist active infinitive is -σαι, in a liquid stem -αι; παιδεῦσαι, πέμψαι, μεῖναι. The infinitive is not augmented, the augment being used only in the indicative mood. The accent is always upon the penult.

8. There is no imperfect infinitive.

9. The ending of the second aorist infinitive is -εῖν. This infinitive always has the circumflex upon the ultima, e.g., λιπεῖν.

10. So far, three of the six principal parts of the Greek verb have

25

been given. These are the first person singular of the present indicative, of the future indicative, and of the aorist indicative. For example: παιδεύω, παιδεύσω, ἐπαίδευσα; λείπω, λείψω, ἔλιπον.

These parts, and others to be learned later, should be practiced together. Rapid identification of any given verb form in Greek depends upon a command of the principal parts.

The first three principal parts of the verbs given in the Vocabularies thus far, with the exception of certain irregular verbs, are given below (the futures of κρίνω and νομίζω will be learned in Lesson 16):

ἄγω, ἄξω, ἤγαγον, lead, drive
γράφω, γράψω, ἔγραψα, write
ἔχω, ἔξω or σχήσω, ἔσχον, have, hold
κρίνω, —, ἔκρινα, judge
νομίζω, —, ἐνόμισα, think
παιδεύω, παιδεύσω, ἐπαίδευσα, educate
πείθω, πείσω, ἔπεισα, persuade
πέμπω, πέμψω, ἔπεμψα, send
πιστεύω, πιστεύσω, ἐπίστευσα, trust
πράττω, πράξω, ἔπραξα, do
φέρω, οἴσω, ἤνεγκον, bear, carry

READING

1. ἴσον ἐστὶν ὀργῇ καὶ θάλαττα καὶ γυνή. 2. οἱ Πέρσαι τὰ τέκνα εἰς ἀλήθειαν ἐπαίδευον. 3. ἐν Ἀθήναις οἱ πολῖται ἐν ταῖς ἐκκλησίαις ἐβούλευον. 4. οἱ Πέρσαι τῷ ἡλίῳ καὶ τῇ σελήνῃ καὶ τῇ γῇ καὶ τοῖς ἀνέμοις ἔθυον. 5. ὁ μὲν ἀγαθὸς ἄνθρωπος ἐκ τοῦ ἀγαθοῦ θησαυροῦ τῆς καρδίας προφέρει τὸ ἀγαθόν, ὁ δὲ πονηρὸς ἐκ τοῦ πονηροῦ τὸ πονηρόν. 6. καὶ σύ, τέκνον!— CAESAR TO BRUTUS, FROM SUETONIUS. 7. Ἀχιλλεὺς ἐπὶ τὸν πόλεμον οὐκ ἐξῇει (went forth), μηνίων (being angry) διὰ Βρισηίδα. ὥστε οἱ Τρῶες θαρσήσαντες (taking courage) ἐκ τῆς πόλεως προῆλθον. οἱ δὲ Ἕλληνες τεῖχος ἔπραττον καὶ τάφρον (ditch). καὶ οἱ Τρῶες τοὺς Ἕλληνας εἰς τὸ τεῖχος ἐδίωκον (pursued).—APOLLODORUS.

Notes: 1. ἴσον, equal [isosceles]; ὀργῇ, dative of respect (Lesson 11); καὶ . . . καὶ, both . . . and. 2. Πέρσαι, Persians; τέκνον, child. 3. ἐκκλησία, assembly [ecclesiastical]; Ἀθῆναι, Athens. 4. σελήνη, moon [selenography]. 5. θησαυροῦ, treasure house [Thesaurus]; καρδία, heart [cardiac]; πρό + φέρει, bring forth. 6. σύ, you (Latin tu). 7. προῆλθον, πρό, forth + ἦλθον, went; Βρισηίδα, accusative of Βρισηίς, Briseïs; ἔπραττον, they built.

26

VOCABULARY

ἀλήθεια, -ας, ἡ, truth
ἄνεμος, -ου, ὁ, wind [anemone]
γῆ, γῆς, γῇ, γῆν, ἡ, earth [geology]
ὀργή, -ῆς, ἡ, temper, anger [orgy]
πόλεμος, -ου, ὁ, war [polemics]
τεῖχος, -ους, τό, wall

πονηρός, -ά, -όν, wicked

βουλεύω, βουλεύσω, ἐβούλευσα, plan
θύω, θύσω, ἔθυσα, sacrifice, sacrifice to (+ dative)
ἦλθον (second aorist of ἔρχομαι), I came, I went (aorist infinitive ἐλθεῖν)
λείπω, λείψω, ἔλιπον, leave
μένω, aorist, ἔμεινα, remain (future to be learned later)
παιδεύω, παιδεύσω, ἐπαίδευσα, teach, educate

διά, preposition + genitive, through (in a spatial sense); + accusative, on account of
ἐκ, preposition + genitive, out of; ἐξ before vowels
ἐπί, preposition + genitive, upon (superposition); + dative, on (proximity), in addition to, for; + accusative, to, against
μέν . . . δέ, used to coordinate members of an antithesis. Often μέν is not translated by a specific word

ENGLISH SENTENCES

1. In Athens they sacrificed to the gods. 2. The king of the Persians remained in the city. 3. The Persians persuade their (the) children to learn (μαθεῖν) the truth. 4. The Athenians came into the city, but the Persians planned to remain and sacrifice to their gods. 5. The wicked king in anger used to remain on the wall. 6. The Athenians were not wise who thought that the winds had come out of the heavens.

REVIEW EXERCISES

I. Translate:

1. ὁ πατὴρ δέκα ἡμερῶν πέμψει τὰ δῶρα τοῖς παισί. 2. οὕτως ἀγαθὸς ἦν ὁ ἀνὴρ ὥστε τοὺς πολίτας ἄριστον αὐτὸν (him) κρίνειν. 3. ἔφη τὸν βασιλέα τὴν γυναῖκα καλὴν εἶναι νομίζειν. 4. οἱ Ἕλληνες ἐν καιρῷ πείσουσι τὰς πόλεις χρήματα τῷ στρατεύματι πέμπειν. 5. ἡ μήτηρ μετὰ τῶν παίδων φέρει δῶρα ἐν χερσὶ τοῖς θεοῖς.

II. Write in Greek:

1. The race of the Greeks thinks a beautiful body is a gift of the

divinities. 2. They trust the king as fair and just. 3. He will do good (things) in the city. 4. The fire is in the army's tents, as they said. 5. The king is the husband of ten wives.

COMPARISON OF ADJECTIVES AND ADVERBS. DECLENSION OF ἡδίων

1. Adjectives with regular comparison form the comparative degree by adding -τερος, -ᾱ, -ον to the stem of the positive, the superlative by adding -τατος, -η, -ον , e.g., δίκαιος, δικαιότερος, δικαιότατος, just.

2. Adjectives in -ος with a long penult keep the omicron of the stem of the positive unchanged; those with a short penult lengthen the omicron to omega before the endings of the comparative and superlative. The penult is counted long if it contains a long vowel or a diphthong, or if it contains a short vowel followed by a double consonant or by two or more consonants. So:

	Positive	Comparative	Superlative
wicked	πονηρός	πονηρότερος	πονηρότατος
noble	ἐσθλός	ἐσθλότερος	ἐσθλότατος
bitter	πικρός	πικρότερος	πικρότατος
but:			
worthy	ἄξιος	ἀξιώτερος	ἀξιώτατος
fearful	φοβερός	φοβερώτερος	φοβερώτατος

3. Several adjectives are compared with -ίων, -ιστος. (For declension of comparatives, see below.)

	M	M,F N	M F N
sweet	ἡδύς[1]	ἡδίων, ἥδιον	ἥδιστος, -η, -ον
beautiful, good	καλός	καλλίων, κάλλιον	κάλλιστος, -η, -ον

4. Several of the commonest adjectives have irregular comparison:

good	ἀγαθός	ἀμείνων, ἄμεινον	ἄριστος, -η, -ον
noble, good	ἀγαθός	βελτίων, βέλτιον	βέλτιστος, -η, ον

[1] For the declension of the positive, ἡδύς, see Lesson 17.

strong, good	ἀγαθός	κρείττων, κρεῖττον	κράτιστος, -η, -ον
bad	κακός	κακίων, κάκιον	κάκιστος, -η, -ον
inferior	κακός	χείρων, χεῖρον	χείριστος, -η, ον
large	μέγας[2]	μείζων, μεῖζον	μέγιστος, -η, -ον
much, many	πολύς[2]	πλείων, πλέον or πλεῖον	πλεῖστος, -η, -ον
easy	ῥάδιος	ῥάων, ῥᾷον	ῥᾷστος, -η, -ον
few	ὀλίγος	ὀλείζων, ὄλειζον	ὀλίγιστος, -η, -ον
small	μικρός	ἐλάττων, ἔλαττον	ἐλάχιστος, -η, -ον
swift	ταχύς	θάττων, θᾶττον	τάχιστος, -η, ον

5. Adverbs are usually formed from adjectives by changing the ων of the genitive plural to ως, e.g., καλός, καλῶς.

6. The comparative of the adverb is the neuter accusative singular of the comparative of the adjective, the superlative the neuter accusative plural of the superlative of the adjective, e.g.,

$$\text{δικαίως} \qquad \text{δικαιότερον} \qquad \text{δικαιότατα}$$

7. The word for *than* is ἤ. When ἤ is used, the second member of a comparison takes the same case as the first. But ἤ may be omitted, in which case the second member of the comparison must be put in the genitive case.

I never saw a better man than Cyrus. οὔποτε εἶδον ἄνδρα ἀμείνονα ἢ Κῦρον or οὔποτε εἶδον ἄνδρα ἀμείνονα Κύρου.

8. The degree of difference with a comparison is expressed by the dative case without a preposition.

Cyrus was ten years younger than his brother. Κῦρος δέκα ἔτεσι νεώτερος ἦν τοῦ ἀδελφοῦ.

9. Learn the declension of ἡδίων, the comparative of the adjective ἡδύς, sweet.[3] Other -ίων comparatives are similarly declined.

SINGULAR		PLURAL	
M, F	N	M, F	N
ἡδίων	ἥδιον	ἡδίονες (ἡδίους)	ἡδίονα (ἡδίω)
ἡδίονος	ἡδίονος	ἡδιόνων	ἡδιόνων
ἡδίονι	ἡδίονι	ἡδίοσι	ἡδίοσι
ἡδίονα (ἡδίω)	ἥδιον	ἡδίονας (ἡδίους)	ἡδίονα (ἡδίω)
ἥδιον	ἥδιον	ἡδίονες	ἡδίονα

[2] For the declension of the positives πολύς and μέγας, see Lesson 18.
[3] The bracketed forms ἡδίω and ἡδίους were commonly used in daily speech, but are less common in literature.

READING

1. σοφὸς Σοφοκλῆς, σοφώτερος δ' Εὐριπίδης, ἀνδρῶν δὲ πάντων Σωκράτης σοφώτατος. 2. καὶ τὸ ὅλον μεῖζον τοῦ μέρους ἐστίν.—EUCLID. 3. οὐκ ἔστι λύπης μεῖζον ἀνθρώποις κακόν. 4. οὐκ ἔσθ' ὑγιείας κρεῖττον οὐδὲν ἐν βίῳ. 5. οὐκ ἔστιν οὐδὲν κτῆμα κάλλιον φίλου. 6. δημοκρατία κρεῖττον τυραννίδος.—PERIANDER. 7. A Theorem of Euclid. παντὸς τριγώνου ὑπὸ τὴν μείζονα γωνίαν ἡ μείζων πλευρὰ ὑποτείνει.

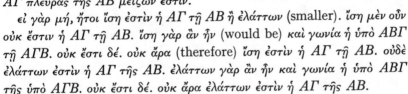

ἔστω τρίγωνον τὸ ΑΒΓ, μείζονα ἔχον (having) τὴν ὑπὸ ΑΒΓ γωνίαν τῆς ὑπὸ ΒΓΑ. λέγω ὅτι καὶ πλευρὰ ἡ ΑΓ πλευρᾶς τῆς ΑΒ μείζων ἐστίν.

εἰ γὰρ μή, ἤτοι ἴση ἐστὶν ἡ ΑΓ τῇ ΑΒ ἢ ἐλάττων (smaller). ἴση μὲν οὖν οὐκ ἔστιν ἡ ΑΓ τῇ ΑΒ. ἴση γὰρ ἂν ἦν (would be) καὶ γωνία ἡ ὑπὸ ΑΒΓ τῇ ΑΓΒ. οὐκ ἔστι δέ. οὐκ ἄρα (therefore) ἴση ἐστὶν ἡ ΑΓ τῇ ΑΒ. οὐδὲ ἐλάττων ἐστὶν ἡ ΑΓ τῆς ΑΒ. ἐλάττων γὰρ ἂν ἦν καὶ γωνία ἡ ὑπὸ ΑΒΓ τῆς ὑπὸ ΑΓΒ. οὐκ ἔστι δέ. οὐκ ἄρα ἐλάττων ἐστὶν ἡ ΑΓ τῆς ΑΒ.

ἐδείχθη (it was shown) δὲ ὅτι οὐδὲ ἴση ἐστίν. μείζων ἄρα ἐστὶν ἡ ΑΓ τῆς ΑΒ. παντὸς ἄρα τριγώνου ὑπὸ τὴν μείζονα γωνίαν ἡ μείζων πλευρὰ ὑποτείνει. ὅπερ ἔδει δεῖξαι (Q.E.D.).

Notes: 1. πάντων, of all. 2. μέρους (genitive), part. 3. λύπης (genitive), pain; κακόν, evil (substantive). 5. κτῆμα, possession. 7. παντός (genitive singular), every; τριγώνου, triangle; μείζονα, greater; γωνία, angle; ὑπό, at; πλευρά, side; ἔστω, let there be (imperative, 3rd singular); ἤτοι, either; ἴση, equal; ἄν, particle not translated (see Lesson 24); ὅπερ, the very thing which.

VOCABULARY

δημοκρατία, -ας, ἡ, democracy
τυραννίς, -ίδος, ἡ, tyranny
ὑγίεια, -ας, ἡ, health [hygiene]

ἡδύς, ἡδεῖα, ἡδύ, sweet, pleasant (for declension, see p. 60)
νέος, -α, -ον, new, young [Neoplatonism]
ὅλος, -η, -ον, whole
οὐδέν, nothing (for declension, see Lesson 37). In a sentence begun with a negative, succeeding negatives are treated as positives. As adjective, no; e.g., οὐδὲν κτῆμα, no possession

ἔστι[ν], there is (emphatic form stressing existence or possibility; see Lesson 12)
λέγω, λέξω, ἔλεξα, say (in indirect discourse, takes a ὅτι clause with the indicative; see Lesson 24); with infinitive, define.
τείνω, aorist ἔτεινα, stretch, extend (ὑποτείνω, subtend)

31

δέ, and, but (postpositive)

εἰ (proclitic), if

ἤ, or, than

ὅτι (conjunction), that (introducing indirect statement); because

οὐδέ, nor, not even, not . . . either

οὖν (postpositive), therefore; now (in narrative sense)

ὑπό, under (preposition with genitive and accusative); by (with genitive, denoting personal agent)

ὡς (with superlative of adjective or adverb), as . . . as possible

The adjectives in paragraphs 3 and 4 are to be learned as part of the vocabulary. Note that the superlative can mean "very" as well as "most."

ENGLISH SENTENCES

1. There exists nothing in life worse than tyranny, as the wisest of all men, Socrates, used to say. 2. The Greeks, therefore, thought that health was the best possession for men. 3. I say that tyranny is the worst thing for men. 4. Democracy did not teach the Greeks to be always calm, neither did tyranny teach them (αὐτούς) to be harsh. 5. They say that health is a pleasant thing for both body and soul. 6. The wise man said that nothing is better than democracy.

REVIEW EXERCISES

I. Translate:

1. ἤλθετε εἰς τὴν τῶν Ἑλλήνων γῆν. 2. ἔθυσαν οἱ στρατιῶται διὰ τὴν τῶν ἀνέμων ὀργήν. 3. ἡ ἀλήθεια οὐκ ἐπαίδευσε τοὺς κακοὺς ἄνδρας. 4. ἔμενον δέκα ἡμέρας ἐν τοῖς τείχεσι διὰ τὸν πόλεμον. 5. οἱ μὲν πονηροὶ πολῖται ἐβούλευσαν λείπειν τοὺς φίλους ἐν τῇ θαλάττῃ, οἱ δὲ ἀγαθοὶ ἔπεμψαν πλοῖα (boats).

II. Write in Greek:

1. The soldiers came from the city into the war. 2. Upon the stone they sacrificed the best of the young men. 3. The Greeks thought that they were brave, but the Persians did not think so. 4. Truth is a wall for the just and fair. 5. He was so wicked that the citizens did not judge him worthy to be king.

32

DEMONSTRATIVES

1. Greek has three demonstrative words which may be used as pronouns or as adjectives: οὗτος, ἐκεῖνος, ὅδε. οὗτος means *this*, or, after an enumeration of two or more persons or things, *the latter*. ἐκεῖνος means *that*, or, after a similar enumeration, *the former*. ὅδε is a weaker demonstrative and means *this* or *that*. Sometimes ὅδε means *the following*, as οὗτος means *the aforesaid*. ὅδε consists of the article plus δε.[1]

2. The declension of these words is as follows:

SINGULAR			PLURAL		
οὗτος	αὕτη	τοῦτο	οὗτοι	αὗται	ταῦτα
τούτου	ταύτης	τούτου	τούτων	τούτων	τούτων
τούτῳ	ταύτῃ	τούτῳ	τούτοις	ταύταις	τούτοις
τοῦτον	ταύτην	τοῦτο	τούτους	ταύτας	ταῦτα
ἐκεῖνος	ἐκείνη	ἐκεῖνο	ἐκεῖνοι	ἐκεῖναι	ἐκεῖνα
ἐκείνου	ἐκείνης	ἐκείνου	ἐκείνων	ἐκείνων	ἐκείνων
ἐκείνῳ	ἐκείνῃ	ἐκείνῳ	ἐκείνοις	ἐκείναις	ἐκείνοις
ἐκεῖνον	ἐκείνην	ἐκεῖνο	ἐκείνους	ἐκείνας	ἐκεῖνα
ὅδε	ἥδε	τόδε	οἵδε	αἵδε	τάδε
τοῦδε	τῆσδε	τοῦδε	τῶνδε	τῶνδε	τῶνδε
τῷδε	τῇδε	τῷδε	τοῖσδε	ταῖσδε	τοῖσδε
τόνδε	τήνδε	τόδε	τούσδε	τάσδε	τάδε

3. When these pronouns are used as demonstrative adjectives, they must be placed in the predicate position, i.e., they stand outside the article-noun group which they modify. Thus, οὗτος ὁ ἄνθρωπος, *this man*, ἐκείνη ἡ κώμη, or ἡ κώμη ἐκείνη, *that village*.

[1] δέ is an enclitic, which explains the apparent anomaly of the accent in several forms. See Lesson 11.

4. Observe that οὗτος has a rough breathing where the article has a rough breathing, a τ where the article has a τ, an ου where the article has an "o" sound, an αυ where the article has an α or η.

READING

1. μέγιστον ὀργῆς ἐστι φάρμακον λόγος. 2. μετὰ δὲ ταῦτα, τούτοις τοῖς θεοῖς ἔθυον. 3. τοῖσδε τοῖς ἀνδράσι μᾶλλον ἢ ἐκείνοις ἐπίστευσα, ὅτι φίλιοί εἰσι τοῖς Ἕλλησιν. 4. λέγουσιν ὅτι οἱ Ἀθηναῖοι θύουσι τοῖς θεοῖς τοῖς τῆς πόλεως. 5. οὗτος ὁ στρατιώτης ὃς ἔπεμψε τῷ στρατηγῷ τὰς ἀσπίδας ἔλεξε τάδε. 6. ὅρκους γυναικὸς εἰς ὕδωρ γράφω. 7. ἀκούσας (having heard) ταῦτα, ἔλεξε τάδε. 8. ὁ Προμηθεὺς πρῶτον μὲν ἀνθρώπους καὶ θηρία ἐποίησε (made). ἔπειτα ὁρῶν (seeing) ὅτι τὰ θηρία πλείονά ἐστι, ἤλλαξέ (changed) τινα (some) εἰς ἀνθρώπους. διὰ δὲ τοῦτο ἔτι εἰσὶν οἳ τὰ μὲν σώματα ἀνθρώπων τὰς δὲ ψυχὰς θηρίων ἔχουσι. 9. Draco the Athenian Lawgiver. Δράκων, ὃς πολίτης ἦν ποτε (once) ἐν ταῖς Ἀθήναις, οὕτω σοφὸς καὶ δίκαιος ἦν ὥστε οἱ Ἀθηναῖοι ἤθελον αὐτὸν (him) νόμους νέους γράφειν. ἀλλὰ χαλεποὶ ἦσαν (were) οἱ νόμοι οὓς ἔγραψεν. ἦν γὰρ ἐν ἐκείνοις τοῖς νόμοις μία (one) ζημία (penalty), θάνατος. οἱ οὖν Ἀθηναῖοι ἔλεγον ὅτι οἱ Δράκοντος νόμοι οὐκ ἀνθρώπου ἦσαν ἀλλὰ δράκοντος.

Notes: 1. φάρμακον, medicine, cure (pharmacist). 3. εἰσι, are (3rd plural, present; Lesson 12). 6. ὅρκους, oaths. 9. δράκοντος, of a serpent.

VOCABULARY

θηρίον, -ου, τό, wild beast
στρατηγός, -οῦ, ὁ, general [strategic]
ὕδωρ, ὕδατος, τό, water [hydroplane]

ἐκεῖνος, -η, -ο, that, the former (of two)
ὅδε, ἥδε, τόδε, this, that
οὗτος, αὕτη, τοῦτο, this, the latter (of two)
πρῶτος, -η, -ον, first; πρῶτον (adverb), at first [protoplasm]

ἐθέλω, ἐθελήσω, ἠθέλησα, wish

ἔπειτα, then, next (conjunction)
ἔτι, still, yet
μᾶλλον, rather, more (comparative of μάλα, very); μᾶλλον . . . ἤ, rather . . . than

ENGLISH SENTENCES

1. They say that there is water in that city in which I wish to remain. 2. Draco thought that the men in Athens wished to have

34

harsh laws. And so he wrote them (αὐτούς). 3. The Greeks did not sacrifice wild beasts to the gods. 4. These generals wished to come into the cities of which they said they were rulers. 5. The old men did not plan to be harsh rather than just. 6. Draco was so noble that it is unjust to say that he was harsh.

REVIEW EXERCISES

I. Translate:

1. οὐδὲν τῆς ὑγιείας ἥδιόν ἐστιν. 2. ἡ δημοκρατία οὐ ῥᾴστη ἐστίν. 3. ἔφυγε δὲ ἡ ὅλη πόλις τὴν τυραννίδα. 4. ὁ οὖν στρατιώτης ἔλεξεν ὅτι τὸ παιδίον κρεῖττον ἦν ἢ ὁ πατήρ. 5. οὐδὲ ἡ ὁδὸς ἔτεινε ὑπὸ τὰ τείχη· ἔλεξεν δὲ ὁ νεανίας ὅτι ἄμεινόν ἐστι τῷ στρατεύματι χρόνον ἐλάττονα μεῖναι.

II. Write in Greek:

1. The army came as quickly as possible. 2. Very many soldiers remained the whole day in their tents. 3. Not even tyranny is stronger than a few just citizens. 4. The wise men said (use λέγω) that health is better than very many possessions. 5. The poets say that the stones of the earth are the fathers of men.

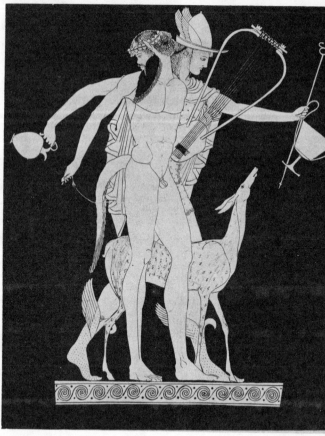

3   A SILEN, HERMES, AND A FAWN

In the Homeric epics the various city-states of Greece are all under kings, and monarchy lasted for centuries. Finally, not long after Delphi had begun its civilizing Apolline teaching, and after the Phoenicians had taught the Greeks their near-perfect alphabet, in most city-states the kings gave way to aristocrats.

The aristocrats carried further the civilizing processes. They enjoyed verse sung to the lyre, and they advanced to new forms, producing that fusion of literature and music which the Greeks called μουσική from the Μοῦσαι (Muses), who were generous in their interests, and inspiring.

The lidded vase above may serve as a symbol of Athens in the fifth century, when democracy was beginning to supplant aristocracy. With its elaborate contrast of the hesitant, snub-nosed, horse-tailed old silen and the dashing, aristocratic young god, the picture is almost too artful an antithesis. A more delicate fawn could not live.

The aristocrats, in their graceful cultivation of mind, hand, eye, and voice, demonstrated to the rest of Greece (and to us) the right balance by which discipline was rigorous without being harsh, and expression was free and strong without loss of precision and control.

INTERROGATIVE AND INDEFINITE PRONOUNS. ENCLITICS. DATIVE AND ACCUSATIVE OF RESPECT

1. The interrogative and indefinite pronouns are declined like nouns of the third declension and are similar in form. The indefinite generally loses its accent. The accent of the interrogative is always the acute over the first syllable; it is never changed to the grave accent.

2. Learn the declension of τίς, τί (interrogative), who? which? what?; and τις, τι (indefinite), anyone, anything, someone, a certain, a, an.

INTERROGATIVE

SINGULAR		PLURAL	
M, F	N	M, F	N
τίς	τί	τίνες	τίνα
τίνος (τοῦ)	τίνος (τοῦ)	τίνων	τίνων
τίνι (τῷ)	τίνι (τῷ)	τίσι	τίσι
τίνα	τί	τίνας	τίνα

INDEFINITE

SINGULAR		PLURAL	
M, F	N	M, F	N
τις	τι	τινές	τινά
τινός (του)	τινός (του)	τινῶν	τινῶν
τινί (τῳ)	τινί (τῳ)	τισί	τισί
τινά	τι	τινάς	τινά

3. The neuter singular accusative of the interrogative (τί) often means *why*?

4. The indefinite pronoun is an enclitic and is postpositive. An enclitic "leans back" upon the preceding word for its accent. The rules

for the accent of enclitics and the words preceding them are as follows:

(a) All monosyllabic enclitics lose their accent.
(b) Dissyllabic enclitics lose their accents except when a paroxytone precedes.
(c) An extra acute accent is added to the ultima of a proparoxytone or a properispomenon when either type of enclitic follows.
(d) An oxytone followed by an enclitic keeps its acute accent. A perispomenon keeps its circumflex.
(e) When two or more enclitics come together, the preceding enclitic or enclitics are normally accented like any other word, but the last of the series remains unaccented.
(f) When a proclitic precedes an enclitic it has an acute accent and the enclitic has none.

The following table will illustrate these rules (s = syllable, e = enclitic syllable):

ś s ś e or ee: ἄνθρωπός τις, ἄνθρωποί τινες
s ś s e but s ś s eê or eé: ἀνθρώπων τις, ἀνθρώπων τινῶν, ἀνθρώπου τινός
s s ś e or ee: ποταμός τις, ποταμοί τινες
ŝ ś e or ee: πλοῖόν τι, πλοῖά τινα
s ŝ e or ee: κωμῶν τις, κωμῶν τινων
ś e: οὔ τις
ś é é ee: εἴ τίς τί ποτε ἀκούει

5. An indefinite relative pronoun ὅστις, whoever, is formed by combining the relative and indefinite pronouns. The relative retains its normal accent, the indefinite has none, but the two are written as one word. It is also used as an indirect interrogative (Lesson 24).

M	F	N
	SINGULAR	
ὅστις	ἥτις	ὅ τι
οὗτινος or ὅτου	ἧστινος	οὗτινος or ὅτου
ᾧτινι or ὅτῳ	ᾗτινι	ᾧτινι or ὅτῳ
ὅντινα	ἥντινα	ὅ τι
	PLURAL	
οἵτινες	αἵτινες	ἅτινα
ὧντινων or ὅτων	ὧντινων	ὧντινων or ὅτων
οἷστισι or ὅτοις	αἷστισι	οἷστισι or ὅτοις
οὕστινας	ἅστινας	ἅτινα

6. Either the dative or the accusative may be used without a preposition to denote the respect in which some statement is true: a man still young in age, ἀνὴρ ἡλικίᾳ ἔτι νέος; swift-footed Achilles, πόδας ὠκὺς Ἀχιλλεύς.

READING

1. τίς ἄρα οὗτός ἐστιν, ὅτι καὶ ὁ ἄνεμος καὶ ἡ θάλαττα ὑπακούει αὐτῷ; St. Mark. 2. τί δέ τις; τί δ᾽ οὔ τις; σκιᾶς ὄναρ ἄνθρωπος.—PINDAR. 3. τί δ᾽ ἄλλο; φωνὴ καὶ σκιὰ γέρων ἀνήρ.—EURIPIDES. 4. ἔστι τις οὕτως ἄφρων ὅστις νομίζει θεοὺς οὐκ εἶναι;—SOCRATES. 5. τί λέγεις ἀρετὴν εἶναι; 6. τυφλὸς τά τ᾽ ὦτα τόν τε νοῦν τά τ᾽ ὄμματ᾽ εἶ.—SOPHO-CLES. 7. ἦν τις ἐν τῇ στρατιᾷ Ξενοφῶν Ἀθηναῖος, ὃς οὔτε στρατηγὸς οὔτε στρατιώτης ἦν.—XENOPHON. 8. Definition of a Ruler. Ἀθηναῖός τις ἠρώτησέ (asked) ποτε τὸν Περικλέα, "ὦ Περίκλεις," ἔφη, "τί ἐστι τὸ πρῶτον ὃ τὸν ἄρχοντα δεῖ ἐν νῷ ἔχειν;" ὁ δὲ ἔφη, "ὅτι ἄνθρωπός ἐστι." "τί δ᾽ ἐστὶ τὸ δεύτερον;" "ὅτι καὶ δεῖ ἄρχειν καλῶς καὶ δικαίως." τέλος δ᾽ ὁ ἀνὴρ ἔλεγε, "τί ἐστι τὸ τρίτον;" καὶ Περικλῆς ἔφη "ὅτι οὐκ ἀεὶ ἄρξει."

Notes: 1. ὑπακούω, heed (+ dative) (cf. ἀκούω, hear [acoustics]); αὐτῷ, him. 2. σκιά, shadow; ὄναρ, dream. 3. φωνή, voice [telephone]; ἄλλο, else. γέρων here is an adjective. 4. ἄφρων, senseless (ἀ + φρήν, mind). 6. τυφλός, blind; ὦτα, accusative plural of οὖς, ὠτός, ear; ὄμμα, -ατος, eye; εἶ, you are (Lesson 12). 8. ὁ δέ refers usually to someone mentioned in the preceding sentence other than the subject.

VOCABULARY

ἀρετή, -ῆς, ἡ, virtue, goodness, excellence
νοῦς, νοῦ, νῷ, νοῦν, νοῦ, ὁ, mind (contracted from νόος)
στρατιά, -ᾶς, ἡ, army (cf. στράτευμα)
τέλος, -ους, τό, end; as adverb, τέλος (accusative) = finally [teleology]

δεύτερος, -α, -ον, second [Deuteronomy]
τίς, τί, who? what? (interrogative)
τις, τι (indefinite), anyone, a (an), someone, a certain, a man
ὅστις, ἥτις, ὅ τι, whoever

ἄρχω, ἄρξω, ἦρξα, rule; often in middle voice (Lesson 25), begin (+ gen.)
δεῖ, it is necessary (impersonal, found also in imperfect ἔδει and infinitive δεῖν). Takes accusative and infinitive

ἄρα, therefore (postpositive)
οὔτε, neither (often correlated with another οὔτε)
ποτέ (enclitic, postpositive), at one time, some time
τε (enclitic, postpositive), and; correlated with another τε, both . . . and
ὦ, O, with vocative. Not translated in English

ENGLISH SENTENCES

1. Who was leading the army into that city? 2. Is there anyone who does not ask (ἐρωτᾷ) what (use form of ὅστις) a ruler ought to keep in mind? 3. What do you think a wise man is? 4. A certain man planned to sacrifice to the gods. 5. Who is so wicked that (ὥστε) he does not at some time speak the truth? 6. It is therefore necessary to think that virtue is the best end in a man's life.

REVIEW EXERCISES

I. For practice in the accentuation of enclitics, decline the following with the indefinite pronoun used as adjective:

ἄνθρωπος   δῶρον   στρατηγός   κλώψ

II. Translate:

1. τοῦτο τὸ θηρίον μᾶλλον κακὸν ἢ καλόν ἐστι. 2. ἐκεῖνον τὸν στρατηγὸν πρῶτον ἔπεμψαν οἱ Ἀθηναῖοι μετὰ τῶν στρατιωτῶν εἰς τὸν πόλεμον. 3. ἔπειτα ἔφερε ὁ παῖς τὸ ὕδωρ τῇ μητρί. 4. οἵδε οἱ νέοι οὐκ ἐθέλουσι πιστεύειν ἐκείνῃ τῇ γυναικί. 5. ἔτι γράφει ὁ δικαστὴς τὴν γνώμην.

III. Write in Greek:

1. These things (use neuter plural of the demonstrative) he will send in addition to those. 2. Out of the city they drove the women and children. 3. On account of that opinion, the citizens will not trust the judges. 4. Boy, the soldier sent the gift. 5. On that day, the rulers of the city will sacrifice to the divinities of the earth and of the sea and of the sky.

THE VERB εἰμί.
THE PRONOUN αὐτός

1. Besides the verbs like παιδεύω, there are a few important verbs whose first person singular present indicative ends in -μι and which for that reason are called μι-verbs or nonthematic verbs, because they contain no thematic vowel. The μι-verbs differ from the ω-verbs in the present, imperfect, and second aorist tenses; otherwise they are similar in inflection to ω-verbs. The μι-verbs fall into three principal classes:

   (a) The *Root* class, in which the personal endings are added directly to the root. Verbs of this type are all irregular and will be presented as they are needed.

   (b) *Reduplicating Present* class, in which the initial consonant is reduplicated with iota (e.g., stem δο-, present δίδωμι).

   (c) The *νυμι*-class, in which the formant -νυ- occurs between the stem and the ending (e.g., δείκ-νυ-μι). This class regularly has a first aorist rather than a second aorist.

2. Learn the following forms of εἰμί, I am (Root class):

Present Indicative	Imperfect Indicative
εἰμί *I am,*	ἦν or ἦ *I was,*
εἶ etc.	ἦσθα etc.
ἐστί(ν)	ἦν
ἐσμέν	ἦμεν
ἐστέ	ἦτε
εἰσί(ν)	ἦσαν

Present Infinitive
εἶναι

3. In the present all indicative forms are enclitic except the second singular. The infinitive is not enclitic.

4. Infinitives in -ναι are regularly accented on the penult.

5. The intensive pronoun αὐτός is declined as follows:

| | SINGULAR | | | PLURAL | |
M	F	N	M	F	N
αὐτός	αὐτή	αὐτό	αὐτοί	αὐταί	αὐτά
αὐτοῦ	αὐτῆς	αὐτοῦ	αὐτῶν	αὐτῶν	αὐτῶν
αὐτῷ	αὐτῇ	αὐτῷ	αὐτοῖς	αὐταῖς	αὐτοῖς
αὐτόν	αὐτήν	αὐτό	αὐτούς	αὐτάς	αὐτά

6. αὐτός has three meanings:

(a) As an intensive pronoun and as an adjective in the predicate position it means *self*, as, αὐτὸς ἔφη, he himself said; εἶδεν τὴν μητέρα αὐτήν, he saw the mother herself; cf. French "le jour même."

(b) Used as an adjective in the attributive position it means *same*, as, we saw the same man, εἴδομεν τὸν αὐτὸν ἄνδρα; cf. French "le même jour."

(c) Used in the oblique cases (i.e., all but the nominative and vocative) it serves as the commonest form of the pronoun of the third person, as, he saw them, εἶδεν αὐτούς; he saw their friends, εἶδεν τοὺς φίλους αὐτῶν.

Learn the following sentence illustrating the three uses: τῇ αὐτῇ ἡμέρᾳ Κῦρος αὐτὸς εἶδεν αὐτούς, on the same day Cyrus himself saw them.

7. Observe that the forms of αὐτός always begin with αὐ and that the accent is always on the last syllable (genitives and datives circumflexed). This will help to distinguish it from οὗτος.

8. The possessive genitive of personal pronouns and partitive genitives occupy the predicate position. ὁ φίλος αὐτοῦ, his friend. οἱ πλεῖστοι τῶν πολιτῶν, most of the citizens.

The possessive genitive of nouns usually occupies the attributive position. ὁ τοῦ σοφιστοῦ φίλος, the professor's friend.

9. ἔστι is often used impersonally in the sense of "it is possible," or "it is allowed," and when so used is followed by the infinitive. ἔστι used without an infinitive stresses the existence of its subject; it is not enclitic.

42

READING

1. ἔστιν ὁ μὲν χείρων ὁ δ' ἀμείνων ἔργον ἕκαστον, / οὐδεὶς δ' ἀνθρώπων αὐτὸς ἅπαντα σοφός. 2. τὸ τῆς Σφιγγὸς αἴνιγμα ἦν τόδε, "τί ἐστι τὸ αὐτὸ τετράπουν καὶ δίπουν καὶ τρίπουν;" 3. τί ἐστι φίλος; ἄλλος ἐγώ. 4. οὐκ ἔστιν οὐδὲν ἀνθρώπῳ χωρὶς θεῶν. 5. τοῖς τῶν αὐτῶν γονέων παισὶ πολλάκις οὐχ οἱ αὐτοὶ τρόποι εἰσίν. 6. εἰρήνη γεωργὸν κἂν πέτραις τρέφει καλῶς, πόλεμος δὲ κἂν πεδίῳ κακῶς. 7. The Two Packs. ἕκαστος ἄνθρωπος δύο πήρας (packs) φέρει, τὴν μὲν ἔμπροσθεν, τὴν δ' ὄπισθεν. καὶ ἑκατέρα κακῶν (faults) μεστή (full) ἐστι. ἡ δὲ ἔμπροσθεν τὰ ἀλλότρια (others') κακὰ φέρει, ἡ δὲ ἑτέρα τὰ αὐτοῦ τοῦ ἀνδρός. διὰ τοῦτο οἱ ἄνθρωποι τὰ ἑαυτῶν (their own) κακὰ οὐχ ὁρῶσι (see), τὰ δὲ ἀλλότρια πάνυ ἀκριβῶς (very keenly) θεῶνται (see).

Notes: 1. ὁ μὲν, see Lesson 3, paragraph 11; ἔργον, accusative of respect; ἅπαντα, in all respects (accusative). 2. Σφιγγός, genitive of Σφίγξ; αἴνιγμα, riddle [enigma]; τετράπουν, four-footed. 3. ἐγώ, I. 4. χωρίς, apart from (adverb with genitive). 5. γονέων, genitive of γονεύς, parent; παισί, dative of possession. 6. γεωργός, farmer [George]; κἂν = καὶ ἐν (crasis).

VOCABULARY

εἰρήνη, -ης, ἡ, peace [Irene]
πεδίον, -ου, τό, plain
πέτρα, -ας, ἡ, rock [Peter, petrify]
τρόπος, -ου, ὁ, character, way, characteristic

ἄλλος, -η, -ο, other, another (declined like αὐτός)
αὐτός, -ή, -ό, self, same, 3rd person pronoun
δύο, two (nominative and accusative)
ἕκαστος, -η, -ον, each (of any number)　} take predicate
ἑκάτερος, -α, -ον, each (of two), both, either } position
ἕτερος, -α, -ον, the other; other (of two) [heterodox]
οὐδείς, no one (for declension, see Lesson 37)

εἶδον, I saw (2nd aorist; infinitive = ἰδεῖν)
εἰμί, be
τρέφω, θρέψω, ἔθρεψα, nourish, care for, rear

ἔμπροσθεν, in front, earlier (adverb)
ὄπισθεν, behind, later (adverb)

ENGLISH SENTENCES

1. The children of the same parents often have (use ἔχω) the same characteristics. 2. You saw once the same men in that city. 3. You thought that those·men were friends. 4. The friend of the ruler himself was in that same plain on which were very large rocks. 5. Who

43

says that the gods did not care for each man well? 6. The character of the other ruler (of the two) was neither noble nor just.

REVIEW EXERCISES

I. Translate:

1. τίς ἄρα ἦλθε μετὰ τούτου τοῦ γέροντος ἐκείνῃ τῇ ἡμέρᾳ; 2. ἔκριναν οἱ δικασταὶ τὸν Ἀθηναῖον οὐ κλῶπα εἶναι. 3. δῶρά τε ἔπεμψε ὁ βασιλεὺς τῷ στρατιώτῃ ὅστις τὴν ἀσπίδα ἤνεγκε. 4. ἐκεῖνος ὁ πολίτης τὸ μὲν σῶμα καλός, τὴν δὲ ψυχὴν πονηρός ἐστι. 5. οὔτε ὁ πατὴρ οὔτε ὁ παῖς ἦλθέ ποτε εἰς τὴν πόλιν.

II. Write in Greek:

1. The excellence of the king's army was very great. 2. In the end, a fair mind is better than a fair body. 3. Whoever came second was inferior. 4. Who shall rule the city of the Athenians? 5. It is therefore necessary that someone write to the boy's father within ten days.

LESSON **13**

MI-VERBS: PRESENT, IMPERFECT, AND FIRST AND SECOND AORIST INDICATIVE ACTIVE OF ἴστημι AND δίδωμι. COMPOUND VERBS

1. As previously explained (Lesson 12), verbs of this class reduplicate the initial consonant of the stem with iota in the present system (present and imperfect tenses). In these tenses the stem vowel is long in the singular and short in the plural. The characteristic personal endings of the μι-inflection are then added directly to the stem. These endings are, for primary tenses: -μι, -ς, -σι, -μεν, -τε, -ασι; for the secondary tenses: -ν, -ς, —, -μεν, -τε, -σαν.

2. Learn the following forms of ἴστημι, to make stand; stem στα:[1]

PRESENT		IMPERFECT	
ἴστημι	*I make stand,*	ἴστην	*I was making stand,*
ἴστης	*etc.*	ἴστης	*etc.*
ἴστησι		ἴστη	
ἴσταμεν		ἴσταμεν	
ἴστατε		ἴστατε	
ἰστᾶσι		ἴστασαν	

PRESENT INFINITIVE: ἰστάναι

SECOND AORIST[2]		FIRST AORIST[2]	
ἔστην	*I stood,*	ἔστησα	*I made stand,*
ἔστης	*etc.*	ἔστησας	*etc.*
ἔστη		ἔστησε	
ἔστημεν		ἐστήσαμεν	
ἔστητε		ἐστήσατε	
ἔστησαν		ἔστησαν	

SECOND AORIST INFINITIVE: στῆναι

FIRST AORIST INFINITIVE: στῆσαι

[1] ἴστημι was originally σίστημι; cf. Latin *sisto*. In Greek an original initial sigma frequently disappears, giving rise to the rough breathing.

[2] The second aorist of ἴστημι is intransitive in meaning; the first aorist has transitive meanings.

45

3. Observe that in the present and imperfect of this verb η is found in the singular, α in the plural.

4. Learn the following forms of δίδωμι, I give:

PRESENT	IMPERFECT	SECOND AORIST
δίδωμι *I give,*	ἐδίδουν *I was giving,*	ἔδωκα[3] *I gave,*
δίδως *etc.*	ἐδίδους *etc.*	ἔδωκας *etc.*
δίδωσι	ἐδίδου	ἔδωκε
δίδομεν	ἐδίδομεν	ἔδομεν
δίδοτε	ἐδίδοτε	ἔδοτε
διδόασι	ἐδίδοσαν	ἔδοσαν

INFINITIVES

διδόναι   δοῦναι

5. The future of μι-verbs is like that of ω-verbs; e.g., στήσω, δώσω.

6. In the following sentences appear some compound verbs, formed by prefixing one or more prepositions to a simple verb. A number of important rules concerning the formation and orthography of such compounds follow:

(a) When a preposition ending in a vowel is prefixed to a verb beginning in a vowel, the final vowel of the preposition is omitted, e.g., ἀπό + ἄγω = ἀπάγω.[4]

(b) If the verb has a rough breathing and the consonant before the elided vowel of the preposition is a mute, the mute must be changed to the aspirated form of its class, e.g., ἐπί + ἵημι = ἐφίημι.

(c) The letter ν is subject to several changes:

Before a labial mute or μ, ν becomes μ, e.g., σύν + πέμπω = συμπέμπω; σύν + μάχομαι = συμμάχομαι.

Before a palatal mute ν becomes γ, e.g., ἐν + γράφω = ἐγγράφω.

Before λ, ν becomes λ, e.g., σύν + λαμβάνω = συλλαμβάνω.

Before σ and ζ, ν drops, e.g., σύν + στρατεύω = συστρατεύω.

(d) Compound verbs are augmented after the prepositional element, and elision occurs before the augment, e.g.,

---

[3] The second aorist singular endings of δίδωμι and those of τίθημι and ἵημι in Lesson 14 are irregular.

[4] περί and πρό are exceptions to this rule.

46

ἀποδίδωμι, ἀπέδωκα; ἀποπέμπω, ἀπέπεμψα. Consonants changed to fit the laws of euphony go back to their original form before the augment, e.g., συμπέμπω, συνέπεμψα.

(e) The accent of a compound verb can never recede beyond the augment, e.g., ἀπάγω, ἀπῆγον. Infinitives and participles retain the accent of the uncompounded forms, e.g., ἀπαγαγεῖν, ἀπάγον.

READING

1. ἐνταῦθα οὖν ἔστησαν οἱ Ἕλληνες. 2. τότε δὲ ἀπέστησαν πρὸς Κῦρον αἱ πόλεις πλὴν Μιλήτου. 3. ὅστις ἄνδρα φίλον μὴ προδίδωσιν, μεγάλην ἔχει τιμὴν ἔν τε βροτοῖς ἔν τε θεοῖσιν κατ' ἐμὸν νόον.—ATTIC SCOLION. 4. ἡ μωρία δίδωσιν ἀνθρώποις κακά. 5. λέγουσιν ὅτι, ἐν ταύτῃ τῇ μάχῃ, τῶν στρατιωτῶν οἱ μὲν ἔφευγον πρὸς τὸ στρατόπεδον, οἱ δὲ ἐνόμιζον αἰσχρὸν εἶναι φυγεῖν. ἀλλὰ ἄλλος ἄλλο λέγει· ἐγὼ (I) δὲ οὐ πιστεύω τοῖς τῶν πολιτῶν λόγοις. 6. ποιητής τις λέγει ὅτι οἱ θεοί, ἐπειδὴ ἐποίησαν (made) τὰ ζῷα (living creatures), ἔδοσαν ἑκάστῳ γέρας τι (a gift). καὶ τοῖς ταύροις (bulls) κέρα (horns) ἔδοσαν, τοῖς δὲ ὄρνισι (birds) πτέρυγας (wings) καὶ τοῖς ἄλλοις ἄλλο τι τοιοῦτον. ἀνθρώποις (humans) δὲ οὐδὲν τοιοῦτον ἔδοσαν, ἀλλὰ τοῖς μὲν ἀνδράσι ἀρετήν, ταῖς δὲ γυναιξὶ κάλλος (beauty). διὰ δὲ ταῦτα ἡ γυνὴ πάντων (of all) κρατίστη ἐστί. οἱ γὰρ ἄνδρες βελτίονές εἰσι τῇ ἀρετῇ. αἱ δὲ γυναῖκες νικῶσι (conquer) τοὺς ἄνδρας τῷ κάλλει.

Notes: 2. ἀφίστημι, go over to; Κῦρον, Cyrus; Μιλήτου, Miletus, a Greek city in Asia Minor. 3. μεγάλην, great; βροτοῖς, mortals; θεοῖσιν = θεοῖς; κατ' ἐμὸν νόον, according to my mind, in my opinion. 4. μωρία, folly [moron, sophomore]. 5. ἄλλος ἄλλο λέγει, one says one thing, another another.

VOCABULARY

μάχη, -ης, ἡ, battle [logomachy]
στρατόπεδον, -ου, τό, camp
τιμή, -ῆς, ἡ, esteem, honor [timocracy]

αἰσχρός, -ά, -όν, disgraceful
τοιοῦτος, τοιαύτη, τοιοῦτο or τοιοῦτον, such

δίδωμι, δώσω, ἔδωκα, give
ἵστημι, στήσω, ἔστησα and ἔστην, stand, set, establish
προδίδωμι, betray
φεύγω, 2nd aorist ἔφυγον, flee

ἐνταῦθα (adverb), here, there

47

ἐπεί, ἐπειδή, when, since, after

πλήν (preposition with genitive), except

πρός, preposition with genitive, from; with dative, near; with accusative, to, against

τότε (adverb), then

ENGLISH SENTENCES

1. The Greeks in Miletus did not revolt, since the king gave them gifts. 2. The general then halted his soldiers near that wall and wished them to remain there. 3. It is folly to betray friends. 4. They said that the poets fled shamefully from that battle. 5. It was never disgraceful to give such a gift to a king. 6. Those who betray their friends do not have honor among the Greeks.

REVIEW EXERCISES

I. Translate:

1. ἔφη ἐν μὲν τῇ θαλάττῃ εἰρήνην εἶναι, ἐν δὲ τῇ πόλει οὔ. 2. ἔμπροσθεν μὲν τὴν θάλατταν εἴδομεν, ὄπισθεν δὲ ἐν τῷ πεδίῳ πέτρας μεγίστας. 3. τί τοὺς ἐκείνου τοῦ παιδὸς τρόπους ἰδεῖν ἠθέλετε; 4. δύο ἵπποι εἰσί· τοῦτον μὲν ἄξομεν, τὸν δὲ ἕτερον τῇ μητρὶ λείψομεν, αὐτὴ γὰρ ἔθρεψεν αὐτόν. 5. οὐδείς ἐστιν οὕτω πονηρὸς τοῖς τρόποις ὥστε μὴ ἐθέλειν φίλους ἔχειν.

II. Write in Greek:

1. Each child bore a gift for his father. 2. These men wish to have peace; the others are planning to go to the wars. 3. We did not think he was wicked, but the judges say that his ways are very bad. 4. Who reared the children of that king? 5. Whoever was in the tent, he was not the thief.

MI-VERBS: PRESENT, IMPERFECT, AND SECOND AORIST INDICATIVE ACTIVE OF τίθημι, ἵημι. PRESENT AND IMPERFECT OF δείκνυμι

1. Learn the following forms of τίθημι, to place; stem, -θε, -θη:[1]

PRESENT	IMPERFECT	SECOND AORIST
τίθημι *I place,*	ἐτίθην *I was placing,*	ἔθηκα[2] *I placed,*
τίθης *etc.*	ἐτίθεις *etc.*	ἔθηκας *etc.*
τίθησι	ἐτίθει	ἔθηκε
τίθεμεν	ἐτίθεμεν	ἔθεμεν
τίθετε	ἐτίθετε	ἔθετε
τιθέασι	ἐτίθεσαν	ἔθεσαν

INFINITIVES

τιθέναι	θεῖναι

2. Learn the following forms of ἵημι, to hurl; stem, ἑ, or ἡ:[1]

PRESENT	IMPERFECT	SECOND AORIST
ἵημι *I hurl,*	ἵην *I was hurling,*	ἧκα[2] *I hurled,*
ἵης *etc.*	ἵεις *etc.*	ἧκας *etc.*
ἵησι	ἵει	ἧκε
ἵεμεν	ἵεμεν	-εἷμεν[3]
ἵετε	ἵετε	-εἷτε
ἱᾶσι	ἵεσαν	-εἷσαν

INFINITIVES

ἱέναι	εἷναι

[1] The original form of τίθημι was θίθημι; that of ἵημι is uncertain. It may be cognate with Latin *iacio.*

[2] The endings in the second aorist singular of τίθημι and ἵημι are irregular.

[3] A hyphen before a form denotes that the form is found only in compounds.

3. Learn the present and imperfect of δείκνυμι. This verb has a regular first aorist, ἔδειξα. Notice that the formant νυ occurs in the present and imperfect only, between the ending and the stem.

PRESENT		IMPERFECT	
δείκνυμι	δείκνυμεν	ἐδείκνυν	ἐδείκνυμεν
δείκνυς	δείκνυτε	ἐδείκνυς	ἐδείκνυτε
δείκνυσι	δεικνύασι	ἐδείκνυ	ἐδείκνυσαν

INFINITIVE
δεικνύναι

READING

1. τὰ δὲ χρήματα ταῦτα κατετίθην. 2. Μίνως τοῖς Κρησὶ νόμους ἔθηκε καὶ ἔλεγεν ὅτι παρὰ Διὸς τοῦ πατρὸς ἔλαβεν αὐτούς. 3. ὁ ἥλιος ἐντίθησι τῇ σελήνῃ τὸ λαμπρόν. 4. Ὦτος καὶ Ἐφιάλτης, οἱ δύο παῖδες τοῦ Ποσειδῶνος, τὴν μὲν Ὄσσαν ἐπὶ τὸν Ὄλυμπον, ἐπὶ δὲ τὴν Ὄσσαν τὸ Πήλιον ἔθεσαν. οὕτω γὰρ ἐνόμιζον εἰς οὐρανὸν ἀναβήσεσθαι (would go up). — APOLLODORUS. 5. ἐπεὶ δὲ εἶδον ἀλλήλους, οἱ Ἕλληνες ἵεσαν τοὺς λίθους. 6. χρόνος δίκαιον ἄνδρα δείκνυσιν μόνος.—SOPHOCLES. 7. οἱ ποιηταὶ ἐπιδεικνύασι τὰ τῶν παλαιῶν ἀνδρῶν ἔργα καὶ πράξεις θαυμαστὰς καὶ λόγους. 8. τῶν Ἑλληνικῶν πόλεων ἡ πόλις τῶν Ἀθηναίων πρώτη νόμους ἐτίθει. 9. ὅπερ ἔδει δεῖξαι (Q. E. D.) — EUCLID. 10. The First Anabasis of Cyrus the Younger. Δαρείου (Darius) καὶ Παρυσάτιδος (Parýsatis) γίγνονται (were born) παῖδες δύο, πρεσβύτερος μὲν Ἀρταξέρξης, νεώτερος δὲ Κῦρος. ἐπειδὴ δὲ Δαρεῖος ὑπώπτευε (suspected) τὴν τελευτὴν (end, cf. τέλος) τοῦ βίου παρεῖναι, ἤθελε τοὺς παῖδας ἰδεῖν. Ἀρταξέρξης μὲν οὖν παρῆν. ἄγγελον δὲ ἔπεμψεν ὁ βασιλεὺς τῷ Κύρῳ ὃς ἔμενεν ἐν τῇ ἀρχῇ ἧς σατράπης (satrap) ἦν. — XENOPHON, Anabasis 1.1 (adapted).

Notes: 2. Μίνως, Minos, legendary king of Crete; Κρησί, dative of Κρῆτες, Cretans; Διός, genitive of Ζεύς, Zeus. 3. ἐντίθησι, from ἐν + τίθημι; σελήνη, moon; λαμπρόν, brightness [lamp]. 4. Ὄσσα, Πήλιον, and Ὄλυμπος are mountains in northern Greece. 7. πράξεις, deeds (declined like πόλις; cf. πράττω). 8. πρώτη: when πρῶτος is used as a predicate adjective, translate "(was) the first (to)." The adverb "first" is πρῶτον. 10. Δαρείου, Παρυσάτιδος are genitives of source; πρεσβύτερος (adjective), elder.

VOCABULARY

ἄγγελος -ου, ὁ, messenger [angel]
ἀρχή, -ῆς, ἡ, province, rule; beginning (cf. ἄρχω)

ἀλλήλων, -οις, -ους, etc. (only in plural), each other [parallel]
Ἑλληνικός, -ή, -όν, Greek

θαυμαστός, -ή, -όν, marvelous [thaumaturgy]
παλαιός, -ά, -όν, ancient [palaeolithic]

δείκνυμι, δείξω, ἔδειξα, show
ἐπιδείκνυμι, show forth, reveal
ἵημι, ἥσω, ἧκα (-εῖμεν), throw, send, hurl
κατατίθημι, pay down, deposit
λαμβάνω, second aorist, ἔλαβον, take, get
πάρειμι (παρά, by side of, + εἰμί), be present
τίθημι, θήσω, ἔθηκα (ἔθεμεν), place, establish

παρά, preposition with genitive, from; with dative, beside; with accusative, to
-περ, often attached to a relative word, means *exactly, the very*, e.g., ὅσπερ, the very one who

ENGLISH SENTENCES

1. We shall pay down that money here; and so no one will say that you took it. 2. The elder son of Darius was king. 3. They inscribed these matters (neuter) on the stones which they took from the king. 4. They were the first to establish laws for the Greeks; and so they got honor. 5. The ancients never betrayed each other. 6. Their friends are the very ones who gave such good things.

REVIEW EXERCISES

I. Translate:

1. οἱ στρατιῶται οἱ ἐν τῷ στρατοπέδῳ οὐκ ἐδίδοσαν τιμὴν τῷ στρατηγῷ. 2. τί οὐκ ἔστη τότε ἡ τῶν Ἑλλήνων στρατιὰ ἐν ἐκείνῃ τῇ μάχῃ; αἰσχρὸν γὰρ ἦν τοὺς ἄλλους προδοῦναι. 3. ἐνταῦθα οὖν ἔφυγε ὁ τοῦ ἄρχοντος παῖς. 4. πρὸς τῷ τείχει ὁ στρατηγὸς ἔστησε τοὺς Ἕλληνας πλὴν τῶν Ἀθηναίων. 5. οἵ τε κακοὶ οἵ τε ἀγαθοὶ ἔφευγον πρὸς τὴν πόλιν.

II. Write in Greek:

1. Who gave such gifts to that harsh woman? 2. Men do not establish a common measure of the beautiful. 3. Such was the opinion of the army which was with the general. 4. Calmness is the best gift which the gods give to the souls of the wise. 5. After the attempt, the army did not wish to remain beneath the walls of the city.

CONTRACT VERBS: τιμάω
AND φιλέω

1. Three groups of verbs in Greek are known as contract verbs. In each of these groups the stem of the verb ends in a vowel which contracts with the personal endings in the present and imperfect tenses. Elsewhere these verbs are regular, save that the final α or ε of the stem is lengthened to η, final ο to ω, in other tenses. The commonest classes are those of verbs having stems ending in -α or -ε. Verbs with -ο stems will be discussed in the following lesson.

2. Contract verbs are extremely regular in their obedience to the rules which govern their contraction. It will repay the student to learn these rules thoroughly, as from them he can construct the contracted forms.

(a) For α-verbs:
    1. Iota of the personal endings, or of the modal sign (Lesson 23), is written as subscript.
    2. α plus any ο sound gives ω(ῳ). An ο prevails over any other sound.
    3. α plus any ε sound gives α (ᾳ).

(b) For ε-verbs:
    1. ε plus ε becomes ει.
    2. ε plus ο becomes ου.
    3. ε before a long vowel or a diphthong is absorbed.[1]

3. In contract verbs, the contracted syllable is accented if either of its components in the uncontracted form was accented. It has a

---

[1] Verbs of two syllables in έω (e.g., πλέω, sail; δέω, want) contract only when the contraction gives ει; otherwise they remain uncontracted.

circumflex if the first of its components had an acute accent, an acute if the second of its components had the acute.

4. For convenience in analyzing the changes in vowels according to the principles of contraction, the following paradigms, consisting of contracted and uncontracted forms, are given (τιμάω, to honor, and φιλέω, to love):

PRESENT		IMPERFECT	
τιμῶ	(τιμάω)	ἐτίμων	(ἐτίμαον)
τιμᾷς	(τιμάεις)	ἐτίμας	(ἐτίμαες)
τιμᾷ	(τιμάει)	ἐτίμα	(ἐτίμαε)
τιμῶμεν	(τιμάομεν)	ἐτιμῶμεν	(ἐτιμάομεν)
τιμᾶτε	(τιμάετε)	ἐτιμᾶτε	(ἐτιμάετε)
τιμῶσι	(τιμάουσι)	ἐτίμων	(ἐτίμαον)

INFINITIVE

τιμᾶν   (τιμάειν)[2]

PRESENT		IMPERFECT	
φιλῶ	(φιλέω)	ἐφίλουν	(ἐφίλεον)
φιλεῖς	(φιλέεις)	ἐφίλεις	(ἐφίλεες)
φιλεῖ	(φιλέει)	ἐφίλει	(ἐφίλεε)
φιλοῦμεν	(φιλέομεν)	ἐφιλοῦμεν	(ἐφιλέομεν)
φιλεῖτε	(φιλέετε)	ἐφιλεῖτε	(ἐφιλέετε)
φιλοῦσι	(φιλέουσι)	ἐφίλουν	(ἐφίλεον)

INFINITIVE

φιλεῖν   (φιλέειν)

READING

A.[3] τίμα τὸν πατέρα σου καὶ τὴν μητέρα σου. — OLD TESTAMENT.

B. ἄλλον τρόπον | ἄλλων ἐγείρει φροντὶς ἀνθρώπων.—FRAGMENTA MELICA ADESPOTA.

1. χαλεπὸν τὸ ποιεῖν, τὸ δὲ κελεῦσαι ῥᾴδιον. 2. οὐ γὰρ δοκεῖν ἄριστος, ἀλλ' εἶναι θέλει. — AESCHYLUS. 3. ὃν οἱ θεοὶ φιλοῦσιν ἀποθνῄσκει νέος. 4. βέλτιόν ἐστι σῶμά γ' ἢ ψυχὴν νοσεῖν. 5. ὀργὴν ἑταίρου καὶ φίλου πειρῶ φέρειν. 6. τῶν φιλοσόφων ἔργον ἐστὶν εἰδέναι τί μὲν βλαβερὸν τί

[2] Properly speaking, the -ειν of the infinitive represented an original ε + εν. Therefore, τιμᾶν = τιμα + ε + εν and there is no iota. So it is τιμᾶν, not τιμᾷν.

[3] Beginning with this lesson sentences designated by A, B, C, and so on, have been included with a view to class discussion. They should be read in class with the instructor. New words found in them are not placed in the lesson vocabularies, but will be found in the general vocabulary.

δὲ ὠφέλιμον ἀνθρώποις. 7. Θεμιστοκλῆς ἐνόμισεν αὐτοὺς τοὺς θεοὺς κωλῦσαι τὸν Ξέρξην τοῦ βασιλεῦσαι καὶ τῆς Ἀσίας καὶ τῆς Εὐρώπης. 8. The North Wind and the Sun. ὁ Βορέας ποτὲ καὶ ὁ ἥλιος ἤριζον (contested) ὁπότερός ἐστι κρείττων. ἰδὼν (seeing) δὲ ἄνθρωπον ἔχοντα (having) ἱμάτιον (cloak), ἔφη ὁ ἥλιος, "τί μάτην (vainly) λέγομεν; ὁρᾷς τὸν ἄνδρα ἐκεῖνον· ὁπότερος ἂν οὖν ἡμῶν (of us) δύνηται (is able) ἐκδῦσαι (to take off) τὸ ἱμάτιον, οὗτος νικήσει." ὁ δὲ ἕτερος ἐπὶ τούτοις ὡμολόγησε (agreed). πρῶτον μὲν οὖν ὁ Βορέας ἔπνευσε (blew), ὁ δὲ ἀνὴρ ἑαυτὸν (himself) τῷ ἱματίῳ ἐκάλυπτε (covered). ἔπειτα δὲ ὁ ἥλιος ἐξῆλθεν (came out). τέλος δὲ ὁ ἀνήρ, θερμὸς (hot) ὤν (being), τὸ ἱμάτιον ἀπέρριψε (threw off).

Notes: 1. τὸ ποιεῖν, "articular infinitive": infinitive with neuter article, used as a substantive in any case, like English gerund. 2. θέλω = ἐθέλω. 4. σῶμα, ψυχήν are accusative of respect; γε (enclitic, postpositive) at least. 5. πειρῶ, try (imperative, 2nd singular). 6. φιλοσόφων, philosophers; εἰδέναι, to know (infinitive); βλαβερόν, harmful; ὠφέλιμον, helpful. 7. Θεμιστοκλῆς, Athenian statesman; κωλύω, prevent, + genitive; τοῦ βασιλεῦσαι, articular infinitive in genitive case; Ἀσίας καὶ Εὐρώπης, Asia and Europe, genitive with verb meaning "rule." 8. ἂν δύνηται (subjunctive) explained in Lesson 22.

VOCABULARY

ἑταῖρος, -ου, ὁ, companion

ὁπότερος, -α, -ον, which (of two)
ῥᾴδιος, -α, -ον, easy

ἀποθνήσκω, 2nd aorist ἀπέθανον, die
βασιλεύω, -σω, ἐβασίλευσα, be king (cf. βασιλεύς)
δοκέω, δόξω, ἔδοξα, seem; 3rd singular, seem best (impersonal) [het- erodox]; think
ἐρωτάω, -ήσω, ἠρώτησα, ask a question
κελεύω, -σω, ἐκέλευσα, order, urge (takes complementary infinitive)
νικάω, -ήσω, ἐνίκησα, conquer, win
νοσέω, be ill
ὁράω, aorist εἶδον, see (imperfect ἑώρων)
ποιέω, -ήσω, ἐποίησα, do, act, make; with two accusatives, do something to someone
τιμάω, -ήσω, ἐτίμησα, honor
φιλέω, love

ENGLISH SENTENCES

1. The gods themselves will order Xerxes to send (infinitive) soldiers. 2. Philosophers point out to men what is harmful to them.

54

3. It is easy to seem to be best, but difficult to be (so). 4. The companions finally asked them (accusative) which of the two seemed swifter. 5. It is not easy to see who came. 6. The mother orders, the father acts.

REVIEW EXERCISES

I. Translate:

1. ὁ ἄγγελος ἔδειξεν ἐκεῖνα τὰ θαυμαστὰ ἃ ἔλαβον οἱ στρατιῶται. 2. κατέθεσαν οἱ πολῖται τὰ χρήματα ἀλλήλοις. 3. ἐπεὶ εἰς τὴν πόλιν ἦλθον ἣ παλαιοτάτη τῆς ἀρχῆς ἦν, πῦρ ἵεσαν εἰς τὰς οἰκίας (houses). 4. οὐ λέξεις ὅστις παρῆν καὶ ἔδειξε τῷ ἄρχοντι τὰ δῶρα; 5. οἱ πολῖται οἱ παρὰ τῷ βασιλεῖ εἰσιν οἵπερ τιθέασι τοὺς νόμους τῇ πόλει.

II. Write in Greek:

1. At (use ἐν) this time, there was a wind upon the sea. 2. The unjust men established new laws which were a misfortune for the citizens. 3. We shall persuade the ruler to give the beautiful stone to the woman. It will give her (αὐτῇ) pleasure. 4. The gods will send sleep as a favor to the old men. 5. The guards stood that day near the body of the king's wife.

In many city-states, the aristocracies were overthrown by aristocratic tyrants, who proved to be stepping-stones to a wide extension of aristocratic privileges and culture. Thus democracy was born in the fifth century, most notably in Athens.

Each city-state (πόλις) was in reality a small territorial state, with a hill fortified for sieges; the citadel thus formed was called the ἀκρόπολις. Here in early days lived the king, who conducted the state worship centered in the temples of the ἀκρόπολις. Round its foot clustered the houses of the citizens, the πολῖται; the compact body of houses was called the ἄστυ. When enemies attacked, the πολῖται abandoned their houses and hurried up into the ἀκρόπολις. In time of peace they commuted daily to their fields in the surrounding countryside, called the χώρα.

In the picture above, the sharp-topped conical hill on the left, Lykabettos, was useless as a citadel, but from early times the hill on the right made a suitable Acropolis. Here the Periclean democracy built the Parthenon (447–432 B.C.), which still dominates in any view of Athens. Below, at the extreme left, stands the almost completely preserved temple of Hephaestus. Between this temple and the Acropolis much of the area was devoted to the public gathering-place or forum (ἀγορά), which contained many of the civic buildings. The Acropolis was reserved for the gods.

In recent years the American School of Classical Studies has excavated the ancient Agora. The modern visitor can tread where Socrates taught, where Saint Paul preached, where in later Roman times the antiquarian Pausanias noted down building after building which has again come to light. At the far side of the Agora (in the middle of the photograph) the School has reconstructed, faithfully in every detail, one of the ancient buildings, for a museum and place of study. Thus the creative energy of Athens, long known from its literature and thought, is now clear also in its architecture, where the tradition of free but disciplined expression, a heritage from the aristocracy, was blended with the new democratic energy.

δηλόω. FUTURE OF LIQUID VERBS.
PERSONAL PRONOUNS

1. The rules for contraction of o-verbs are:
   (a) o plus ε, o, or ου becomes ου.
   (b) o plus η or ω becomes ω.
   (c) o plus any iota diphthong becomes οι, except in the present infinitive (= -οῦν).

2. Learn the conjugation of the following tenses of δηλόω, show:

Present	Imperfect	Present Infinitive
δηλῶ *I show,*	ἐδήλουν *I was showing,*	δηλοῦν
δηλοῖς *etc.*	ἐδήλους *etc.*	
δηλοῖ	ἐδήλου	
δηλοῦμεν	ἐδηλοῦμεν	
δηλοῦτε	ἐδηλοῦτε	
δηλοῦσι	ἐδήλουν	

3. Verbs whose stems end in a liquid (λ, μ, ν, ρ) have a future like the present of -εω contract verbs: e.g., μένω, future μενῶ, μενεῖς, μενεῖ, μενοῦμεν, μενεῖτε, μενοῦσι. There is often a change in the verb stem in the future; e.g., φαίνω, future φανῶ; βάλλω, future βαλῶ; ἀγγέλλω, future ἀγγελῶ.

4. Verbs in -ίζω drop the ζ and form a contract future similar to that of liquid verbs; e.g., νομίζω, future νομιῶ (aorist ἐνόμισα).

5. Attic Future. In Attic Greek certain verbs in -έω and -άω drop the σ of the future and contract the ε or the α as in the present, e.g., καλέω, future καλῶ, καλεῖς, etc.; ἐλαύνω (stem ἐλα-), future ἐλῶ, ἐλᾷς, etc. All verbs in -άννυμι have such futures in -άω, e.g., σκεδάννυμι (scatter), future σκεδῶ, σκεδᾷς, etc.

6. It should be remembered that verbs whose stem ends in a liquid form their first aorists without σ, e.g., μένω, first aorist ἔμεινα. Cf. Lesson 8.

57

7. Learn the declension of the personal pronouns of the first and second persons:

<table>
<tr><th colspan="2">FIRST PERSON</th><th colspan="2">SECOND PERSON</th></tr>
<tr><th>SINGULAR</th><th>PLURAL</th><th>SINGULAR</th><th>PLURAL</th></tr>
<tr><td>ἐγώ</td><td>ἡμεῖς</td><td>σύ</td><td>ὑμεῖς</td></tr>
<tr><td>ἐμοῦ (μου)</td><td>ἡμῶν</td><td>σοῦ (σου)</td><td>ὑμῶν</td></tr>
<tr><td>ἐμοί (μοι)</td><td>ἡμῖν</td><td>σοί (σοι)</td><td>ὑμῖν</td></tr>
<tr><td>ἐμέ (με)</td><td>ἡμᾶς</td><td>σέ (σε)</td><td>ὑμᾶς</td></tr>
</table>

In the oblique cases of the singular the shorter forms of ἐγώ are enclitic; forms of σύ are found both as accented and as enclitic forms.

8. The pronoun of the third person is customarily supplied by the oblique cases of αὐτός. Cf. Lesson 12.

9. The possessive genitive of the personal pronoun takes the predicate position. Cf. Lesson 12.

READING

A. πατρὸς σωφροσύνη μέγιστον τέκνοις παράγγελμα. — DEMOCRITUS.
B. αἱ δεύτεραί πως φροντίδες σοφώτεραι. — EURIPIDES.
1. ὁ χρόνος τὰ ἄδηλα δηλοῖ. 2. οὐκ ἔστιν ἡδέως (happily) ζῆν ἄνευ τοῦ φρονίμως καὶ καλῶς καὶ δικαίως ζῆν, οὐδὲ φρονίμως καὶ καλῶς καὶ δικαίως ἄνευ τοῦ ἡδέως ζῆν. εἰ δέ τῳ μὴ ἔξεστι ζῆν φρονίμως καὶ καλῶς καὶ δικαίως, οὐκ ἔστι τοῦτον ἡδέως ζῆν. 3. ὁ θεὸς καὶ ἡ φύσις οὐδὲν μάτην ποιοῦσιν. 4. τὴν γυναῖκα τὴν σώφρονα οὐ δεῖ τὰς τρίχας ξανθὰς ποιεῖν. 5. ἀποβαλεῖτε τὴν ἀρετὴν ἣν ἐλάβετε ἀπὸ τῶν πατέρων ὑμῶν; 6. ὁμονοοῦντες ἰσχυροὶ μενοῦμεν. 7. Πλάτων φησὶ τὰς Μούσας ἐν ταῖς ψυχαῖς τῶν εὐφυῶν οἰκεῖν. 8. ἀξιοῖς ἄλλο τι ἢ ἀποθανεῖν; — LYSIAS
9. The Trumpeter. στρατιῶταί τινες οἳ ἐνίκησαν τοὺς πολεμίους σαλπιγ-κτὴν (trumpeter) ἔλαβον. ἐπεὶ δὲ ἔμελλον ἀποκτείνειν αὐτόν, "ὦ ἄνδρες," ἔφη, "μὴ ἀποκτείνητέ (do not kill) με. ἐγὼ γὰρ ὑμᾶς οὐκ ἀπέκτεινα. ὁρᾶτε ὅτι οὐδὲν ὅπλον (weapon) ἔχω, εἰ μὴ τὴν σάλπιγγα ταύτην." οἱ δὲ ἔλεξαν, "διὰ αὐτὸ τοῦτο δίκαιος εἶ ἀποθανεῖν, ὅτι σὺ μὲν αὐτὸς οὐ πολεμεῖς, τοὺς δὲ ἄλλους εἰς μάχην ἐγείρεις (arouse)."

Notes: ἄδηλος (adjective), unrevealed, unclear (cf. δηλόω). 2. ἄνευ, without (+ genitive); φρονίμως, wisely. ἔστι, it is (not) possible. 3. φύσις, nature (cf. φύω, to grow); μάτην, in vain. 4. σώφρων, σώφρονος, modest, wise; θρίξ, τριχός, hair; ξανθός, yellow. 6. ὁμονοοῦντες, by agreeing. 7. Μοῦσαι, the Muses; εὐφυής, well-born (declension, Lesson 17); φησί, says. 9. εἰ μή, except; οἱ δέ, the soldiers; πολεμεῖς, you fight (cf. πόλεμος).

VOCABULARY

πολέμιοι, -ων, οἱ, the enemy (substantive use of the adjective πολέμιος, -α, -ον, hostile)

ἰσχυρός, -ά, -όν, strong

ἀξιόω, -ώσω, ἠξίωσα, expect, demand
ἀποκτείνω, ἀποκτενῶ, ἀπέκτεινα, kill
βάλλω, βαλῶ, ἔβαλον, throw, pelt [ballistics]
δηλόω, -ώσω, ἐδήλωσα, reveal, make clear (δῆλος)
ἐλαύνω, ἐλῶ, ἤλασα, drive, ride, march
ἔξεστιν, it is possible, permissible (impersonal; + dative or accusative and infinitive)
ζάω, ζήσω, imperfect. ἔζων, live (contracts into η, not α; infinitive ζῆν)
καλέω, καλῶ, ἐκάλεσα, call, summon
μέλλω, μελλήσω, ἐμέλλησα, to be about to (with complementary infinitive, regularly future)
νοέω, νοήσω, ἐνόησα, think (often compounded; cf. νοῦς)
οἰκέω, -ήσω, ᾤκησα, live in, dwell [economy]

ENGLISH SENTENCES

1. It is possible to live justly and happily and do good things for men. 2. We shall remain here with our friends for a few days. 3. I shall show you what it is to live well; and so you also will live happily among your friends. 4. We ourselves expect to live since we are strong. 5. You say that the enemy are about to dwell in our province. 6. A trumpeter aroused his soldiers, and so they fought the enemy.

REVIEW EXERCISES

I. Translate:

1. ὁ τοῦ Ἕλληνος ἑταῖρος ἔδοξεν ὕδωρ ὁρᾶν, ἀλλὰ τῷ νῷ ἐνόσει. 2. ὁ δαίμων τὰ θηρία ἐν καιρῷ ἐνίκα. 3. οὐ δοκεῖ ῥᾴδιον εἶναι τιμᾶν βασιλέα πονηρόν. 4. ἐρωτᾷ ἡ γυνὴ ὁπότερος ὁποτέραν φιλεῖ. 5. ὁ βασιλεὺς τότε ἀπέθνῃσκε καὶ ἐκέλευσε τὸν παῖδα βασιλεύειν ἐσθλῶς καὶ ἀγαθὰ ποιεῖν τοὺς πολίτας.

II. Write in Greek:

1. Race or money, which do you honor more? 2. We were ill and did not wish to come; nor did it seem best to remain with the others. 3. The general asked which wind was blowing. 4. I think the man's temper will get the better of his mind. 5. I saw that the ruler had left his shield upon that stone.

ADJECTIVES IN -ύς, -εῖα, -ύ, AND -ής, -ές.
CONTRACT ADJECTIVES

1. Many important adjectives in Greek have the endings -ύς, -εῖα, -ύ, typified by ἡδύς, sweet, which follows:

	SINGULAR			PLURAL	
M	F	N	M	F	N
ἡδύς	ἡδεῖα	ἡδύ	ἡδεῖς	ἡδεῖαι	ἡδέα
ἡδέος	ἡδείας	ἡδέος	ἡδέων	ἡδειῶν	ἡδέων
ἡδεῖ	ἡδείᾳ	ἡδεῖ	ἡδέσι	ἡδείαις	ἡδέσι
ἡδύν	ἡδεῖαν	ἡδύ	ἡδεῖς	ἡδείας	ἡδέα
ἡδύ	ἡδεῖα	ἡδύ	ἡδεῖς	ἡδεῖαι	ἡδέα

2. Another important group of adjectives is that with the ending -ής in the masculine and feminine nominative singular and -ές in the neuter. Learn the declension of ἀσφαλής, safe. Note the contractions in the genitive and dative singular and the genitive plural, similar to those in γένος (Lesson 7).

SINGULAR		PLURAL	
M, F	N	M, F	N
ἀσφαλής	ἀσφαλές	ἀσφαλεῖς	ἀσφαλῆ
ἀσφαλοῦς	ἀσφαλοῦς	ἀσφαλῶν	ἀσφαλῶν
ἀσφαλεῖ	ἀσφαλεῖ	ἀσφαλέσι	ἀσφαλέσι
ἀσφαλῆ	ἀσφαλές	ἀσφαλεῖς	ἀσφαλῆ
ἀσφαλές	ἀσφαλές	ἀσφαλεῖς	ἀσφαλῆ

3. A few adjectives of the first and second declensions are contracted. The nominative and vocative singular is -οῦς, -ῆ (-ᾶ), -οῦν; the accusative singular -οῦν, -ῆν (-ᾶν), -οῦν. Otherwise they have the same endings as ἀγαθός or ἄξιος, but are circumflexed on the ultima throughout, e.g., χρυσοῦς, χρυσῆ, χρυσοῦν, golden, and ἀργυροῦς, ἀργυρᾶ, ἀργυροῦν, silver. See paradigms on pages 160–161.

4. Elision. When one word ending in a short vowel is immediately followed by another word beginning with a vowel, the last vowel of the first word is sometimes omitted and an apostrophe written in its place. This is called *elision*, e.g., ἀλλ' ἄγε for ἀλλὰ ἄγε.

5. Crasis. Occasionally the final vowel or diphthong of a word is contracted with the initial vowel of the following word and the two words are written as one. A smooth breathing is placed over the contracted vowel. This is called *crasis*, e.g., ταὐτά for τὰ αὐτά.

READING

A. οὐ μετανοεῖν ἀλλὰ προνοεῖν χρὴ τὸν ἄνδρα τὸν σοφόν.— EPICHARMUS.

B. γλυκὺς ἀπείρῳ πόλεμος.

1. πολλάκις χαλεπόν ἐστι τῶν ἀληθῶν τὰ ψευδῆ χωρίζειν. 2. ἀγαθὸν οὐ τὸ μὴ ἀδικεῖν ἀλλὰ τὸ μηδὲ ἐθέλειν. — DEMOCRITUS. 3. τὸ μὲν ἀληθὲς πικρόν ἐστι τοῖς ἀνοήτοις, τὸ δὲ ψευδὲς γλυκύ. 4. παιδεία τοῖς μὲν εὐτυχέσι κόσμος ἐστί, τοῖς δὲ δυστυχέσι καταφυγή. 5. βραχεῖα τέρψις ἡδονῆς κακῆς. 6. γαστὴρ παχεῖα λεπτὸν οὐ τίκτει νόον. 7. ὁ ποιητὴς τραχεῖαν ἐκάλει τῆς ἀρετῆς τὴν ὁδόν. 8. ἡ παιδεία ὁμοία ἐστὶ χρυσῷ στεφάνῳ. 9. τἀληθῆ λέγοντες οὐκ ἀεὶ τοὺς ἀνθρώπους εὐφραίνομεν. 10. πλεῖστοι τοι ὄντες εὐγενεῖς εἰσιν κακοί.

Notes: 1. χωρίζω, separate (cf. χωρίς); ἀληθῶν, genitive of separation. 3. ἀνοήτοις, foolish. 4. καταφυγή, refuge. 5. τέρψις, enjoyment. 6. γαστήρ, belly; παχεῖα, thick; λεπτόν, fine. 7. τραχεῖα, rough. 9. λέγοντες, participle of λέγω (Lesson 19); εὐφραίνομεν, gladden. 10. τοι, you know (colloquial); ὄντες, being, participle of εἰμί (Lesson 19).

VOCABULARY

παιδεία, -ας, ἡ, education, training
στέφανος, -ου, ὁ, crown, wreath

ἀληθής, -ές, true
ἀργυροῦς, -ᾶ, -οῦν, silver
βραχύς, -εῖα, -ύ, short, brief
γλυκύς, -εῖα, -ύ, sweet, pleasant
δυστυχής, -ές, ill-starred, unfortunate
εὐγενής, -ές, well-born
εὐτυχής, -ές, fortunate
ὅμοιος, -α, -ον, similar, like
πικρός, -ά, -όν, bitter
χρυσοῦς, -ῆ, -οῦν, golden
ψευδής, -ές, false

ἀδικέω, -ήσω, ἠδίκησα, be unjust, harm
τίκτω, 2nd aorist ἔτεκον, bring forth
χρή (impersonal), it is necessary (takes accusative and infinitive)

μηδέ, nor, not even, not . . . either (used instead of οὐδέ where μή would
be used instead of οὐ; cf. Lesson 6)

ENGLISH SENTENCES

1. It is not difficult to point out the truth to them. 2. Truth is often
pleasant even to the unfortunate. 3. It is necessary to tell the truth,
and to speak briefly (βραχέως). 4. Education never harmed any one.
5. A crown is a pleasant thing to the well-born. 6. It is bitter to do
harm, but pleasant to wish to do good to someone.

REVIEW EXERCISES

I. Translate:

1. ἀποκτενοῦμεν τοὺς πολεμίους οἳ λίθοις ἔβαλον τὰς γυναῖκας καὶ
τοὺς παῖδας ἡμῶν ἐπὶ τοῦ τείχους. 2. τί ἀξιοῖς λαβεῖν εἰ ἔξεστι διδόναι
σοί τι; 3. οὐκ ἰσχυρά ἐστιν ἡ μήτηρ αὐτοῦ. οὐκ οὖν μέλλει ζήσειν εἰς τὸ τοῦ
πολέμου τέλος. 4. εἴ τι νοεῖς περὶ τοῦ πολέμου, δοκεῖ μοι ἄμεινον εἶναι
δηλοῦν αὐτὸ τοῖς στρατηγοῖς. 5. τίνες οἰκοῦσιν ἐν τῇ γῇ ἐκείνῃ μεθ' ὑμῶν;

II. Write in Greek:

1. He thinks that the Greeks will scatter our enemies. 2. In our
land the wind is always strong. 3. Who will call you on the day of the
battle? 4. The boys will drive your horses into the camp. 5. We shall
remain with our friends upon the wall.

DECLENSION OF πᾶς. μέγας, AND πολύς

1. Learn the declension of the irregular adjectives πᾶς, all,[1] μέγας, great, and πολύς, much, many.

	SINGULAR			PLURAL	
M	F	N	M	F	N
πᾶς	πᾶσα	πᾶν	πάντες	πᾶσαι	πάντα
παντός	πάσης	παντός	πάντων	πασῶν	πάντων
παντί	πάσῃ	παντί	πᾶσι	πάσαις	πᾶσι
πάντα	πᾶσαν	πᾶν	πάντας	πάσας	πάντα
μέγας	μεγάλη	μέγα	μεγάλοι	μεγάλαι	μεγάλα
μεγάλου	μεγάλης	μεγάλου	μεγάλων	μεγάλων	μεγάλων
μεγάλῳ	μεγάλῃ	μεγάλῳ	μεγάλοις	μεγάλαις	μεγάλοις
μέγαν	μεγάλην	μέγα	μεγάλους	μεγάλας	μεγάλα
πολύς	πολλή	πολύ	πολλοί	πολλαί	πολλά
πολλοῦ	πολλῆς	πολλοῦ	πολλῶν	πολλῶν	πολλῶν
πολλῷ	πολλῇ	πολλῷ	πολλοῖς	πολλαῖς	πολλοῖς
πολύν	πολλήν	πολύ	πολλούς	πολλάς	πολλά

READING

A. ἀνδρὶ σοφῷ πᾶσα γῆ βατή· ψυχῆς γὰρ ἀγαθῆς πατρὶς ὁ ξύμπας κόσμος.—DEMOCRITUS.

B. μέγα βιβλίον μέγα κακόν.—CALLIMACHUS.

C. οὐ παντὸς ἀνδρὸς εἰς Κόρινθόν ἐσθ' ὁ πλοῦς.

1. χρόνος τὰ κρυπτὰ πάντα πρὸς τὸ φῶς φέρει.—MENANDER. 2. ὁ βίος πολλὰ ἔχει παράδοξα. 3. οὐ πολλά, ἀλλὰ πολύ. 4. νῦν ὑπὲρ πάντων ὁ ἀγών ἐστιν.—AESCHYLUS. 5. ἐν τῷ ἐν Δελφοῖς ἱερῷ χρυσοῖ καὶ

---

[1] When πᾶς means *all*, it has the predicate position (πᾶσαι αἱ πόλεις); when it means *whole*, it has the attributive position (ἡ πᾶσα πόλις); used without the article it means *every*.

ἀργυροῖ κρατῆρες ἦσαν. 6. ἔλεγε δὲ τῷ Θεμιστοκλεῖ ὁ διδάσκαλος,
Οὐδὲν ἔσῃ, παῖ, σὺ (you) μικρόν, ἀλλὰ μέγα πάντως ἀγαθὸν ἢ κακόν.

7. The Medes and Persians under Xerxes attack at Thermopylae.
ἐπειδὴ δὲ οἱ Πέρσαι ἦσαν ἐγγὺς τῶν ἐν Θερμοπύλαις Ἑλλήνων, Ξέρξης
ἐνόμιζεν ἐκείνους ὀλίγων ἡμερῶν ἀπιέναι (would withdraw). οἱ δὲ οὐκ
ἐποίουν τοῦτο. ἐν νῷ οὖν εἶχεν ὁ βασιλεὺς τοὺς στρατιώτας πέμπειν ἐπὶ
τοὺς πολεμίους. ἐκέλευσεν δὲ τοὺς Μήδους λαβεῖν τινας τῶν Ἑλλήνων
αἰχμαλώτους (captives) καὶ ἀπάγειν πρὸς ἑαυτόν (himself). πρῶτον
μὲν οὖν οἱ Μῆδοι ἐπολέμουν τοῖς Ἕλλησι καὶ οὐδὲν κακὸν αὐτοὺς ἐποίησαν.
διὰ δὲ ταῦτα δῆλον ἦν οὐ μόνον τῷ Ξέρξῃ ἀλλὰ καὶ πᾶσιν ὅτι πολλοὶ μὲν
ἄνθρωποί εἰσιν ὀλίγοι δὲ ἄνδρες.—HERODOTUS (adapted).

Notes: 2. παράδοξα, contrary to expectation (δόξα, cf. δοκέω). 5. Δελφοῖς,
Delphi (dative); κρατήρ, mixing bowl. 6. ἔσῃ, you will be; παῖ, my boy
(vocative). 7. κακὸν αὐτοὺς ἐποίησαν, did harm to them (two accusatives);
οὐ μόνον, not only (adverbial).

VOCABULARY

ἀγών, -ῶνος, ὁ, contest (cf. ἄγω) [agony]
βιβλίον, -ου, τό, book
διδάσκαλος, -ου, ὁ, teacher, master
ἱερόν, -οῦ, τό, temple (i.e., sacred place) [hierophant, hierarchy]
φῶς, φωτός, τό, light [photograph]

δῆλος, -η, -ον, evident
κρυπτός, -ή, -όν, hidden (cf. κρύπτω) [crypt]
μέγας, μεγάλη, μέγα, large, great
πᾶς, πᾶσα, πᾶν, all, every; singular in attributive position, entire
πολύς, πολλή, πολύ, much; plural, many

ἀπάγω, lead back
πίπτω, 2nd aorist ἔπεσον, fall

ἐγγύς (adverb + genitive), near
νῦν (temporal adverb), now
πάντως (adverb), wholly
ὑπέρ, preposition with genitive, over, in behalf of (for); with accusative,
  over

ENGLISH SENTENCES

1. All the Greeks went to Thermopylae and fought with (ἐμα-
χέσαντο + dative) many Persians. 2. King Xerxes had a large
army. 3. For the whole day they tried (ἐπειρῶντο) to conquer the
Lacedaemonians. 4. Of all the Greeks at Thermopylae, every Spartan

64

fell. 5. Life has many paradoxes and much evil. 6. When Xerxes first came into Greece, he thought that the Greek soldiers would betray their country.

REVIEW EXERCISES

I. Translate:

1. ἔδωκεν ὁ κλὼψ δῶρα χρυσᾶ ὡς πλεῖστα τοῖς δικασταῖς. 2. τἀν τῇ πόλει ὡς πικρότατα ἦν τοῖς πολίταις. 3. οὐκ ἀεὶ ἥδιον τὸ ἀληθὲς τοῦ ψευδοῦς ἐστιν. 4. ὁ τοῦ ἄρχοντος βίος δέκα ἡμέραις βραχίων ἦν ἢ ὁ τοῦ ἀδελφοῦ αὐτοῦ. 5. χρὴ νομίζειν τὸ μὲν ἀδικεῖν πικρόν, τὸ δὲ δίκαια πράττειν γλυκύ.

Note: 5. See note on articular infinitive, page 54.

II. Write in Greek:

1. Education is the noblest gift of the fortunate. 2. The fairest crown of democracy is justice. 3. Education makes the unfortunate similar to the well-born. 4. Tyranny seemed the easiest thing to most of the citizens. 5. It is a very bitter thing to see men give more (things) to the false than to the true.

PRESENT, FUTURE, AND SECOND AORIST PARTICIPLES ACTIVE OF Ω- AND CONTRACT VERBS

1. Learn the declension of the present participle of the verb εἰμί, to be.

| | SINGULAR | | | PLURAL | |
M	F	N	M	F	N
ὤν	οὖσα	ὄν	ὄντες	οὖσαι	ὄντα
ὄντος	οὔσης	ὄντος	ὄντων	οὐσῶν	ὄντων
ὄντι	οὔσῃ	ὄντι	οὖσι	οὔσαις	οὖσι
ὄντα	οὖσαν	ὄν	ὄντας	οὔσας	ὄντα

2. The accent of participles is persistent, like that of adjectives.

3. Learn the declension of the present active participle παιδεύων, educating, and of the second aorist active participle λιπών, leaving or having left, noting the accent of the latter. All second aorist participles are so accented.

M	F	N	M	F	N
παιδεύων	παιδεύουσα	παιδεῦον	λιπών	λιποῦσα	λιπόν
παιδεύοντος	παιδευούσης	παιδεύοντος	λιπόντος	λιπούσης	λιπόντος
παιδεύοντι	παιδευούσῃ	παιδεύοντι	λιπόντι	λιπούσῃ	λιπόντι
παιδεύοντα	παιδεύουσαν	παιδεῦον	λιπόντα	λιποῦσαν	λιπόν
παιδεύοντες	παιδεύουσαι	παιδεύοντα	λιπόντες	λιποῦσαι	λιπόντα
παιδευόντων	παιδευουσῶν	παιδευόντων	λιπόντων	λιπουσῶν	λιπόντων
παιδεύουσι	παιδευούσαις	παιδεύουσι	λιποῦσι	λιπούσαις	λιποῦσι
παιδεύοντας	παιδευούσας	παιδεύοντα	λιπόντας	λιπούσας	λιπόντα

4. The future active participle, παιδεύσων, is declined exactly like the present active participle.

5. Learn the declensions of the following participles of contract verbs: τιμῶν, honoring, φιλῶν, loving, and δηλῶν, showing (declined like φιλῶν), which are similar to those of the verbs given above, save for the contraction of the stem vowels with the endings.

M	F	N	M	F	N
τιμῶν	τιμῶσα	τιμῶν	φιλῶν	φιλοῦσα	φιλοῦν
τιμῶντος	τιμώσης	τιμῶντος	φιλοῦντος	φιλούσης	φιλοῦντος
τιμῶντι	τιμώσῃ	τιμῶντι	φιλοῦντι	φιλούσῃ	φιλοῦντι
τιμῶντα	τιμῶσαν	τιμῶν	φιλοῦντα	φιλοῦσαν	φιλοῦν
τιμῶντες	τιμῶσαι	τιμῶντα	φιλοῦντες	φιλοῦσαι	φιλοῦντα
τιμώντων	τιμωσῶν	τιμώντων	φιλούντων	φιλουσῶν	φιλούντων
τιμῶσι	τιμώσαις	τιμῶσι	φιλοῦσι	φιλούσαις	φιλοῦσι
τιμῶντας	τιμώσας	τιμῶντα	φιλοῦντας	φιλούσας	φιλοῦντα

READING

A. ὁ ἄνθρωπος φύσει πολιτικὸν ζῷον.—ARISTOTLE, *Politics*.

B. ὁ κόσμος σκηνή, ὁ βίος πάροδος. ἦλθες, εἶδες, ἀπῆλθες.

1. πιστεύειν δεῖ τοῖς μαθοῦσιν. 2. ὁ μὲν δὴ θεός, ὥσπερ καὶ ὁ παλαιὸς λόγος, ἀρχήν τε καὶ τελευτὴν καὶ μέσα τῶν ὄντων πάντων ἔχει.—PLATO. 3. αἱ Γοργόνες θυγατέρες ἦσαν Φόρκυος καὶ Κητοῦς. εἶχον δὲ κεφαλὰς μὲν περιεσπειραμένας δρακοῦσι ὀδόντας δὲ μεγάλους καὶ χεῖρας χαλκᾶς καὶ πτέρυγας χρυσᾶς. τοὺς δὲ ἰδόντας αὐτάς, λίθους ἐποίουν. 4. ἡ Κύπρις τὴν Κύπριν ἐνὶ Κνίδῳ εἶπεν ἰδοῦσα / φεῦ, φεῦ, ποῦ γυμνὴν εἶδέ με Πραξιτέλης;—GREEK ANTHOLOGY. 5. The Battle of Thermopylae (continued). ἔπειτα δὲ ὁ Ξέρξης ἔπεμψεν τοὺς Πέρσας οἳ ἦσαν βέλτιστοι καὶ κράτιστοι τῶν στρατιωτῶν πάντων. τούτους δὲ οἱ τότε ἐκάλουν τοὺς ἀθανάτους (Immortals), ὧν ἦρχεν Ὑδάρνης. ἐπεὶ δὲ οὗτοι ἐπολέμουν τοῖς Λακεδαιμονίοις καὶ τοῖς συμμάχοις (allies) οὐδὲν πλέον ἐποίουν τοῦ στρατεύματος τοῦ Μηδικοῦ, ἀλλὰ τὰ αὐτά, οἱ δὲ Λακεδαιμόνιοι ἐμάχοντο (fought) ἀξίως λόγου (notably) καὶ ἔπιπτον αὐτῶν τῶν Σπαρτιατῶν (Spartans) ἐνταῦθα ὀλίγοι.—HERODOTUS (adapted).

Notes: 2. τε . . . καὶ, both . . . and; τελευτή, end (cf. τέλος). 3. θυγάτηρ, daughter; Φόρκυος καὶ Κητοῦς, Phorcys and Ceto; περιεσπειραμένας δράκουσι, wreathed with snakes [spiral]; χαλκᾶς, of bronze (adjective); πτέρυξ, wing [pterodactyl]; χρυσᾶς, of gold (adjective). 4. Κύπρις, Aphrodite; τὴν Κύπριν ἐνὶ (= ἐν) Κνίδῳ = the statue of Aphrodite in Cnidus by Praxiteles; φεῦ, φεῦ, expression of amazement, "my, my!" ἰδοῦσα, 2nd aorist active participle feminine of εἶδον. 5. ἔπειτα, then.

67

VOCABULARY

κεφαλή, -ῆς, ἡ, head [brachycephalic]
ὀδούς, ὀδόντος, ὁ, tooth [orthodontist]

γυμνός, -ή, -όν, naked [gymnasium]
μέσος, -η, -ον, middle; in predicate position, middle of [Mesozoic]

εἶπον, second aorist, I said; aorist infinitive εἰπεῖν, participle εἰπών
μανθάνω, second aorist ἔμαθον, learn, know [mathematics]

δή, surely, indeed, of course (postpositive)
ποῦ, where?
ὥσπερ, just as

ENGLISH SENTENCES

1. I said that I had seen (aorist) the Gorgons; but they did not make me a stone. 2. Finally Xerxes ordered his men to conquer the enemy. 3. When he had left the soldiers there, he sent the general into the city. 4. What did Hippias ('Ιππίας) say when his tooth fell out at (in) Marathon (Μαραθῶνι)? 5. He knew when he saw this that he would surely not conquer Greece (τὴν Ἑλλάδα). 6. Plato (ὁ Πλάτων) said that god controls all things that exist.

REVIEW EXERCISES

I. Translate:

1. πολλοὶ στρατιῶται ἦσαν ἐν τῷ ἀγῶνι. 2. δῆλον ἔδοξεν εἶναι ὅτι ὁ διδάσκαλος τὸ μέγα βιβλίον ἐν τῷ ἱερῷ οὐκ ἔλιπε. 3. πάντες οἱ νέοι νῦν ἐθέλουσι τόδε τὸ θηρίον λαμβάνειν. 4. ὁ ἄρχων πρῶτος ὑπὲρ τῶν πολιτῶν πολλὰς ἀσπίδας ἀργυρᾶς τῇ θεῷ ἀνέθηκε (dedicated). 5. ταῦτα τὰ κρυπτὰ εἰς φῶς ἔτι ἀπάξομεν.

II. Write in Greek:

1. The soldier who stood near the general is wholly bad. 2. The few seem to wish to show the truth to the many, but the latter are unwilling to receive it. 3. All the children love this teacher more than that one. 4. He thinks (use δοκεῖ) he will conquer the great king. 5. The book was so large that the teacher could not carry it.

FIRST AORIST ACTIVE PARTICIPLE OF Ω-VERBS.
PRESENT AND SECOND AORIST PARTICIPLES ACTIVE OF *MI*-VERBS

1. Learn the declension of the first aorist active participle, παιδεύσας, having educated:

M	F	N
παιδεύσας	παιδεύσασα	παιδεῦσαν
παιδεύσαντος	παιδευσάσης	παιδεύσαντος
παιδεύσαντι	παιδευσάσῃ	παιδεύσαντι
παιδεύσαντα	παιδεύσασαν	παιδεῦσαν
παιδεύσαντες	παιδεύσασαι	παιδεύσαντα
παιδευσάντων	παιδευσασῶν	παιδευσάντων
παιδεύσασι	παιδευσάσαις	παιδεύσασι
παιδεύσαντας	παιδευσάσας	παιδεύσαντα

2. Similarly are declined the present active participle of ἵστημι, ἱστάς, -ᾶσα, -άν, causing to stand, the second aorist active participle, στάς, having stood, and the first aorist active participle, στήσας, having caused to stand.

3. The present and second aorist active participles of τίθημι, τιθείς, placing, and θείς, having placed, are declined as follows:

PRESENT			SECOND AORIST		
M	F	N	M	F	N
τιθείς	τιθεῖσα	τιθέν	θείς	θεῖσα	θέν
τιθέντος	τιθείσης	τιθέντος	θέντος	θείσης	θέντος
τιθέντι	τιθείσῃ	τιθέντι	θέντι	θείσῃ	θέντι
τιθέντα	τιθεῖσαν	τιθέν	θέντα	θεῖσαν	θέν
τιθέντες	τιθεῖσαι	τιθέντα	θέντες	θεῖσαι	θέντα
τιθέντων	τιθεισῶν	τιθέντων	θέντων	θεισῶν	θέντων
τιθεῖσι	τιθείσαις	τιθεῖσι	θεῖσι	θείσαις	θεῖσι
τιθέντας	τιθείσας	τιθέντα	θέντας	θείσας	θέντα

Similarly to τιθείς are declined the participles of ἵημι: present, ἱείς, ἱεῖσα, ἱέν, throwing, and second aorist, -εἷς, -εἷσα, -ἕν (only in compounds).

4. The present and second aorist active participles of δίδωμι, διδούς, giving, and δούς, having given, are declined as follows:

| PRESENT | | | SECOND AORIST | | |
M	F	N	M	F	N
διδούς	διδοῦσα	διδόν	δούς	δοῦσα	δόν
διδόντος	διδούσης	διδόντος	δόντος	δούσης	δόντος
διδόντι	διδούσῃ	διδόντι	δόντι	δούσῃ	δόντι
διδόντα	διδοῦσαν	διδόν	δόντα	δοῦσαν	δόν
διδόντες	διδοῦσαι	διδόντα	δόντες	δοῦσαι	δόντα
διδόντων	διδουσῶν	διδόντων	δόντων	δουσῶν	δόντων
διδοῦσι	διδούσαις	διδοῦσι	δοῦσι	δούσαις	δοῦσι
διδόντας	διδούσας	διδόντα	δόντας	δούσας	δόντα

READING

A. πολλὰ πιὼν καὶ πολλὰ φαγὼν καὶ πολλὰ κακ᾽ εἰπὼν/ἀνθρώπους κεῖμαι, Τιμοκρέων ῾Ρόδιος.—SIMONIDES.

B. φιλεῖ δὲ τῷ κάμνοντι συσπεύδειν θεός.—AESCHYLUS.

1. λίαν φιλῶν σεαυτὸν οὐχ ἕξεις φίλον. 2. τοῖς ἀεὶ ἀληθεύσασι πάντες πιστεύσουσιν. 3. καλῶς ἐποίησεν οὕτως τελευτήσας τὸν βίον.—LYSIAS. 4. Γοργὼ ἡ Λεωνίδου γυνὴ παραδιδοῦσα τῷ υἱῷ τὴν ἀσπίδα ἔλεγεν, "ἢ ταύτην ἢ ἐπὶ ταύτῃ." 5. οἱ ᾽Επιδάμνιοι πέμψαντες εἰς Δελφοὺς ἠρώτησαν τὸν θεὸν εἰ παραδοῖεν τοῖς Κορινθίοις τὴν πόλιν. 6. ἡ δοῦσα πάντα καὶ κομίζεται τύχη. 7. θεοῦ διδόντος οὐδὲν ἰσχύει φθόνος, καὶ μὴ διδόντος οὐδὲν ἰσχύει πόνος. 8. Μαχάων τὸ τοῦ Μενελάου τραῦμα ἰάσατο φάρμακα ἐπιτιθείς. 9. ὁ εὖ διαθεὶς τὸν ἑαυτοῦ οἶκον καὶ τὰ τῆς πόλεως πράγματ᾽ εὖ ἂν διαθείη. 10. οἱ τάλαντα ἐπὶ τάλαντα ἐπιθέντες ὑπὸ τῶν πενήτων φθονοῦνται. 11. Λύσανδρος τῶν ᾽Αθηνῶν κρατήσας εὐθὺς μετέστησε τὴν πολιτείαν, τριάκοντα μὲν ἄρχοντας καθιστὰς ἐν ἄστει δέκα δ᾽ ἐν τῷ Πειραιεῖ. 12. An Incident During the March of The Ten Thousand. ὁ δὲ φεύγει εἰς τὸ ἑαυτοῦ στράτευμα, καὶ εὐθὺς παραγγέλλει (commanded) εἰς τὰ ὅπλα. καὶ τοὺς μὲν ὁπλίτας αὐτοῦ ἐκέλευσε μεῖναι, τὰς ἀσπίδας πρὸς τὰ γόνατα (knees) θέντας, αὐτὸς δὲ λαβὼν τοὺς ἱππέας (cavalry) οἳ ἦσαν αὐτῷ ἐν τῷ στρατεύματι πλείους ἢ τετταράκοντα, τούτων δὲ οἱ πλεῖστοι Θρᾷκες (Thracians), ἤλαυνεν (charged) ἐπὶ τοὺς Μένωνος· οἱ δὲ καὶ ἕστασαν ἀποροῦντες (perplexed) τῷ πράγματι.

70

Notes: 1. σεαυτόν, yourself (reflexive pronoun); 2. ἀληθεύω, speak the truth. 4. Γοργώ, Gorgo, a Spartan woman; Λεωνίδου, genitive of Λεωνίδας. 5. 'Επιδάμνιοι, people of Epidamnus; Κορινθίοις, people of Corinth; παραδοῖεν (optative), they should give. 6. κομίζεται (middle), takes away. 7. Θεοῦ διδόντος, if God gives (genitive absolute, cf. Lesson 21; similarly μὴ διδόντος); ἰσχύω, avail. 8. Μαχάων, Machaon; Μενελάου, of Menelaus; τραῦμα, wound; ἰάσατο (1st aorist middle), from ἰάομαι, heal. 9. ἑαυτοῦ (reflexive), his own; πράγματα, affairs; ἂν διαθείη, would arrange. 10. πένης, -ητος, a poor man; φθονοῦνται (passive) are envied. 11. Λύσανδρος, Lysander, who captured Athens; 'Αθηνῶν, genitive of 'Αθῆναι, Athens; μετέστησε, changed; πολιτεία, government; καθιστάς, placing; ἄστει, dative of ἄστυ, the citadel of Athens; Πειραιεῖ, dative of Πειραιεύς, Piraeus, port of Athens. 12. ὁ refers to Clearchus, one of Cyrus' generals; ὁπλίτας, hoplites; Μένωνος, genitive of Μένων, Menon, one of Cyrus' generals; τετταράκοντα, forty; ἕστασαν (2nd pluperfect), stood.

VOCABULARY

οἶκος, -ου, ὁ, house
ὅπλον, -ου, τό, weapon; plural, arms
πόνος, -ου, ὁ, labor, toil
τάλαντον, -ου, τό, a talent (measure of value, worth about $1100)
τύχη, -ης, ἡ, fate, luck
υἱός, -οῦ, ὁ, son
φάρμακον, -ου, τό, drug
φθόνος, -ου, ὁ, jealousy, envy

διατίθημι, dispose, arrange
ἐπιτίθημι, apply; add
κομίζω, κομιῶ, ἐκόμισα, bring, accompany; middle (rarely), take away
κρατέω, conquer, be powerful over (+ genitive)
παραδίδωμι, give over, surrender
τελευτάω, come to the end (τελευτή), die, bring to an end

εὖ (adverb), well
εὐθύς (adverb), at once
λίαν (adverb), too much, very
τριάκοντα, thirty

ENGLISH SENTENCES

1. The wife of Leonidas, sending her son into battle, ordered him not (use μὴ) to surrender his shield. 2. Clearchus and Menon who were (i.e., being) generals of Cyrus, ordered their cavalry to conquer the enemy. 3. Machaon applied drugs to the bodies of many men who fought near Troy (Τροία, -ας, ἡ). 4. The father, dying, gave over his arms to his son. 5. Fortune gives many evil things, but much good. 6. When Cyrus gave orders, the Thracians charged against the enemy.

REVIEW EXERCISES

I. Translate:

1. οἱ νέοι γυμνοὶ ὄντες εἰς μέσον τὸν ἀγῶνα κατέστησαν (entered).
2. εἶπον ὅτι ὁ τῆς Γοργόνος ὀδούς ǀ μείζων ἢ ἀνθρώπου κεφαλὴ ἦν. 3. τοὺς
σοφοὺς καλοῦντες, οἱ πολῖται ἔμαθον τί δεῖ ποιεῖν. 4. ποῦ δὴ πεσόντες
ἀπέθανον οἱ τῆς στρατιᾶς ἄρχοντες; 5. τέλος ἄρα ἐλθόντες τινὲς ὥσπερ
νικῶντες τοὺς τῆς πόλεως γέροντας ἐκάλεσαν.

II. Write in Greek:

1. The excellence of the boy's mind was greater than that of his
father's. 2. Who is that man who ruled the city for ten days?
3. Neither those who were in the city nor those who were by the sea
learned anything new. 4. Calling their mother, the children remained
near the fire. 5. Fleeing the Greeks, he fell into the midst of the
Gorgons.

USES OF THE PARTICIPLE

1. One of the salient characteristics of Greek is the variety and frequency of its uses of the participle. These uses fall into three main divisions—the attributive, the circumstantial, and the supplementary.

2. The attributive participle is one used simply as an adjective, usually with the article, e.g., the reigning Cyrus, ὁ βασιλεύων Κῦρος.

Very often the noun is omitted and the participle is used as a substantive, sometimes with modifiers, e.g., those who flee, οἱ φεύγοντες; those who came from the city, οἱ ἐκ τῆς πόλεως ἐλθόντες; in the land which was once Messenia, ἐν τῇ Μεσσηνίᾳ ποτὲ οὔσῃ γῇ; against the islands called those of Aeolus, ἐπὶ τὰς Αἰόλου νήσους καλουμένας.

3. The circumstantial participle is used to set forth any circumstances or conditions attendant upon the action of the main verb. It may express time, cause, manner, means, condition, concession, purpose, or any other attendant circumstance, and is most conveniently translated into English by means of an English clause expressing one of these relationships. Examples follow:

When he had come into the city, he wrote a letter. εἰς τὴν πόλιν ἐλθών, ἔγραψεν ἐπιστολήν.

Since he had boats, he escaped. πλοῖα ἔχων, ἀπέφυγεν.

By slaying the guard, he escaped. τὸν φύλακα ἀποκτείνας, ἀπέφυγεν.

If he seizes the city, he will conquer.[1] τὴν πόλιν λαβών, νικήσει.

For many, although they talk smoothly, have no sense. πολλοὶ γάρ, καίπε εὖ λέγοντες, οὐκ ἔχουσι νοῦν.

He came to persuade the king. ἦλθεν (ὡς) τὸν βασιλέα πείσων.

---

[1] The negative with the conditional participle is μή.

73

The last example illustrates the fact that ὡς may be used with the future participle to express purpose. The negative is μή; in this construction the negative is very rare.

4. ὡς is used with the participle in Greek to indicate that the writer is giving the presumed reason or purpose of the subject, but does not himself assume responsibility for the correctness of the facts. Compare the Latin use of *quod* with the subjunctive. A somewhat clumsy but useful rule-of-thumb translation of ὡς with the participle is *on the ground that*. τὸν ἄνδρα ἀπέκτεινε ὡς προδιδόντα τὸν βασιλέα. He slew the man on the ground that he was betraying the king.

5. The supplementary participle is used to supplement or complete the meaning of certain verbs. Particularly important are the uses with τυγχάνω, to happen; λανθάνω, to escape notice; φθάνω, to anticipate. Study carefully the following examples:

ἐτύγχανε παρών. He happened to be present.
ἔλαθεν εἰς τὴν πόλιν ἐλθών. He came into the city without being seen.
ἔφθασε τοὺς πολεμίους τὸν λόφον λαβών.[2] He captured the hill ahead of the enemy.

6. A noun and a participle may be used in the genitive case in an absolute construction corresponding to the Latin ablative absolute:

τῶν παιδίων παρόντων, ἀπέθανεν ὁ πατήρ. While the children were present, the father died.

7. The present participle represents action continuous with, often contemporary with, that of the main verb. The aorist represents a single act, often prior to that of the main verb. The future participle is usually employed only to express purpose, and is often, as stated above, accompanied by ὡς. In the supplementary participle the tense of the participle represents the type or stage of an action, the present usually being used for a continuous action or state, the aorist for a single act.

[2] φθάνω and λανθάνω may take direct objects.

74

8. After verbs of sense perception and certain other important verbs meaning *to know*, *to remember*, indirect discourse is often expressed by the participle; usually its subject is in the accusative, but if the subject of the participle is that of the main verb, the participle is in the nominative. The tense of the participle is that of the original verb in the direct statement.

I see that Cyrus is riding up. ὁρῶ Κῦρον προσελαύνοντα.
I hear that the enemy fled. ἀκούω τοὺς πολεμίους ἀποφυγόντας.

When the participle refers to an actual fact, as usually in indirect discourse, its negative is οὐ, when it refers to a condition or a general statement, its negative is μή.

(With these verbs, indirect discourse may also be expressed by ὅτι with the indicative; cf. Lesson 24.)

READING

A. ἦν Λακεδαιμόνιος, Χίλων σοφός, ὃς τάδ' ἔλεξε / μηδὲν ἄγαν· καιρῷ πάντα πρόσεστι καλά.—CRITIAS.

B. μελέτη τὸ πᾶν.

C. Ἑλλήνων προμαχοῦντες Ἀθηναῖοι Μαραθῶνι / χρυσοφόρων Μήδων ἐστόρεσαν δύναμιν.—SIMONIDES.

1. οὐδεὶς ποιῶν πονηρὰ λανθάνει θεόν.—MENANDER. 2. Ἕλληνες ὄντες βαρβάροις δουλεύσομεν; 3. ἀνὴρ γὰρ ὅστις ἥδεται λέγων ἀεί, ἔλαθεν ἑαυτὸν τοῖς συνοῦσιν ὢν βαρύς.—SOPHOCLES. 4. ἄνθρωποι τὸν θάνατον φεύγοντες διώκουσιν.—DEMOCRITUS. 5. φίλους ἔχων ἐνόμιζε θησαυροὺς ἔχειν. 6. Πύρρων οὐδὲν ἔφη διαφέρειν ζῆν ἢ τεθνάναι. εἰπόντος δέ τινος, "τί οὖν οὐκ ἀποθνήσκεις;" ἔφη, "ὅτι οὐδὲν διαφέρει." 7. ὁ Ἀλέξανδρος ηὐδαιμόνισε τὸν Ἀχιλλέα ὅτι Ὅμηρον κήρυκα εἰς τὴν ἔπειτα μνήμην ἔχων ἔτυχεν.—ARRIAN. 8. οἱ ἐν τῇ πόλει ἔπεμψαν ἄνδρας λέξοντας ὅτι διδόασι πάντα τὰ ὅπλα τοῖς Λακεδαιμονίοις.—XENOPHON.

Notes: 2. βαρβάροις, dative with δουλεύειν, be slaves to. 3. ἥδεται (deponent), takes pleasure (+ participle); ἔλαθεν (gnomic aorist); ἑαυτόν (reflexive), himself. 5. θησαυρός, treasure [Thesaurus]. 6. Πύρρων, Pyrrho, a philosopher; διαφέρω, make a difference (its object, οὐδέν, is an inner accusative); τεθνάναι, perfect infinitive of ἀποθνήσκω. 7. εὐδαιμονίζω, consider fortunate (cf. εὐδαίμων); Ἀχιλλέα, from Ἀχιλλεύς, Achilles; Ὅμηρος, Homer; ἔπειτα, future; μνήμη, remembrance (cf. μιμνήσκω, recall).

VOCABULARY

βάρβαρος, -ov, ὁ, foreigner, often a Persian [barbarian]
κῆρυξ, κήρυκος, ὁ, messenger, herald

βαρύς, -εῖα, -ύ, heavy, tiresome [baritone]; declined like ἡδύς (Lesson 17)

διώκω, διώξω, ἐδίωξα, pursue
λανθάνω, λήσω, ἔλαθον, escape notice of (+ participle); deceive, elude
σύνειμι, be with (+ dative)
τυγχάνω, second aorist ἔτυχον, happen to (+ participle); happen upon, meet, get (+ genitive)

σύν (+ dative), with

ENGLISH SENTENCES

1. After saying (use participle) this to the soldiers, the general went away (ἀπῆλθεν) from the camp. 2. The messengers who happened to be with the old men escaped their notice going away. 3. He saw the herald bringing the letter of the barbarians. 4. Although they were near the king, they did not pursue him. 5. When someone said, "Where is the messenger?" the foreigner replied, "He went away." 6. The herald heard that Cyrus was pursuing the foreigners, who were fleeing.

REVIEW EXERCISES

I. Translate:

1. τὰ ὅπλα τῷ τοῦ ἄρχοντος υἱῷ ἐν τῷ οἴκῳ παραδούς, τάλαντον ἔλαβε. 2. πόνον πόνῳ ἐπιθείς, εὖ διέθηκε τὰ χρήματα. 3. τῷ σοφῷ ὕπνος πόνου φάρμακον ἐδόκει. 4. τῶν πολεμίων κρατήσας καὶ τὴν πέτραν ἐν τῷ πεδίῳ ὡς τρόπαιον (trophy) λιπών, εὐθὺς εἰρήνην τῇ πόλει ἐκόμισε. 5. ὁ βασιλεὺς τελευτῶν, λίαν τὸν νεώτερον υἱὸν φιλῶν, τὴν ἀρχὴν καὶ τριάκοντα τάλαντα αὐτῷ ἔδωκε· ὁ δὲ ἀδελφὸς διὰ φθόνον ἐκεῖνον ἀπέκτεινε.

II. Write in Greek:

1. Leaving her children behind, the mother fled to the city. 2. I saw them giving the money to the slave. 3. Not having cared for the children well, the father must not expect honor. 4. Why, having thirty talents, does he wish to get more? 5. I shall not hand over the drugs to a dying man.

PRESENT AND AORIST SUBJUNCTIVE
ACTIVE. FUTURE MORE VIVID
AND PRESENT GENERAL CONDITIONS

1. Learn the present subjunctive of the verb εἰμί, to be: ὦ, ᾖς, ᾖ, ὦμεν, ἦτε, ὦσι.

2. Similar to these forms are the subjunctives of nearly all verbs, both in present and aorist. In all its tenses and voices, the subjunctive has the characteristic long vowels ω and η. The subjunctive has the same stem as the indicative of its tense and voice. The subjunctive never has an augment. There is no future subjunctive.

PRESENT	FIRST AORIST	SECOND AORIST	PRESENT	PRESENT
παιδεύω	παιδεύσω	λίπω	φιλῶ	δεικνύω
παιδεύῃς	παιδεύσῃς	λίπῃς	φιλῇς	δεικνύῃς
παιδεύῃ	παιδεύσῃ	λίπῃ	φιλῇ	δεικνύῃ
παιδεύωμεν	παιδεύσωμεν	λίπωμεν	φιλῶμεν	δεικνύωμεν
παιδεύητε	παιδεύσητε	λίπητε	φιλῆτε	δεικνύητε
παιδεύωσι	παιδεύσωσι	λίπωσι	φιλῶσι	δεικνύωσι

	PRESENT			SECOND AORIST	
ἱστῶ	τιθῶ	ἱῶ	στῶ	θῶ	-ῶ
ἱστῇς	τιθῇς	ἱῇς	στῇς	θῇς	-ῇς
ἱστῇ	τιθῇ	ἱῇ	στῇ	θῇ	-ῇ
ἱστῶμεν	τιθῶμεν	ἱῶμεν	στῶμεν	θῶμεν	-ῶμεν
ἱστῆτε	τιθῆτε	ἱῆτε	στῆτε	θῆτε	-ῆτε
ἱστῶσι	τιθῶσι	ἱῶσι	στῶσι	θῶσι	-ῶσι

3. τιμάω, δηλόω, and δίδωμι differ in subjunctive endings from the verbs in paragraph 2. (Cf. the rules for contraction given in Lessons 15 and 16.)

77

PRESENT	PRESENT	PRESENT	SECOND AORIST
τιμῶ	δηλῶ	διδῶ	δῶ
τιμᾷς	δηλοῖς	διδῷς	δῷς
τιμᾷ	δηλοῖ	διδῷ	δῷ
τιμῶμεν	δηλῶμεν	διδῶμεν	δῶμεν
τιμᾶτε	δηλῶτε	διδῶτε	δῶτε
τιμῶσι	δηλῶσι	διδῶσι	δῶσι

4. The subjunctive, which generally refers in time to the future, may be used in a subordinate clause if the sequence is primary. After main verbs in the secondary tenses the optative is used, although the subjunctive is sometimes found in place of the optative. Thus Greek has a *sequence of moods*, whereas Latin has a *sequence of tenses*.

5. Since the subjunctive refers commonly to the future, its tenses have no temporal significance. The present is used for a continued act, the aorist for a single act.

6. The subjunctive is used in two classes of conditions:

(a) More Vivid Future Conditions. These make a definite and unqualified statement (one that is more "vivid" in that it is more likely to take place) about some future event. They follow this formula:

PROTASIS (*if* clause)	APODOSIS (conclusion)
ἐάν (= εἰ + ἄν) or ἄν or ἤν plus subjunctive (present or aorist)	future indicative or equivalent, sometimes imperative

If he comes, we shall conquer, ἐὰν ἔλθῃ, νικήσομεν.

(b) Present General Conditions. These state some general fact (one which is always true) in present time. Their formula follows:

PROTASIS	APODOSIS
ἐάν or ἄν or ἤν plus subjunctive (present or aorist)	present indicative

If Cyrus is general, the soldiers (always) conquer, ἐὰν Κῦρος στρατηγὸς ᾖ, οἱ στρατιῶται νικῶσι.

(c) In both these conditions, the protasis may be introduced by a relative pronoun or adverb instead of ἐάν—by ἐπειδάν, ὅταν (when, whenever), ὅπου ἄν (wherever), ὃς ἄν, ὅστις ἄν (whoever), etc.

7. In conditions the negative of the protasis is μή, that of the apodosis usually οὐ.

READING

A. μικραὶ χάριτες ἐν καιρῷ μέγισται τοῖς λαμβάνουσιν.—DEMOCRITUS.

B. ποιητὴς δὲ ἅτινα ἂν γράφῃ μετ' ἐνθουσιασμοῦ καὶ ἱεροῦ πνεύματος, καλὰ κάρτα ἐστίν.—DEMOCRITUS.

1. ἐὰν ἔχωμεν χρήμαθ', ἕξομεν φίλους. 2. κύνες καταβαΰζουσιν ὧν ἂν μὴ γιγνώσκωσιν.—HERACLITUS. 3. ἀεὶ καλὸς πλοῦς ἐσθ' ὅταν φεύγῃς κακά.—SOPHOCLES. 4. A. "τίς ἐστιν οὗτος;" B. "ἰατρός." A. "ὡς κακῶς ἔχει/ἅπας ἰατρός, ἐὰν κακῶς μηδεὶς ἔχῃ."—PHILEMON. 5. Aristides the Just is Ostracized. λέγουσιν οἱ Ἀθηναῖοι ὅτι τῶν ἀγροίκων τις, ἀγράμματος (unlettered, ἀ + γράφω) ὤν, δοὺς τὸ ὄστρακον (sherd) τῷ Ἀριστείδῃ ἐν τῇ ἀγορᾷ (οὐ γὰρ ἐγίγνωσκε ὅστις ἦν), ἠξίωσε τὸ ὄνομα "'Ἀριστείδην" ἐγγράφειν. ὁ δὲ θαυμάσας ἠρώτησεν ὅ τι κακὸν αὐτὸν Ἀριστείδης ἐποίησεν. ὁ δὲ ἄνθρωπος "οὐδέν," ἔφη, "οὐδὲ γιγνώσκω τὸν ἄνδρα, ἀλλὰ χαλεπῶς φέρω πανταχοῦ (everywhere) 'τὸν δίκαιον' ἀκούων." ταῦτα δὴ ἀκούσας Ἀριστείδης ἐνέγραψέ τε τὸ ὄνομα τῷ ὀστράκῳ καὶ ἀπέδωκεν.

Notes: 2. καταβαΰζω, bark at (+ genitive). 3. πλοῦς, sailing, voyage (cf. πλέω, sail); ἐσθ' = ἐστι before rough breathing. 4. μηδείς, for οὐδείς where μή would be used instead of οὐ. 5. ἐγγράφειν from ἐν + γράφειν (Lesson 13).

VOCABULARY

ἀγορά, -ᾶς, ἡ, marketplace, assembly
κύων, κυνός, ὁ, dog [cynic]
ὄνομα, ὀνόματος, τό, name (cf. ὀνομάζω) [homonym]

ἄγροικος, -η, -ον, rustic
ἅπας, ἅπασα, ἅπαν, all, every (like πᾶς)

ἀκούω, aorist ἤκουσα, hear [acoustics]
ἀποδίδωμι, give back
γιγνώσκω, know [gnomic] (future and aorist to be learned later)
θαυμάζω, —, ἐθαύμασα, marvel at, wonder [thaumatology] (future to be learned later)
ποιέω + two accusatives, do something to somebody
κακῶς ἔχω, be badly off, be ill
χαλεπῶς φέρω, be annoyed

ὡς (adverb modifying adverb), how

79

Μεγακλῆς ἱπποκράτους
Megakles (son) of Hippocrates
Ostracized in 486/5 B.C.

Ἀριστείδης Λυσιμάχου
Aristides (son) of Lysimachus
Ostracized in 482/1 B.C.

Θεμισθοκλῆς Νεοκλέους
Themistocles (son) of Neocles

Θεμισθοκλῆς (corrected
to Θεμιστοκλῆς) Φρεάρhιος
Themistocles of (the deme) Phrearrhos

Ostracized in 472/1 B.C.

The very word "politics" shows its origin. Politics in a πόλις needed no stimulation: man is by nature, said Aristotle, a political animal.

One problem of democracy was the danger that a strong man might again succeed in mastering the state as a tyrant. To avert this danger by legal means, the Athenians invented the institution of ostracism, which was simply a popular balloting on pieces of broken clay pottery (ὄστρακα) — the waste paper of ancient Greece. Provided as many as 6000 ὄστρακα were cast, the man named on a plurality of them was required to leave the country for ten years. No law required a voter to inscribe his own ballot; it was unsigned. Ostracism was thus open to manipulation, and finally was abandoned, though long after the righteous Aristides (above) was ostracized.

The actual writing is the old Attic letters used before 403/2 B.C., altered in the captions to the later forms. Some citizens were uncertain about spellings, and whether to use the demotic (Themistocles Phrearrhios) or the patronymic (all others).

ENGLISH SENTENCES

1. If you are badly off, you will call a doctor. 2. Whenever they are annoyed at someone, their friends ask them who did something evil to them. 3. If he hears the enemy, he orders his soldiers to flee. 4. If I do not have friends, I know that I am badly off. 5. He who (ὅστις) knows the truth will do justly (do just things) to all men. 6. The rustic happened to give a sherd to Aristides and asked him to write on it.

REVIEW EXERCISES

I. Translate:

1. ὁ παῖς ἔλαθε τὸν πατέρα τὸ δῶρον τῇ μητρὶ διδούς. 2. εἶδον τοὺς βαρβάρους τὸν κήρυκα ἀποκτείνοντας. 3. τοὺς λίθους βαρεῖς ὄντας οὐκ ἐθελήσουσιν οἱ στρατιῶται εἰς τὸ στρατόπεδον φέρειν. 4. τοὺς τὴν πόλιν προδόντας νομίζομεν ἐκείνῳ τῷ πολίτῃ συνεῖναι. 5. τοῦ βασιλέως ἐλθόντος, ἔτυχεν ὁ ἄρχων τοὺς ἵππους διώκων.

II. Write in Greek:

1. I see that the battle is very hard for those who are with the king. 2. The general will honor those who went into the enemy's camp unseen. 3. Here the Greeks stood, for it did not escape them that to flee was disgraceful. 4. All except the Athenian betrayed those who were with them. 5. Near the general stood the herald of the barbarians.

THE OPTATIVE. PURPOSE CLAUSES

WITH ἵνα, ὡς, AND ὅπως

1. The *optative*, which takes its name from its chief independent use, that of expressing a wish, is the mood used in secondary sequence in many constructions.

2. The endings of this mood are of two kinds:

   (a) The -ι type, found in the present, future, and the first and second aorists active of regular verbs.

   (b) The -ιη type, found in the present of contract verbs and the present and second aorist of μι-verbs, except those in -νυμι.

3. Learn the following optatives:

   (a) Regular verbs (-ι type):

Present	Present	Future
παιδεύοιμι	δεικνύοιμι	παιδεύσοιμι
παιδεύοις	δεικνύοις	παιδεύσοις
παιδεύοι[1]	δεικνύοι	παιδεύσοι
παιδεύοιμεν	δεικνύοιμεν	παιδεύσοιμεν
παιδεύοιτε	δεικνύοιτε	παιδεύσοιτε
παιδεύοιεν	δεικνύοιεν	παιδεύσοιεν

First Aorist	Second Aorist
παιδεύσαιμι	λίποιμι
παιδεύσαις or παιδεύσειας[2]	λίποις
παιδεύσαι[1] or παιδεύσειε	λίποι
παιδεύσαιμεν	λίποιμεν
παιδεύσαιτε	λίποιτε
παιδεύσαιεν or παιδεύσειαν	λίποιεν

[1] It should be remembered that final αι and οι in the optative mood are counted long in determining the accent. Cf. Lesson 2.

[2] The forms in -ειας, -ειε, and -ειαν are more common in Attic Greek.

(b) Contract and μι-verbs (-ιη type):

PRESENT

τιμῴην	φιλοίην[3]	ἱσταίην	τιθείην[4]	διδοίην	εἴην, (from εἰμί)
τιμῴης	φιλοίης	ἱσταίης	τιθείης	διδοίης	εἴης
τιμῴη	φιλοίη	ἱσταίη	τιθείη	διδοίη	εἴη
τιμῷμεν	φιλοῖμεν	ἱσταῖμεν	τιθεῖμεν	διδοῖμεν	εἶμεν or εἴημεν
τιμῷτε	φιλοῖτε	ἱσταῖτε	τιθεῖτε	διδοῖτε	εἶτε or εἴητε
τιμῷεν	φιλοῖεν	ἱσταῖεν	τιθεῖεν	διδοῖεν	εἶεν or εἴησαν

SECOND AORIST

σταίην, etc.   θείην, etc.   δοίην etc.   εἴην, etc. (from ἵημι)

In the plural of all these verbs, longer forms with iota followed by -ημεν, -ητε, -ησαν are found. Cf. the optative of εἰμί.

4. One of the commonest ways of expressing purpose in Greek is by a clause introduced by ἵνα, ὡς, or ὅπως, followed by the subjunctive after a primary tense of the main verb, by an optative after a secondary tense.[5] Negative purpose is expressed by ἵνα μή, ὡς μή, ὅπως μή, or μή.

He is come to teach Cyrus. ἥκει ἵνα Κῦρον παιδεύῃ.

He came to teach Cyrus. ἦλθεν ἵνα Κῦρον παιδεύοι.

5. The optative, either present or aorist, may be used either with or without εἴθε or εἰ γάρ to express a possible wish. The negative is μή.

εἴθε Κῦρος ἔλθοι. Would that Cyrus would come! or, May Cyrus come!

6. Wishes impossible of realization are expressed by εἴθε or εἰ γάρ with the imperfect indicative for present time, with the aorist indicative for past time. The negative is μή.

εἴθε Κῦρος παρῆν. Would that Cyrus were here!

READING

A. Ὦ φίλε Πάν τε καὶ ἄλλοι ὅσοι τῇδε θεοί, δοίητέ μοι καλῷ γενέσθαι τἄνδοθεν· ἔξωθεν δ' ὅσα ἔχω, τοῖς ἐντὸς εἶναί μοι φίλια. πλούσιον δὲ νομίζοιμι τὸν σοφόν. τὸ δὲ χρυσοῦ πλῆθος εἴη μοι ὅσον μήτε φέρειν μήτε ἄγειν δύναιτ' ἄλλος ἢ ὁ σώφρων.—PLATO, Phaedrus.

[3] Similarly to φιλοίην conjugate the optative δηλοίην from δηλόω.
[4] Similarly to τιθείην conjugate the optative ἱείην from ἵημι.
[5] Even after secondary tenses of the main verb, the subjunctive is sometimes used in purpose clauses.

83

1. Σωκράτης ἔφη τοὺς μὲν πολλοὺς ἀνθρώπους ζῆν ἵνα ἐσθίωσιν, αὐτὸς δὲ ἐσθίειν ἵνα ζῇ.—XENOPHON. 2. ἂν καλὸν ἔχῃ τις σῶμα καὶ ψυχὴν κακήν, καλὴν ἔχει ναῦν καὶ κυβερνήτην κακόν. 3. πρῶτος ἤγγειλα Κῦρον στρατεύοντα ἐπ᾽ αὐτόν. 4. οἱ Ἀθηναῖοι πολλὰς ναῦς εἷλον καὶ πέντε τούτων αὐτοῖς σὺν ἀνδράσιν. 5. ὁ δὲ Ἀλκιβιάδης ἰδὼν τοὺς Ἀθηναίους οὐκ ἔχοντας σῖτον, ἔπειθεν αὐτοὺς ἀπὸ τοῦ κακοῦ χωρίου ἀπελθεῖν ὡς σῖτον ἕλοιεν. οἱ δὲ στρατηγοὶ ἐκέλευσαν αὐτὸν ἀπελθεῖν· αὐτοὶ γὰρ νῦν στρατηγεῖν, οὐκ ἐκεῖνον. 6 ἅμα φεύγοντες ἀπέβαλον τὰ ὅπλα καίπερ ἡμῶν οὐ διωκόντων. 7. κατέκαυσαν ὡς πλείστας τῶν νεῶν ὅπως μὴ οἱ Πέρσαι εἰς τὰς νήσους εἰσπλέοιεν.

Notes: 2. κυβερνήτης, pilot (cf. Latin *gubernator*; governor). 3. στρατεύω, carry on a campaign (cf. στρατιά, etc.): participle in indirect discourse. 5. ἰδών, aorist participle of ὁράω (vocabulary, Lesson 24); στρατηγεῖν, infinitive in implied indirect statement following ἐκέλευσαν. 7. κατακαίω, burn up [caustic]; ἡ νῆσος, island [Dodecanese]; εἰσπλέοιεν, dissyllabic verbs in -εω do not contract e with o sounds (cf. Lesson 15).

VOCABULARY

ναῦς, νεώς, ἡ, ship [Latin *navis, nauta*] (declension continues νηΐ, ναῦν; νῆες, νεῶν, ναυσί, ναῦς)
πλῆθος, -ους, τό, number, amount, crowd [plethora]
σῖτος, -ου, ὁ, food, grain
χωρίον, -ου, -τό, place, spot

ὅσος, -η, -ον, how much, how great, as much, as great; who (relative; indirect interrogative)

ἀγγέλλω, ἀγγελῶ, ἤγγειλα, report (cf. ἄγγελος); takes participle or ὅτι clause in indirect statement
αἱρέω, αἱρήσω, εἷλον (infinitive ἑλεῖν, participle ἑλών), take
ἐσθίω, 2nd aorist ἔφαγον, eat [esophagus]
πλέω, aorist ἔπλευσα, sail (cf. πλοῦς)

ἅμα, at the same time; together with (+dative)
ἵνα (conjunction), in order that
καίπερ, although (with participle)
ὅπως (conjunction), in order that
πέντε, five

ὡς (conjunction), in order that

ENGLISH SENTENCES

1. He fled that he might not fare badly. 2. They sent the messengers to report that Cyrus was plotting against (ἐπιβουλεύω + dative) the king. 3. He will write the letter in order that the king may kill

84

the men who plotted against him. 4. If you do not eat anything, you will not live. 5. When the ship sails to that place, the men will take food. 6. Alcibiades ordered the Athenians to get food from some other place.

REVIEW EXERCISES

I. Translate:

1. κακῶς ἔχει κύων ὅστις ἂν ἀκούῃ μέν τινα, μηδένα δὲ ὁρᾷ. 2. ὅ τι ἂν γιγνώσκῃ ὁ ἄγγελος, λέξει ὅταν εἰς τὴν ἀγορὰν ἔλθῃ. 3. ὁ βασιλεὺς ἐθέλει μαθεῖν τὸ ὄνομα ἅπαντος ἀνδρὸς ὅστις ἂν τὰ χρήματα μὴ ἀποδιδῷ. 4. θαυμάζει τε καὶ χαλεπῶς φέρει ὅταν ἀκούῃ ὡς οἱ πολῖται ἐκ τοῦ πολέμου ἔφυγον. 5. καταθήσω τὰ χρήματα ἵνα λαμβάνῃς τὸ παλαιὸν βιβλίον ὃ ἔδειξε σοὶ ὁ γέρων.

II. Write in Greek:

1. They are throwing rocks at the boys in order to drive them out of the agora. 2. Whenever the ruler comes into his province, he takes presents from the greatest citizens. 3. What is the name of the wonderful book which you are giving to your brother? Why did you not show it to us?   Whoever is present must stand when the general speaks.   If we do not give back the dog, the boys will be annoyed.

LESSON **24**

FUTURE LESS VIVID AND
PAST GENERAL CONDITIONS.
INDIRECT DISCOURSE WITH ὅτι
AND ὡς. INDIRECT QUESTIONS

1. Future Less Vivid Conditions. These conditions, sometimes known as "should-would" conditions, describe a remote or doubtful possibility in the future. They follow this formula:

PROTASIS	APODOSIS
εἰ + optative (present or aorist)	optative (present or aorist) + ἄν

If the enemy should come, you would fight. εἰ οἱ πολέμιοι ἔλθοιεν, πολεμοῖτε ἄν.

The particle ἄν usually follows a negative, a verb, or some other emphatic word.

2. Past General Conditions. These state some general truth about the past. Their formula is:

PROTASIS	APODOSIS
εἰ + optative (present or aorist)	imperfect indicative

If Cyrus was general, his soldiers won. εἰ στρατηγοίη Κῦρος, ἐνίκων οἱ στρατιῶται αὐτοῦ.

In these conditions, as in Future More Vivid and Present General conditions (cf. Lesson 22, paragraph 6c), a relative pronoun or adverb may be used in place of εἰ.

3. As with the subjunctive, the tenses of the optative describe the type or aspect of an action rather than its time. The present stands for continuous or repeated action, the aorist for a single act. The one exception to this rule is explained in the following paragraph.

4. In addition to indirect discourse expressed by the infinitive or the participle, Greek has a third manner of expressing this construction. After many verbs of saying (e.g., λέγω, εἶπον) and perceiving, the indirect statement may be expressed by a clause introduced by the conjunction ὅτι or ὡς. After a primary tense of the introductory verb, the main verb of the indirect statement remains unchanged in tense or mood from that of the direct statement. But after a secondary tense of the introductory verb, the main verb of the indirect statement *may* be changed to the optative of its original tense. In this construction the tenses of the optative have a real temporal significance. This is almost the only case in which the future optative is used in Greek.

Cyrus is writing. *Κῦρος γράφει.*
He says that Cyrus is writing. *λέγει ὅτι Κῦρος γράφει.*
He said that Cyrus was writing. *ἔλεξεν ὅτι Κῦρος γράφοι* (or *γράφει*).

Cyrus came. *Κῦρος ἦλθε.*
He says that Cyrus came. *λέγει ὅτι Κῦρος ἦλθε.*
He said that Cyrus had come. *ἔλεξεν ὅτι Κῦρος ἔλθοι* (or *ἦλθεν*).

Cyrus will come. *Κῦρος ἥξει.*
He says that Cyrus will come. *λέγει ὅτι Κῦρος ἥξει.*
He said that Cyrus would come. *ἔλεξεν ὅτι Κῦρος ἥξοι* (or *ἥξει*).

5. Subordinate clauses in indirect discourse, both in the infinitive and in the ὅτι construction, are governed by the following rules:

(a) In primary sequence they remain unchanged.
(b) In secondary sequence, if the verb of a subordinate clause is in a primary tense of the indicative or is in the subjunctive, it *may* be changed to the corresponding tense of the optative, ἄν dropping out; but secondary tenses of the indicative are not changed.

ἐὰν Κῦρος ἔλθῃ, νικήσομεν. If Cyrus comes, we shall be victorious.
ἔλεγεν ὅτι εἰ Κῦρος ἔλθοι, νικήσοιμεν. He said that if Cyrus came, we should be victorious (or *ἔφη εἰ Κῦρος ἔλθοι, ἡμᾶς νικήσειν*).

6. It is important to observe that, unlike English, Greek keeps the tense of the direct in the indirect statement, even when the introductory verb is in the past.

7. Indirect questions follow the same rule as does the ὅτι construction.

They ask them who they are. ἐρωτῶσιν αὐτοὺς τίνες εἰσίν.
They asked them who they were. ἠρώτων αὐτοὺς τίνες εἶεν (or εἰσίν).

8. The apodosis of a *future less vivid condition* may be used independently of its protasis to express a possibility, e.g., Κῦρος ἔλθοι ἄν, Cyrus might (or would) come. This is called the *potential optative*.

When the potential optative appears in indirect discourse, it is treated as follows:

(a) With the ὅτι construction it remains unchanged. ἔλεγεν ὅτι Κῦρος ἔλθοι ἄν.
(b) With the infinitive construction it becomes the infinitive with ἄν. ἔφη Κῦρον ἐλθεῖν ἄν.
(c) With the participial construction it becomes the participle with ἄν. ἤκουσε Κῦρον ἐλθόντα ἄν.

READING

A. ἁ δὲ χεὶρ τὰν χεῖρα νίζει· δός τι καὶ λάβοις τί κα.—EPICHARMUS.

B. εἴ τις ὑπερβάλλοι τὸ μέτριον, τὰ ἐπιτερπέστατα ἀτερπέστατα ἂν γίγνοιτο.—DEMOCRITUS.

1. πάντων χρημάτων μέτρον ἐστὶν ἄνθρωπος, τῶν μὲν ὄντων ὡς ἔστιν, τῶν δὲ οὐκ ὄντων ὡς οὐκ ἔστιν.—PROTAGORAS. 2. μικροῖς πόνοις τὰ μεγάλα πῶς ἕλοι τις ἄν; 3. εἰ μὴ γαμοίη ἄνθρωπος, οὐκ ἂν ἔχοι κακά.—MENANDER. 4. εἴης φορητὸς οὐκ ἄν, εἰ πράττοις καλῶς. 5. The Soldiers Are Attacked by "Boulimy" (i.e., ox-hunger, a not very scientific term for exhaustion). τῇ δὲ ὑστεραίᾳ ἤλαυνον διὰ χιόνος (snow) πολλῆς ἐπὶ τὸν Εὐφράτην ποταμόν, καὶ διέβαινον (crossed) αὐτόν. ἐντεῦθεν δὲ ἤλαυνον ἡμέραν ὅλην διὰ χιόνος, καὶ πολλοὶ τῶν ἀνθρώπων ἐβουλιμίασαν. Ξενοφῶν δὲ ἠγνόει ὅ τι τὸ πάθος (matter) εἴη. εἶπε δέ τις αὐτῷ ὅτι οἱ ἄνθρωποι βουλιμιῶεν, καὶ ὅτι χρὴ αὐτοὺς φαγεῖν τι. ὁ δὲ Ξενοφῶν ἀκούσας ταῦτα, περιῄει (went around) περὶ τὸ στρατόπεδον, καὶ εἴ πού τι ὁρῴη βρωτόν (edible), διεδίδου τοῖς βουλιμιῶσιν. ἐπειδὴ δὲ φάγοιεν οἱ ἄνθρωποι, ἀνίσταντο (they got up) καὶ οὐ πολὺ ὕστερον ἤλαυνον.—XENOPHON, *Anabasis* (adapted).

Notes: 1. μέτρον, measure (cf. τὸ μέτριον, the mean, i.e., "measured") [thermometer]. 2. πόνοις, dative of means. 4. φορητός, endurable (cf. φέρω) [semaphore].

88

VOCABULARY

πάθος, -ους, τό, experience, suffering
πατρίς, -ίδος, ἡ, native land, country
ποταμός, -οῦ, ὁ, river

ὑστεραῖος, -α, -ον, the next, later; τῇ ὑστεραίᾳ = the next day
ὕστερος, -α, -ον, later [hysteron proteron]

ἀγνοέω, -ήσω, ἠγνόησα, not know, be ignorant (cf. γιγνώσκω) [agnostic]
γαμέω, γαμῶ, ἔγημα, marry [monogamous]
διαδίδωμι, give around, divide (διά in compound suggests distribution)
ἐλαύνω, ἐλῶ, ἤλασα, march, drive (future conjugated like τιμάω present)
ὁράω, 2nd aorist εἶδον, see
πράττω καλῶς, fare well, do well

ἐντεῦθεν, from here, from there (-θεν as suffix denotes place from which)
που (indefinite adverb, enclitic) somewhere (cf. ποῦ)
πῶς, how?

ENGLISH SENTENCES

1. How would you conquer? 2. The general divided the money in order that the soldiers might not be annoyed and do him some harm. 3. Whenever the general conquered, he sacrificed to the gods of his native land. 4. Someone said that if a man should not marry, he would have troubles (πράγματα). 5. Whoever did not know the truth did not fare well. 6. Xenophon said that if the men ate something, they would march faster.

REVIEW EXERCISES

I. Translate:

1. ἡ ναῦς ἔπλευσεν ὡς σῖτον κομιοῦσα ἵνα ἐσθίοιεν οἱ πολῖται. 2. ἐὰν τὸ χωρίον ἐκεῖνο ἕλωσιν οἱ στρατιῶται, εὐθὺς πέμψουσιν ἑταῖρον ὡς τῷ στρατηγῷ ἀγγέλλῃ. 3. οἱ ἄρχοντες ἐρωτῶσι τὸ πλῆθος ὅσοις δοκεῖ ῥᾴδιον εἶναι τοὺς πολεμίους νικᾶν. 4. καίπερ γέρων ὤν, ἅμα τοῖς νέοις τὰ ὅπλα ἔλαβε. 5. πέντε στρατιώτας ἐκέλευσαν μετὰ τοῦ στρατηγοῦ πλεῖν, ἵνα, εἰ δέοι, ὑπὲρ τῆς πατρίδος ἀποθάνοιεν.

II. Translate:

1. If the wicked man is king, the wise will not remain in the city. 2. Do you not see which is ill and which is cowardly? 3. What did the soldiers do in order that the city should thus honor them? 4. They will kill as many as are unwilling to sail. 5. They do not love the new companion whom the commander gave them.

89

THE MIDDLE AND PASSIVE VOICES.
PRESENT INDICATIVE,
MIDDLE AND PASSIVE.
FUTURE INDICATIVE MIDDLE.
CLAUSES EXPRESSING FEAR

1. Besides the active and passive voices, Greek has a third voice, the *middle*. It represents the subject as acting either upon himself (reflexive) or in his own interest (e.g., λούω, I wash, λούομαι, I take a bath). The special meanings of the middle voice of many verbs must be learned by experience. Some middle verbs are transitive and take objects, but rarely or never appear in active forms. These are known as deponent verbs.

2. The forms of the middle and passive voices are identical in the present, imperfect, perfect, and pluperfect tenses. In the aorist and future there are separate forms for the middle and passive.

3. The personal endings of the middle voice differ from those of the active, and the primary and secondary middle endings differ from one another. The primary endings are:[1]

SINGULAR	PLURAL
-μαι	-μεθα
-σαι	-σθε
-ται	-νται

INFINITIVE
-σθαι

[1] In the second singular of -ω and contract verbs the -σ- of the ending is dropped and the -ε- of the verb theme contracts with the -αι to form -η or -ει (or, in -άω verbs, -ᾷ).

90

4. Learn the following forms:

<table>
<tr><td>PRESENT
MIDDLE AND PASSIVE</td><td>FUTURE
MIDDLE</td></tr>
<tr><td>παιδεύ-ο-μαι</td><td>παιδεύ-σ-ο-μαι</td></tr>
<tr><td>παιδεύ-ει (η)</td><td>παιδεύ-σ-ει (η)</td></tr>
<tr><td>παιδεύ-ε-ται</td><td>παιδεύ-σ-ε-ται</td></tr>
<tr><td>παιδευ-ό-μεθα</td><td>παιδευ-σ-ό-μεθα</td></tr>
<tr><td>παιδεύ-ε-σθε</td><td>παιδεύ-σ-ε-σθε</td></tr>
<tr><td>παιδεύ-ο-νται</td><td>παιδεύ-σ-ο-νται</td></tr>
</table>

INFINITIVE

παιδεύ-ε-σθαι   παιδεύ-σ-ε-σθαι

PRESENT MIDDLE AND PASSIVE

τιμῶμαι	φιλοῦμαι	δηλοῦμαι	ἵσταμαι	τίθεμαι²	δίδομαι
τιμᾷ	φιλεῖ (-ῇ)	δηλοῖ	ἵστασαι	τίθεσαι	δίδοσαι
τιμᾶται	φιλεῖται	δηλοῦται	ἵσταται	τίθεται	δίδοται
τιμώμεθα	φιλούμεθα	δηλούμεθα	ἱστάμεθα	τιθέμεθα	διδόμεθα
τιμᾶσθε	φιλεῖσθε	δηλοῦσθε	ἵστασθε	τίθεσθε	δίδοσθε
τιμῶνται	φιλοῦνται	δηλοῦνται	ἵστανται	τίθενται	δίδονται

INFINITIVE

τιμᾶσθαι	φιλεῖσθαι	δηλοῦσθαι	ἵστασθαι	τίθεσθαι	δίδοσθαι

5. All future middles are regularly formed upon the stem of the future active, e.g., παιδεύσομαι, τιμήσομαι, ποιήσομαι, στήσομαι, etc. Liquid verbs have future middles of contract form similar to the present middle of -έω verbs, e.g., κρινοῦμαι.

6. Some verbs, like εἰμί, have no future active, only the future middle. Learn the future of εἰμί, ἔσομαι:

SINGULAR	PLURAL	INFINITIVE
ἔσομαι	ἐσόμεθα	ἔσεσθαι
ἔσει (-η)	ἔσεσθε	
ἔσται	ἔσονται	

7. Middle participles have the endings -μενος, -μένη, -μενον.³ They are declined like ἀγαθός. Learn the following present middle participles: παιδευόμενος, τιμώμενος, φιλούμενος, δηλούμενος, ἱστάμενος, τιθέμενος, διδόμενος.

Learn the future middle participles: παιδευσόμενος, τιμησόμενος, ποιησόμενος, δηλωσόμενος, στησόμενος, θησόμενος, and δωσόμενος.

² Similar to τίθεμαι is the present middle and passive of ἵημι, ἵεμαι.
³ The accent of the feminine genitive plural of -μενος participles is on the penult.

8. Verbs of fearing, when referring to an event feared in the future, are followed by object clauses which are introduced by μή for an affirmative and μὴ οὐ for a negative fear. After a primary tense of the verb of fearing the subjunctive is used in the object clause, after a secondary tense usually the optative, though the subjunctive is permissible.

I fear that Cyrus may not come. δέδοικα μὴ Κῦρος οὐκ ἔλθῃ.
They feared that the enemy might win. ἐδεδοίκεσαν μὴ οἱ πολέμιοι νικήσειαν.

When a verb of fearing refers to an event feared in the present or past, it is followed by μή (or μὴ οὐ) and the indicative. δέδοικα μὴ οἱ πολέμιοι ἐνίκησαν, I fear that the enemy may have won.

9. A verb of fearing may be followed by an object infinitive. φοβήσεται ἀδικεῖν αὐτούς, he will be afraid to injure them.

READING

A. ἀπὸ νεότητος δὲ ἀρξαμένους δεῖ μανθάνειν.—PROTAGORAS.

B. νόσος δειλοῖσιν ἑορτή. οὐ γὰρ ἐκπορεύονται ἐπὶ πρᾶξιν.—ANTIPHON.

C. ὦ ξεῖν', ἀγγέλλειν Λακεδαιμονίοις ὅτι τῇδε / κείμεθα, τοῖς κείνων ῥήμασι πειθόμενοι.—SIMONIDES.

1. ὁ μὲν νομοθέτης νόμους τίθησιν, ὁ δὲ δῆμος νόμους τίθεται. 2. ἐν νυκτὶ βουλὴ τοῖς σοφοῖς γίγνεται. 3. οὐδεὶς μετ' ὀργῆς ἀσφαλῶς βουλεύεται. 4. ἡ Αἴγυπτος δῶρον τοῦ Νείλου ποταμοῦ λέγεται. 5. νεανίας ποτὲ ὃς κακῶς εἶχε διὰ νόσον τινὰ ἔλεγε τῷ ἰατρῷ ὡς τοσαύτην νόσον ἔχοι ὥστε μὴ δύνασθαι μήτε καθῆσθαι μήτε κατακεῖσθαι μήτε στῆναι. ὁ δὲ ἰατρός, "οὐδέν," ἔφη, "ἄλλο σοι λοιπόν ἐστιν ἢ κρέμασθαι (hang yourself)" 6. A Homily on Fear. οἱ μὲν γὰρ φοβούμενοι μὴ φύγωσι τὴν πατρίδα καὶ οἱ μέλλοντες πολεμεῖν δείσαντες μὴ νικῶνται, κακῶς πράττουσιν· καὶ δὴ καὶ οἱ φοβούμενοι δουλείαν (slavery) καὶ δεσμούς (bonds), οὗτοι οὔτε σῖτον οὔτε ἄλλο ἀγαθόν τι οὐδὲν λαβεῖν δύνανται διὰ τὸν φόβον. οὕτω πάντων τῶν δεινῶν ὁ φόβος μάλιστα καταπλήττει (confuses) τὴν ψυχήν.

Notes: 1. νομοθέτης, lawgiver (νόμος, τίθημι); δῆμος, the people [democracy]. 2. βουλή, counsel, plan; σοφοῖς, dative of reference. 5. νόσος (ἡ), disease, cf. νοσέω; λοιπός, left, remaining (cf. λείπω); κτλ, καὶ τὰ λοιπά = et cetera. 6. φύγωσι, be exiled from; νικῶνται, be overcome.

92

VOCABULARY

νύξ, νυκτός, ἡ, night

φόβος, -ου, ὁ, fear (cf. φοβερός)

δεινός, -ή, -όν, terrible, clever (cf. δείδω) [dinosaur]

βουλεύω, -σω, ἐβούλευσα, counsel, plan; in middle, plan for one's self

γίγνομαι, γενήσομαι, ἐγενόμην (Lesson 26), become, be proved to be, be born (deponent), cf. γένος

δείδω, aorist ἔδεισα, perfect δέδοικα (Lesson 31), fear (present not used in Attic)

δύναμαι, δυνήσουαι, be able (deponent) [dynamite] (a proverb)

ἔρχομαι, ἐλεύσομαι, ἦλθον, come, go

κάθημαι, sit (present and imperfect only; deponent)

κεῖμαι, κείσομαι, lie (deponent; used as perfect passive of τίθημι); κατάκειμαι, lie down

φοβέομαι, φοβήσομαι, fear (deponent) [claustrophobia]

μάλιστα (adverb), very much, most, especially (superlative of μάλα)

τοσοῦτος, τοσαύτη, τοσοῦτο, so much, so great; plural, so many (cf. τοιοῦτος)

ENGLISH SENTENCES

1. The citizens of Athens feared that they might not go back to their native land. 2. Kings established laws in order that men might do justly to each other. 3. He feared that the philosophers would not be kings. 4. They are afraid to sit when the king is standing. (Use genitive absolute.) 5. Those who counsel well would not fear any terrible things. 6. At night even the brave become fearful.

REVIEW EXERCISES

I. Translate:

1. μετὰ τὰ πάθη τὰ ἐκείνου τοῦ ἀνδρός, πῶς ἂν ἐθέλοι τις τὴν γυναῖκα ταύτην γαμεῖν; 2. εἴθε μὴ ἐλαύνοιεν ἡμᾶς εἰς τόνδε τὸν ποταμόν. 3. ὅτε ἔλθοι ὁ ἄρχων, ἡδέως ἂν ἴδοιεν αὐτὸν οἱ στρατιῶται. 4. εἴ που τὰ χρήματα ὁρῴη, τῇ ὑστεραίᾳ τοὺς φίλους εἰς τὸν οἶκον καλοίη ἄν. 5. ὅστις ἔλθοι, οὐκ ἐξῆν αὐτῷ ἐκεῖνο τὸ πάθος δηλοῦν.

II. Write in Greek:

1. He said that he would slay the soldiers who revealed these things to the enemy. 2. He does not know who pelted the ruler with stones. 3. We are asking with whom that woman dwelt afterwards. 4. The clever thieves are about to capture the money of the commander. 5. It would be better that we live, even though being slaves.

93

IMPERFECT MIDDLE AND PASSIVE AND SECOND AORIST MIDDLE. TEMPORAL CLAUSES

1. The secondary middle endings are:

-μην	-μεθα
-σο[1]	-σθε
-το	-ντο

2. Learn the following forms:

IMPERFECT M–P   SECOND AORIST MIDDLE

ἐπαιδευόμην	ἐλιπόμην	ἐδόμην	ἐθέμην	-εἵμην
ἐπαιδεύου	ἐλίπου	ἔδου	ἔθου	-εἶσο
ἐπαιδεύετο	ἐλίπετο	ἔδοτο	ἔθετο	-εἶτο
ἐπαιδευόμεθα	ἐλιπόμεθα	ἐδόμεθα	ἐθέμεθα	-εἵμεθα
ἐπαιδεύεσθε	ἐλίπεσθε	ἔδοσθε	ἔθεσθε	-εἶσθε
ἐπαιδεύοντο	ἐλίποντο	ἔδοντο	ἔθεντο	-εἶντο
INFINITIVE λιπέσθαι[2]		δόσθαι	θέσθαι	-έσθαι
PARTICIPLE λιπόμενος		δόμενος	θέμενος	-έμενος

IMPERFECT MIDDLE AND PASSIVE

ἐτιμώμην	ἐφιλούμην	ἐδηλούμην	ἐτιθέμην[3]	ἱστάμην	ἐδιδόμην
ἐτιμῶ	ἐφιλοῦ	ἐδηλοῦ	ἐτίθεσο	ἵστασο	ἐδίδοσο
ἐτιμᾶτο	ἐφιλεῖτο	ἐδηλοῦτο	ἐτίθετο	ἵστατο	ἐδίδοτο
ἐτιμώμεθα	ἐφιλούμεθα	ἐδηλούμεθα	ἐτιθέμεθα	ἱστάμεθα	ἐδιδόμεθα
ἐτιμᾶσθε	ἐφιλεῖσθε	ἐδηλοῦσθε	ἐτίθεσθε	ἵστασθε	ἐδίδοσθε
ἐτιμῶντο	ἐφιλοῦντο	ἐδηλοῦντο	ἐτίθεντο	ἵσταντο	ἐδίδοντο

[1] In the second singular of most verbs the -σ is dropped and the -ο contracts with the -ε- of the theme of the imperfect and second aorist to -ου; and with the -α of the first aorist to -ω.

[2] Note the accent of λιπέσθαι.

[3] ἱέμην, from ἵημι, is conjugated like ἐτιθέμην.

3. Temporal Clauses:

(a) When πρίν follows an affirmative clause it means *before* and takes the infinitive with subject accusative. When the subject of the main clause and of the infinitive is the same, the subject of the infinitive may be omitted, if it is unemphatic.

The Greeks conquered before Cyrus died. οἱ Ἕλληνες ἐνίκησαν πρὶν Κῦρον ἀποθανεῖν.

(b) πρίν meaning *until* (after a negative clause), and ἔστε, ἕως, and μέχρι, which always mean *until* or *while*, take the following construction:

1. To denote a definite past act they take the indicative, usually aorist. The same is true of ἐπεί and ἐπειδή, *when, after*. Note that the Greek uses the aorist where the English usually uses the pluperfect.

They did not flee until Cyrus had died. οὐκ ἔφυγον πρὶν Κῦρος ἀπέθανεν.

They fought until they had conquered the enemy. ἐμάχοντο ἔστε ἐνίκησαν τοὺς πολεμίους.

When they had loosed the horses, they fled. ἐπειδὴ ἔλυσαν τοὺς ἵππους, ἀπέφυγον.

2. When they denote a future or repeated act, they take a construction analogous to that of the protasis of more and less vivid future conditions:

In primary sequence they take the subjunctive with ἄν. They are waiting until he comes. μένουσιν ἕως ἂν ἔλθῃ.

In secondary sequence they take the optative without ἄν. They were waiting until he should come. ἔμενον ἕως ἔλθοι. They remained as long as we were writing. ἔμενον ἕως γράφοιμεν.

READING

A. θεὸς δ' ἁμαρτάνουσιν οὐ παρίσταται.—MENANDER.

B. ὅταν σπεύδῃ τις αὐτός, χὠ θεὸς συνάπτεται.—AESCHYLUS.

C. ὁ νόμος βούλεται μὲν εὐεργετεῖν βίον ἀνθρώπων· δύναται δὲ ὅταν αὐτοὶ βούλωνται πάσχειν εὖ· τοῖσι γὰρ πειθομένοισι τὴν ἰδίην ἀρετὴν ἐνδείκνυται.—DEMOCRITUS.

1. κακῆς ἀπ' ἀρχῆς γίγνεται τέλος κακόν.—EURIPIDES. 2. περιμένετε ἔστ' ἂν ἐγὼ ἔλθω. 3. ὁπότε ὥρα εἴη ἀρίστου, ἀνέμενεν αὐτοὺς ἔστε φάγοιέν τι.—XENOPHON. 4. καὶ ταῦτα ἐποίουν μέχρι σκότος ἐγένετο.—XENOPHON. 5. ἐπεὶ δὲ ἐξῆλθεν, ἐξήγγειλε τοῖς φίλοις τὴν κρίσιν τοῦ Ὀρόντα ὡς ἐγένετο.—XENOPHON. 6. ἔχω δὲ πολλὴν οὐσίαν καὶ πλούσιος καλοῦμαι ὑπὸ πάντων, μακάριος δ' ὑπ' οὐδενός.—MENANDER.ᵛ 7.—Themistocles and the Cock Fight. ὅτε Θεμιστοκλῆς ἐπὶ τοὺς βαρβάρους ἐξῆγε τοὺς Ἀθηναίους, ἀλεκτρυόνας (cocks) εἶδεν μαχομένους. ἰδὼν δὲ ἐπέστησε (halted) τοὺς ἄνδρας καὶ ἔλεγε πρὸς αὐτούς, "οὗτοι μὲν οὐχ ὑπὲρ πατρίδος οὐδὲ ὑπὲρ τῶν θεῶν κακῶς πάσχουσιν, οὐδὲ ὑπὲρ δόξης (glory) οὐδὲ ὑπὲρ ἐλευθερίας (freedom) οὐδὲ ὑπὲρ παίδων, ἀλλ' ὑπὲρ τοῦ μὴ ἡττηθῆναι (be beaten) ἕκαστος μηδὲ εἶξαι (yield) τῷ ἑτέρῳ ὁ ἕτερος." ταῦτα δὴ εἰπὼν ἐποίησε τοὺς Ἀθηναίους πολὺ προθυμοτέρους εἰς τὴν μάχην.—AELIAN (adapted).

Notes: C. τοῖσι πειθομένοισι, Ionic dative plural. 2. περιμένω = wait around (imperative). 3. ἄριστον (τό), lunch; ἀναμένω, wait for. 4. σκότος, darkness. 5. κρίσις, trial (cf. κρίνω, κριτής); Ὀρόντας (genitive in -α), a Persian traitor in the Anabasis. 6. οὐσία (cf. οὖσα), substance, property; ὑπό, by (Lesson 30); οὐδενός, genitive of οὐδείς (Lesson 37). 7. πάσχουσιν, suffer.

VOCABULARY

ἵππος, -ου, ὁ, ἡ, horse
πατρίς, -ίδος, ἡ, native land
ὥρα, -ας, ἡ, time, season [hour]

ἴδιος, -α, -ον, private, one's own personal (cf. ἰδιώτης, private individual) [idiot, idiom]
μακάριος, -α, -ον, blessed, happy
πλούσιος, -α, -ον, wealthy
πρόθυμος, -ον, eager (πρό + θυμός, spirit; cf. ἄθυμος, disheartened)

ἁμαρτάνω, ἁμαρτήσομαι, ἥμαρτον, miss a mark (+ genitive); err (cf. ἁμαρτία, sin)
βούλομαι, βουλήσομαι, wish
εὐεργετέω, do good to (+accusative; εὖ + ἔργον)
μάχομαι, μαχοῦμαι, fight (+ dative)
σπεύδω, -σω, ἔσπευσα, hasten, be eager

ἔστε, until, while
ἕως, until, while
μέχρι, until, while
ὁπότε and ὅτε, when, whenever
πρίν, before, until
ὡς, how

ENGLISH SENTENCES

1. I shall order them to go away when it seems best to me. 2. They wished to advise (συμβουλεύω + dative) their friends well whenever they erred. 3. He did not hurry until he saw the soldiers. 4. Solon (ὁ Σόλων) wished to see the end of a man's life before he called him happy. 5. We never err when we do good to someone. 6. Whoever was eager to fight for his native land was held in honor.

REVIEW EXERCISES

I. Translate:

1. φοβούμεθα μὴ τῆς νυκτὸς ἔλθωσιν οἱ πολέμιοι εἰς τὴν πατρίδα. 2. δεινὸς μὲν καὶ πικρός, βραχὺς δὲ γίγνεται ὁ θανάτου φόβος. 3. ἡ παιδεία, καίπερ οὐ γλυκεῖα οὖσα, πολλὰ καὶ ἀγαθὰ τοῖς εὐγενέσι δύναται τίκτειν. 4. ἔρχονται οἱ ἀληθεῖς φίλοι ὡς βουλεύσοντες εὖ ποιεῖν τοὺς ἐν δεινοῖς κειμένους. 5. κάθηται ὁ γέρων τοῖς νεανίαις μάλιστα λόγους δηλῶν ἀληθεῖς.

II. Write in Greek:

1. We fear that the city will not give the crown to the brave but to the fortunate. 2. The false can become pleasant to those who fear the truth, for of these there are too many in our country. 3. It is not safe to sit when the king is standing. 4. They asked who was cleverest to plan the war. 5. Whoever knows the truth will plan the best.

FIRST AORIST MIDDLE.
REFLEXIVE PRONOUNS.
CONTRARY-TO-FACT CONDITIONS

1. Learn the following forms:

FIRST AORIST MIDDLE

ἐπαιδευσάμην	ἐπαιδευσάμεθα
ἐπαιδεύσω	ἐπαιδεύσασθε
ἐπαιδεύσατο	ἐπαιδεύσαντο

INFINITIVE	PARTICIPLE
παιδεύσασθαι	παιδευσάμενος, -μένη, -μενον

2. The reflexive pronoun is a compound of the stems of the personal pronouns with αὐτός. In the singular of the first and second persons and throughout the third person the forms are written as one word. The ἐ- of the third person comes from an old reflexive form. Note the rough breathing of the contracted forms of the third person, by which they are distinguished from the forms of αὐτός.

3. Learn the following forms:

FIRST PERSON (*myself*)		SECOND PERSON (*yourself*)	
M	F	M	F
		SINGULAR	
ἐμαυτοῦ	ἐμαυτῆς	σεαυτοῦ (σαυτοῦ)	σεαυτῆς (σαυτῆς)
ἐμαυτῷ	ἐμαυτῇ	σεαυτῷ (σαυτῷ)	σεαυτῇ (σαυτῇ)
ἐμαυτόν	ἐμαυτήν	σεαυτόν (σαυτόν)	σεαυτήν (σαυτήν)
		PLURAL	
ἡμῶν αὐτῶν	ἡμῶν αὐτῶν	ὑμῶν αὐτῶν	ὑμῶν αὐτῶν
ἡμῖν αὐτοῖς	ἡμῖν αὐταῖς	ὑμῖν αὐτοῖς	ὑμῖν αὐταῖς
ἡμᾶς αὐτούς	ἡμᾶς αὐτάς	ὑμᾶς αὐτούς	ὑμᾶς αὐτάς

M (*himself*)   F (*herself*)   N (*itself*)

SINGULAR

ἑαυτοῦ	(αὑτοῦ)	ἑαυτῆς	(αὑτῆς)	ἑαυτοῦ	(αὑτοῦ)
ἑαυτῷ	(αὑτῷ)	ἑαυτῇ	(αὑτῇ)	ἑαυτῷ	(αὑτῷ)
ἑαυτόν	(αὑτόν)	ἑαυτήν	(αὑτήν)	ἑαυτό	(αὑτό)

PLURAL

ἑαυτῶν	(αὑτῶν)	ἑαυτῶν	(αὑτῶν)	ἑαυτῶν	(αὑτῶν)
ἑαυτοῖς	(αὑτοῖς)	ἑαυταῖς	(αὑταῖς)	ἑαυτοῖς	(αὑτοῖς)
ἑαυτούς	(αὑτούς)	ἑαυτάς	(αὑτάς)	ἑαυτά	(αὑτά)

4. The possessive adjectives are ἐμός, σός, ἡμέτερος, ὑμέτερος. They are declined like ἀγαθός and ἄξιος, and are put in the attributive position. The possessive adjective of the third person is usually supplied by the possessive genitive of αὐτός, i.e., αὐτοῦ, αὐτῆς, αὐτῶν.

5. The possessive genitive of the reflexive pronoun has the attributive position, but the possessive genitive of the personal pronoun has the predicate position (cf. Lesson 16), e.g., ὁ ἐμαυτοῦ πατήρ, ὁ πατήρ μου.

6. The rules for contrary-to-fact conditions follow:

PRESENT

PROTASIS	APODOSIS
εἰ + imperfect indicative	imperfect indicative + ἄν

PAST

εἰ + aorist indicative	aorist indicative + ἄν

7. The following examples illustrate the above rules:

If I had money, I should keep horses. εἰ χρήματα εἶχον, ἔτρεφον ἄν ἵππους.

If Cyrus had not died, the Greeks would not have come home. εἰ Κῦρος μὴ ἀπέθανεν, οὐκ ἄν ἦλθον οἴκαδε οἱ Ἕλληνες.

READING

A. διὰ γὰρ τὸ θαυμάζειν οἱ ἄνθρωποι καὶ νῦν καὶ τὸ πρῶτον ἤρξαντο φιλοσοφεῖν.—ARISTOTLE.

B. πολυμαθίη νόον ἔχειν οὐ διδάσκει· Ἡσίοδον γὰρ ἄν ἐδίδαξε καὶ Πυθαγόρην αὖτίς τε Ξενοφάνεά τε καὶ Ἑκαταῖον· . . . εἶναι γὰρ ἓν τὸ σοφόν, ἐπίστασθαι γνώμην.—HERACLITUS.

1. ὦ Μένανδρε καὶ βίε, πότερος ἄρ' ὑμῶν πότερον ἀπεμιμήσατο;

99

2. μαινόμεθα πάντες ὁπόταν ὀργιζώμεθα.—PHILEMON. 3. ἑξηκοντούτης
Διονύσιος ἐνθάδε κεῖμαι / Ταρσεύς, μὴ γήμας· εἴθε δὲ μηδ' ὁ πατήρ.
   4. πολλοί τοι πλουτοῦσι κακοί, ἀγαθοὶ δὲ πένονται,
      ἀλλ' ἡμεῖς τούτοις οὐ διαμειψόμεθα
      τῆς ἀρετῆς τὸν πλοῦτον, ἐπεὶ τὸ μὲν ἔμπεδον αἰεί,
      χρήματα δ' ἀνθρώπων ἄλλοτε ἄλλος ἔχει.—SOLON.
   5. Socrates Discusses Democracy. "Δημοκρατία, οἶμαι, γίγνεται
ὅταν οἱ πένητες (the poor) νικήσαντες τοὺς μὲν ἀποκτείνωσι τῶν ἑτέρων,
τοὺς δὲ ἐκβάλωσι, τοῖς δὲ λοιποῖς ἐξ ἴσου (equally) μεταδῶσι πολιτείας
τε καὶ ἀρχῶν." "ἔστι γάρ (surely)," ἔφη ὁ Ἀδείμαντος, "αὕτη ἡ κατάστασις (establishment) δημοκρατίας, ἐάν τε καὶ διὰ ὅπλων γένηται
ἐάν τε καὶ διὰ φόβον." "τίνα δὴ οὖν τρόπον," ἦν δ' ἐγώ (said I), "οὗτοι
οἰκοῦσι; καὶ ποία τις ἡ τοιαύτη αὖ πολιτεία; οὐκοῦν πρῶτον μὲν δὴ
ἐλεύθεροι οἱ ἄνθρωποι, καὶ ἐλευθερίας ἡ πόλις μεστὴ καὶ παρρησίας
(free speech) γίγνεται, καὶ ἐξουσία (opportunity) ἐν αὐτῇ ποιεῖν ὅ τι
τις βούλεται;" "λέγεταί γε δή," ἔφη. "ὅπου δέ γε ἐξουσία εἴη, δῆλόν
ἐστιν ὅτι ἕκαστος ἂν τὸν βίον κατασκευάζοιτο (arrange) ἐν αὐτῇ ὅστις
ἕκαστον ἀρέσκοι (please)." "δῆλον." "παντοδαποὶ (of all sorts) δὴ
ἄν, οἶμαι, ἐν ταύτῃ τῇ πολιτείᾳ μάλιστα γίγνοιντο ἄνθρωποι." "πῶς γὰρ
οὔ (why not?);" "κινδυνεύει (is likely)," ἦν δ' ἐγώ, "καλλίστη αὕτη
τῶν πολιτειῶν εἶναι."—PLATO (abridged).

Notes: 1. ἀπομιμέομαι, imitate [mimic]. 2. μαίνομαι, be mad (crazy);
ὁπόταν = ὁπότε + ἄν; ὀργίζομαι, be angry (for subjunctive form see next
lesson). 3. ἑξηκοντούτης, sixty years old; Ταρσεύς (adjective), of Tarsus;
γήμας, participle of γαμέω; εἴθε, oh that . . . (Lesson 23). 4. πλουτέω, cf.
πλοῦτος; τοι, you know; πένομαι, be poor; διαμείβομαι, take in exchange
for; ἔμπεδον, secure; ἄλλοτε, sometimes (take with ἄλλος ἀνθρώπων, as ἄλλος
ἄλλο, Lesson 13); αἰεί = ἀεί. 5. μεταδίδωμι, give a share of; πολιτεία,
government; ἀρχῶν, offices; ἐάν τε . . . ἐάν τε, whether . . . or; τρόπον, in
(what) way; μεστή, full of.

VOCABULARY

ἐλευθερία, -ας, ἡ, freedom (ἐλεύθερος, adjective, free)

ποῖος, -α, -ον, of what sort?
πότερος, -α, -ον, which (of two)?

δῆλος εἰμί+participle, be plainly, manifestly
διδάσκω, διδάξω, ἐδίδαξα, teach [didactic]
ἐπίσταμαι, know, know how to
οἶμαι and οἴομαι, οἰήσομαι (imperfect ᾤμην) think

αὖ, on the other hand, again (postpositive)
ἐνθάδε, here
ὅπου, where (in relative clauses and indirect questions; cf. ποῦ)
οὐκοῦν, to introduce a question, "is it not true that . . . ?"; therefore

ENGLISH SENTENCES

1. Which of the two would best arrange his life in such a state?
2. Socrates (ὁ Σωκράτης) said that a democracy is a government of such a sort that all the citizens know both how to rule and to be ruled. 3. If the Athenians had not killed Socrates, Plato would not have written the *Phaedo*. 4. It would be a terrible thing if good men were not happy. 5. It is better for us (accusative) to teach ourselves. 6. Is it not true that many evil men are poor?

REVIEW EXERCISES

I. Translate:

1. πρὶν μάχεσθαι, οἱ στρατιῶται ἔσπευσαν τὴν τοῦ στρατηγοῦ ἵππον πρὸς τὸν ποταμὸν ἀπάγειν· ὥρα γὰρ ἦν ὕδωρ αὐτῇ διδόναι. 2. οὐ βουλόμεθα εὐεργετεῖν αὐτοὺς πρὶν ἂν δῆλοι ὦσιν ἡμᾶς φιλοῦντες. 3. ἐμάχοντο τὴν ὅλην ἡμέραν ἔστε ἐνίκησαν τοὺς πολεμίους. 4. τὰ χρήματα αὐτοῦ τὰ ἴδια κρυπτὰ εἶχεν· οὐ γὰρ πρόθυμος ἦν πάντας τοὺς ἑταίρους πλουσίους ποιεῖν. 5. ἁμαρτάνεις ἐκεῖνον τὸν διδάσκαλον μακάριον νομίζων· οὐδεὶς γὰρ τῶν παίδων ἐν τῷ ἀγῶνι ἐνίκησεν.

II. Write in Greek:

1. I do not think he will bring the hidden talents out of the temple into the light as long as many are near him. 2. Now every man will fight for the city until he falls. 3. Who is wholly happy if he does not have a friend? 4. Every Athenian was a soldier before he became truly a citizen. 5. When we had come to a great river, we fought.

6   ART IN THE CITY-STATE: A BRONZE FOUNDRY

The outside of the fifth-century Athenian drinking cup above shows scenes in the casting of bronze statues: the kiln, with a boy behind working the bellows; on the wall, models, spare parts, and tools. To the right, a life-size statue is being pounded together. In the center below, two workmen smooth down a bronze warrior. The workmen are made small to show that the statue is twice life-size. The surface of bronze statues was not turned green and dull, but was left polished and gleaming; and marble statues were not left cold and white, but were touched with bright colors.

LESSON **28**

PRESENT MIDDLE AND PASSIVE
AND AORIST MIDDLE SUBJUNCTIVE.
THE HORTATORY SUBJUNCTIVE

---

1. The subjunctive, being associated with primary tenses (cf. Lesson 22), always has primary endings. Learn the following tenses:

PRESENT MIDDLE AND PASSIVE SUBJUNCTIVE

παιδεύωμαι	τιμῶμαι	φιλῶμαι	δηλῶμαι	τιθῶμαι[1]	διδῶμαι
παιδεύῃ	τιμᾷ	φιλῇ	δηλοῖ	τιθῇ	διδῷ
παιδεύηται	τιμᾶται	φιλῆται	δηλῶται	τιθῆται	διδῶται
παιδευώμεθα	τιμώμεθα	φιλώμεθα	δηλώμεθα	τιθώμεθα	διδώμεθα
παιδεύησθε	τιμᾶσθε	φιλῆσθε	δηλῶσθε	τιθῆσθε	διδῶσθε
παιδεύωνται	τιμῶνται	φιλῶνται	δηλῶνται	τιθῶνται	διδῶνται

AORIST MIDDLE SUBJUNCTIVE

FIRST AORIST   SECOND AORIST

FIRST AORIST	SECOND AORIST				
παιδεύσωμαι	λίπωμαι	θῶμαι	δῶμαι	-ῶμαι
παιδεύσῃ	λίπῃ	θῇ	δῷ	-ῇ
παιδεύσηται	λίπηται	θῆται	δῶται	-ῆται
παιδευσώμεθα	λιπώμεθα	θώμεθα	δώμεθα	-ώμεθα
παιδεύσησθε	λίπησθε	θῆσθε	δῶσθε	-ῆσθε
παιδεύσωνται	λίπωνται	θῶνται	δῶνται	-ῶνται

2. The *hortatory subjunctive*, usually in the first person plural, is used to express a request or a proposal (negative μή). νῦν ἀκούωμεν τοῦ ἀνδρός, now let us listen to the man.

READING

A. ἔστι που νέων ξύνεσις καὶ γερόντων ἀξυνεσίη· χρόνος γὰρ οὐ διδάσκει φρονεῖν ἀλλ’ ὡραίη τροφὴ καὶ φύσις.—DEMOCRITUS.

B. οἴῳ τις ἂν τὸ πλεῖστον τῆς ἡμέρας συνῇ, τοιοῦτον ἀνάγκη γενέσθαι καὶ αὐτὸν τοὺς τρόπους.—ANTIPHON.

[1] Similar to τιθῶμαι are ἱστῶμαι from ἵστημι and ἱῶμαι from ἵημι.

1. μέγα νομίζομεν κέρδος ἐὰν ἀλλήλοις ὠφέλιμοι γιγνώμεθα.— SOCRATES. 2. ἐμοὶ δὲ ἔστι φωνή τις ἥ, ὅταν γένηται, ἀεὶ ἀποτρέπει με.—SOCRATES. 3. μὴ φύγωμεν, ἀλλ' ἀποθάνωμεν μαχόμενοι ὑπὲρ τῆς πατρίδος. 4. μετὰ δὲ τὸ δεῖπνον ἔτυχον ἐν περιπάτῳ ὄντες πρὸ τοῦ στρατοπέδου Πρόξενος καὶ Ξενοφῶν. καὶ προσελθὼν ἄνθρωπός τις ἠρώτησε τοὺς προφύλακας ποῦ ἂν ἴδοι Πρόξενον. ἐπεὶ δὲ Πρόξενος εἶπεν ὅτι "αὐτός εἰμι ὃν ζητεῖς," εἶπεν ὁ ἄνθρωπος τάδε, "ἔπεμψέ με 'Αριαῖος πιστὸς ὢν Κύρῳ καὶ σοὶ εὔνους, καὶ κελεύει φυλάττεσθαι μή σοι ἐπιθῶνται νυκτὸς οἱ βάρβαροι. ἔστι δὲ στράτευμα πολὺ ἐν τῷ πλησίον παραδείσῳ. καὶ παρὰ τὴν γέφυραν τοῦ Τίγρητος ποταμοῦ πέμψαι κελεύει φυλακήν, ὡς Τισσαφέρνης διανοεῖται αὐτὴν λῦσαι τῆς νυκτός, ἐὰν δύνηται, ἵνα μὴ διαβῆτε (cross) τὸν ποταμόν."—XENOPHON (adapted). 5. ἦν δέ τις ἐν τῇ στρατιᾷ Ξενοφῶν 'Αθηναῖος, ὃς οὔτε στρατηγὸς οὔτε λοχαγὸς (captain) οὔτε στρατιώτης ὢν συνηκολούθει. Πρόξενος δὲ αὐτὸν μετεπέμψατο οἴκοθεν ξένος ὢν ἀρχαῖος. ὑπισχνεῖτο δὲ αὐτῷ εἰ ἔλθοι φίλον αὐτὸν Κύρῳ ποιήσειν, ὃν αὐτὸς ἔφη κρείττονα ἑαυτῷ (to himself) νομίζειν τῆς πατρίδος. —XENOPHON (adapted).

Notes: 1. κέρδος (τό), gain, advantage; ὠφέλιμοι, helpful. 4. περίπατος, walk [peripatetic]; προφύλαξ, sentry (cf. φυλάττω); ὅτι is sometimes used to introduce a direct quotation (= quotation marks); πιστός, loyal friend (cf. πιστεύω); εὔνους, friendly (εὖ + νοῦς); ἐπιτίθημι, attack (middle); παράδεισος, park, woods [paradise]; γέφυρα, bridge; φυλακή, a guard (φυλάττω); διανοέομαι, intend, have in mind (νοῦς). 5. συνακολουθέω, follow along [acolyte]; μεταπέμπομαι, summon; οἴκοθεν, from home (οἶκος, house); ἔλθοι, cf. Lesson 24, § 5; κρείττονα, more important.

VOCABULARY

ἀνάγκη, -ης, ἡ, necessity, fate; (it is) necessary

δεῖπνον, -ου, τό, meal, dinner

ξένος, -ου, ὁ, friend in a foreign country; guest; stranger; mercenary soldier [xenophobia]

φωνή, ῆς, ἡ, voice [phonograph]

ἀρχαῖος, -α, -ον, ancient, old (ἀρχή) [archaeology]

ζητέω, -ήσω, ἐζήτησα, seek

λύω, λύσω, ἔλυσα, loose, destroy [analysis]

τρέπω, τρέψω, ἔτρεψα, turn [protreptic]; ἀποτρέπω, turn aside

ὑπισχνέομαι, ὑποσχήσομαι, ὑπεσχόμην, promise

φυλάττω, φυλάξω, ἐφύλαξα, guard; middle, be on guard against [prophylactic]

ἀπό (preposition with genitive), from

πρό (preposition with genitive), before, in front of

ὡς (conjunction), because

104

ENGLISH SENTENCES

1. I asked in what manner they were helpful. 2. The messenger thinks that the enemy will attack the city as quickly as possible. 3. Let us consult about (περί + genitive) the battle which we shall fight. 4. If you promise to seek the truth, we will watch out for you. 5. Socrates says that he has a voice within himself which often turns him away. 6. There was a certain Xenophon in the army who went with Cyrus to conquer the king of the Persians.

REVIEW EXERCISES

I. Translate:

1. εἰ οἱ πολῖται τὴν ἐλευθερίαν ἐφίλησαν, οὐκ ἂν οἶμαι αὐτοὺς ἐκεῖνον τὸν βασιλέα ἑλέσθαι. 2. οὐκοῦν δεῖ ἐπίστασθαι μανθάνειν ἐὰν διδάσκειν ἐθέλῃς; 3. ἡ μήτηρ μόνους πέντε ὀδόντας ἐν τῇ κεφαλῇ εἶχεν, τούτων δὲ ὁ μέσος χρυσοῦς ἦν. 4. πότερος τῶν νεανιῶν γυμνὸς εἰς τὴν ἀγορὰν ἔπεσεν; 5. εἶπον μὲν δή τινες ὅτι οἱ στρατιῶται ἐνθάδε τοῖς πολεμίοις ἐμαχέσαντο· ἐγὼ δ᾽ αὖ ἀπὸ τοῦ ἐμαυτοῦ πατρὸς ἤκουσα ὅτι οἱ πολῖται οὐκ ἔμαθον ὅπου ἡ μάχη ἐγένετο.

II. Write in Greek:

1. If the old man had teeth, he would take more food. 2. Where did you learn to take care of your own horse? 3. If the stone had not fallen, the soldier would not have known that the enemy were coming. 4. What sort of freedom did that ruler give his own city? 5. Indeed I do not think that he ruled just as his father did.

THE MIDDLE AND PASSIVE OPTATIVE

The optative, being usually associated with secondary tenses, has secondary endings even in the present. Learn the following tenses:

(a) Present Middle and Passive:

παιδευ-οί-μην	τιμ-ῴ-μην	φιλ-οί-μην[1]	τιθεί-μην	ἱεί-μην	ἱσταί-μην
παιδεύ-οι-ο	τιμ-ῷ-ο	φιλ-οῖ-ο	τιθεῖ-ο	ἱεῖ-ο	ἱσταῖ-ο
παιδεύ-οι-το	τιμ-ῷ-το	φιλ-οῖ-το	τιθεῖ-το	ἱεῖ-το	ἱσταῖ-το
παιδευ-οί-μεθα	τιμ-ῴ-μεθα	φιλ-οί-μεθα	τιθεί-μεθα	ἱεί-μεθα	ἱσταί-μεθα
παιδεύ-οι-σθε	τιμ-ῷ-σθε	φιλ-οῖ-σθε	τιθεῖ-σθε	ἱεῖ-σθε	ἱσταῖ-σθε
παιδεύ-οι-ντο	τιμ-ῷ-ντο	φιλ-οῖ-ντο	τιθεῖ-ντο	ἱεῖ-ντο	ἱσταῖ-ντο

(b) Middle:

FIRST AORIST	FUTURE	SECOND AORIST		
παιδευ-σα-ί-μην	παιδευ-σ-οί-μην	λιπ-οί-μην	θε-ί-μην[2]	δο-ί-μην
παιδεύ-σα-ι-ο	(like	(like	(like	(like
παιδεύ-σα-ι-το	παιδευοίμην)	παιδευοίμην)	τιθείμην)	φιλοίμην)
παιδευ-σα-ί-μεθα				
παιδεύ-σα-ι-σθε				
παιδεύ-σα-ι-ντο				

READING

A. πρῶτον, οἶμαι, τῶν ἐν ἀνθρώποις ἐστὶ παίδευσις. ὅταν γάρ τις πράγματος τὴν ἀρχὴν ὀρθῶς ποιήσηται, εἰκὸς καὶ τὴν τελευτὴν ὀρθῶς γίγνεσθαι. καὶ γὰρ τῇ γῇ οἷον ἄν τις τὸ σπέρμα ἐναρόσῃ, τοιαῦτα καὶ τὰ ἔκφορα δεῖ προσδοκᾶν. καὶ ἐν νέῳ σώματι ὅταν τις τὴν παίδευσιν γενναίαν ἐναρόσῃ, ζῇ τοῦτο καὶ θάλλει διὰ παντὸς τοῦ βίου.—ANTIPHON.

I. πεινῶν φάγοι ἂν ὁπότε βούλοιτο.—XENOPHON. 2. οἱ Ἠλεῖοι ἔπειθον αὐτοὺς μὴ ποιεῖσθαι μάχην πρὶν οἱ Θηβαῖοι παραγένοιντο.—XENOPHON. 3. ἐθήρευεν ἀφ' ἵππου ὁπότε γυμνάσαι βούλοιτο ἑαυτόν.—XENOPHON. 4. ἐπεὶ δὲ Κῦρος ἀπέθανεν, οὔτε βασιλεῖ ἀντιποιούμεθα τῆς

[1] διδοίμην (from δίδωμι) and δηλοίμην (from δηλόω) are like φιλοίμην.
[2] εἵμην (from ἵημι) is like θείμην.

ἀρχῆς οὔτ' ἔστιν ὅτου ἕνεκα βουλοίμεθα ἂν τὴν βασιλέως χώραν κακῶς
ποιεῖν, οὐδ' αὐτὸν ἀποκτεῖναι ἂν ἐθέλοιμεν· πορευοίμεθα δ' ἂν οἴκαδε, εἴ
τις ἡμᾶς μὴ λυποίη.—XENOPHON. 5. The Persians' View of the
Olympic Games. ἐπεὶ οἱ Μῆδοι ἐν Ἑλλάδι ἦσαν, ἧκον ἐπ' αὐτοὺς ἄνδρες
τινὲς Ἀρκάδες ὡς αὐτομολήσοντες (desert). τούτων δὲ ἐλθόντων πρὸ
τοῦ βασιλέως, οἱ Πέρσαι ἐπύθοντο περὶ τῶν Ἑλλήνων ὅ τι νῦν ποιοῖεν. οἱ
δὲ αὐτόμολοι εἶπον ὅτι Ὀλύμπια ἄγοιεν (holding the Olympic games),
καὶ θεωροῖεν ἀγῶνας καὶ γυμνικοὺς καὶ ἱππικούς. καὶ ταῦτα ἀκούσαντες οἱ
Πέρσαι ἠρώτησαν ὅ τι τὸ ἆθλον εἴη περὶ ὅτου ἀγωνίζονται (contest).
οἱ δὲ εἶπον ὅτι στέφανος (wreath) κοτίνου (wild olive) ἐστίν. ἔπειτα τῶν
Περσῶν τις ἔφη, "ποίους ἐπ' ἄνδρας μαχούμεθα, οἳ οὐ περὶ χρημάτων τὸν
ἀγῶνα ποιοῦνται, ἀλλὰ περὶ ἀρετῆς;"—HERODOTUS (adapted).

Notes: 1. πεινάω, be hungry. 2. ἔπειθον, conative imperfect, tried to persuade. 3. θηρεύω (θηράω), hunt (cf. θηρίον, θήρ [wild beast]); γυμνάζω
exercise (γυμνός). 4. ἀντιποιέομαι, contend with; οὔτ' ἔστιν ὅτου ἕνεκα, there
is no reason why (cf. οὐκ ἔστιν ὅστις, there is no one who, etc.); λυποίη, cf.
λύπη, pain.

VOCABULARY

ἆθλον, -ου, τό, prize [athletic]
Ἑλλάς, -άδος, ἡ, Greece [Hellas]
χώρα, -ας, ἡ, country, land (cf. χωρίον)

ἥκω, ἥξω (imperfect ἧκον), have come, arrive, come
θεωρέω, watch, view [theory]
πορεύομαι, -σομαι, proceed, go [pore]
πυνθάνομαι, πεύσομαι, ἐπυθόμην, inquire, learn (often takes participle in
  indirect discourse)

ἀντί, preposition with genitive, instead of, for, in place of
ἕνεκα, on account of (preposition + genitive; follows its noun)
οἴκαδε, (to) home, homeward (οἰκία); suffix -δε denotes place to which
  (cf. -θεν)
περί, preposition with genitive, for, concerning; with dative and accusative, around, about

ENGLISH SENTENCES

1. Xenophon, who was an old friend of Proxenus, went along with
him in order to fight the Persians. 2. They learned that they were in
Greece. 3. He inquired why they wished to view the country. 4.
Proxenus (ὁ Πρόξενος) said that Xenophon would go home when he
had seen the country of the Persians. 5. The prize for which they

contested (ἠγωνίζοντο) was excellence rather than money. 6. The guards asked the man who was seeking (use participle) Proxenus who he was.

REVIEW EXERCISES

I. Translate:

1. τῶν στρατιωτῶν τὸ στρατόπεδον φυλαττόντων, εἰς τὴν τοῦ βασιλέως σκηνὴν ἔλθωμεν καὶ τὸν παῖδα λύωμεν. 2. ἠκούσαμεν τὴν τῆς μητρὸς φωνὴν ἡμᾶς εἰς δεῖπνον καλούσης. 3. ἀνάγκη γὰρ ἦν καὶ τὰ ὅπλα καὶ τὰ φάρμακα πρὸ τῆς μάχης διατιθέναι· οὐ γὰρ δῆλόν ἐστι πότερος νικήσει, πόνος ἢ εὐχή. 4. τάλαντον τῷ τοῦ υἱοῦ δώρῳ ἐπιθείς, οὐκ εὖ ἐποίησεν. 5. λίαν φοβούμενοι, τοὺς ξένους ἀπὸ τῆς πατρίδος οὐκ ἔτρεψαν.

II. Write in Greek:

1. It is by bringing arms and food and not by surrendering the city that you will conquer the foe. 2. When he died, the king promised to leave thirty talents to his younger son. 3. It is not (the part) of those who conquer to surrender their arms. 4. Because of an old jealousy, the woman was seeking a poison for her husband. 5. From his tent the general came at once to the house because he wished to seize the letters.

THE AORIST PASSIVE
AND THE FUTURE PASSIVE.
DATIVE OF MEANS AND
GENITIVE OF PERSONAL AGENT

1. In the aorist and future tenses there are separate forms for the passive voice as distinguished from the middle. The sign of both the first aorist and the first future passive is the suffix θη (in the indicative and infinitive) or θε (in the subjunctive, optative, and participle) added directly to the stem of the verb. There is the usual augment in the aorist indicative. In the subjunctive the ε is contracted with the regular subjunctive endings of the active voice, as the accent shows. In the optative, the ε combines with the -ιη- optative forms to make endings similar to the optative of εἰμί. The infinitive ending is -ναι, and the accent is on the penult, as is regularly the case with infinitives which have that ending. Before the θ of the aorist passive suffix a labial mute is changed to φ (ἐλείφθην), a palatal mute to χ (ἐπράχθην); a dental mute or ζ is changed to σ (ἐπείσθην). Most verbs have an aorist passive of this type, but a few consonant stems, like βλάπτω, have what is known as a second aorist passive without the θ of the regular suffix.

2. Learn the following forms:

FIRST AORIST PASSIVE

INDICATIVE	SUBJUNCTIVE	OPTATIVE
ἐπαιδεύθην, *I was*	παιδευθῶ	παιδευθείην
ἐπαιδεύθης *educated,*	παιδευθῇς	παιδευθείης
ἐπαιδεύθη etc.	παιδευθῇ	παιδευθείη
ἐπαιδεύθημεν	παιδευθῶμεν	παιδευθεῖμεν or παιδευθείημεν
ἐπαιδεύθητε	παιδευθῆτε	παιδευθεῖτε or παιδευθείητε
ἐπαιδεύθησαν	παιδευθῶσι	παιδευθεῖεν or παιδευθείησαν

INFINITIVE: παιδευθῆναι

109

SECOND AORIST PASSIVE

INDICATIVE	SUBJUNCTIVE	OPTATIVE
ἐβλάβην, *I was*	βλαβῶ	βλαβείην
ἐβλάβης *harmed,*	βλαβῇς	βλαβείης
ἐβλάβη *etc.*	βλαβῇ	βλαβείη
ἐβλάβημεν	βλαβῶμεν	βλαβεῖμεν
ἐβλάβητε	βλαβῆτε	βλαβεῖτε
ἐβλάβησαν	βλαβῶσι	βλαβεῖεν

INFINITIVE: βλαβῆναι

3. Learn the declension of the first aorist passive participle:[1]

M	F	N
παιδευθείς	παιδευθεῖσα	παιδευθέν
παιδευθέντος	παιδευθείσης	παιδευθέντος
παιδευθέντι	παιδευθείσῃ	παιδευθέντι
παιδευθέντα	παιδευθεῖσαν	παιδευθέν
παιδευθέντες	παιδευθεῖσαι	παιδευθέντα
παιδευθέντων	παιδευθεισῶν	παιδευθέντων
παιδευθεῖσι	παιδευθείσαις	παιδευθεῖσι
παιδευθέντας	παιδευθείσας	παιδευθέντα

4. Means or instrument is expressed by the dative case without a preposition. ἀπέκτεινε τὸν ἵππον λίθῳ, he killed the horse with a stone.

5. Personal agent with the passive voice is generally expressed by the genitive with ὑπό. ἐκολάσθη ὑπὸ Κύρου, he was punished by Cyrus.

6. The first future passive is formed by the unaugmented first aorist passive stem plus the -σ- of the future, the thematic vowels, and the middle personal endings. Study the following:

FIRST FUTURE PASSIVE

INDICATIVE	OPTATIVE	INFINITIVE	PARTICIPLE
παιδευθήσομαι	παιδευθησοίμην	παιδευθήσεσθαι	παιδευθησόμενος
παιδευθήσει or -ῃ	παιδευθήσοιο		
παιδευθήσεται	παιδευθήσοιτο		
παιδευθησόμεθα	παιδευθησοίμεθα		
παιδευθήσεσθε	παιδευθήσοισθε		
παιδευθήσονται	παιδευθήσοιντο		

SECOND FUTURE PASSIVE

INDICATIVE	OPTATIVE	INFINITIVE	PARTICIPLE
βλαβήσομαι, etc.	βλαβησοίμην, etc.	βλαβήσεσθαι	βλαβησόμενος

[1] Similarly the second aorist participle of βλάπτω: βλαβείς, -έντος, βλαβεῖσα, -ης, βλαβέν, -έντος.

READING

A. ἱστορίας γὰρ ἐὰν ἀφέλῃ τις τὸ "διὰ τί" καὶ "πῶς" καὶ "τίνος χάριν ἐπράχθη τὸ πραχθέν" καὶ "πότερα εὔλογον ἔσχε τὸ τέλος," τὸ καταλειπόμενον αὐτῆς ἀγώνισμα μὲν μάθημα δ' οὐ γίνεται· καὶ παραυτίκα μὲν τέρπει, πρὸς δὲ τὸ μέλλον οὐδὲν ὠφελεῖ τὸ παράπαν.—POLYBIUS.

B. Σῶσος καὶ Σωσώ, Σῶτερ, σοὶ τόνδ' ἀνέθηκαν,
Σῶσος μὲν σωθείς, Σωσὼ δ' ὅτι Σῶσος ἐσώθη.—SIMONIDES.

1. περιεμένομεν ἑκάστοτε ἕως ἀνοιχθείη τὸ δεσμωτήριον· ἐπειδὴ δὲ ἀνοιχθείη, εἰσῇμεν.—PLATO. 2. χαλεπὸν χρήματα συναγείρασθαι, χαλεπώτερον δὲ φυλακὴν τούτοις περιθεῖναι.—ANAXARCHUS. 3. ἡδὺ δὲ καὶ τὸ πυθέσθαι.—HESIOD. 4. ἐν τοιούτοις δὲ πράγμασι ὄντες, συμβουλευόμεθά σοι τί χρὴ ἡμᾶς ποιεῖν περὶ ὧν λέγεις. σὺ οὖν πρὸς θεῶν συμβούλευσον ἡμῖν ὅ τι σοι δοκεῖ κάλλιστον καὶ ἄριστον εἶναι· ὥστε ἐν Ἑλλάδι περί σου λεχθήσεται ὅτι "τοῖς Ἕλλησι συμβουλευομένοις συνεβούλευσεν τάδε."— XENOPHON. 5. Λακεδαιμονίων γὰρ εἰ ἡ πόλις ἐρημωθείη (abandoned [hermit]), λειφθείη δὲ τά τε ἱερὰ καὶ τῆς κατασκευῆς τὰ ἐδάφη (the foundations of buildings), πολλὴν ἂν οἶμαι ἀπιστίαν (disbelief) τῆς δυνάμεως, προελθόντος πολλοῦ χρόνου, τοῖς ἔπειτα πρὸς τὸ κλέος αὐτῶν εἶναι . . . Ἀθηναίων δὲ τὸ αὐτὸ τοῦτο παθόντων, διπλασίαν (double) ἂν τὴν δύναμιν εἰκάζεσθαι ἀπὸ τῆς φανερᾶς ὄψεως (appearance) τῆς πόλεως ἢ ἔστιν.—THUCYDIDES.

Notes: 1. ἑκάστοτε, on each occasion (ἕκαστος, τότε); δεσμωτήριον, prison (cf. δεσμός, fetter); εἰσῇμεν, we went in (εἶμι). 4. συμβούλευσον, 1st aorist active imperative, 2nd singular; λεχθήσεται, from λέγω. 5. τοῖς ἔπειτα, cf. οἱ τότε; αὐτῶν, the Spartans'; παθόντων (πάσχω), experiencing.

VOCABULARY

δύναμις, -εως, ἡ, power; force (of troops; cf. δύναμαι)
κλέος, -ους, τό, fame

φανερός, -ά, -όν, plain, obvious

ἀγείρω, aorist active ἤγειρα, aorist passive ἠγέρθην, collect (ἀγορά)[2]
ἀνοίγνυμι and ἀνοίγω, ἀνοίξω, ἀνέῳξα, ἀνεῴχθην, open
εἰκάζω, -άσω, ἤκασα, ἠκάσθην, liken, conjecture (εἰκός, it is likely) [icon]
συμβουλεύω, give advice to; middle, consult with (seeking advice for oneself) (+ dative)

ἑκάστοτε (adverb), on each occasion (ἕκαστος + τότε)
πρὸς θεῶν, in the name of the gods! (in an appeal)

[2] The aorist passive will be added to the principal parts of important verbs from this lesson on. Complete parts of such verbs already given will be found in the general vocabulary.

ENGLISH SENTENCES

1. They consulted with the Persians in order that they might go home. 2. When the Greeks had been collected, they attacked as strongly as possible. 3. He was sent by the king to advise the generals before opening the letters. 4. The Athenians got greater fame, after time had gone on, than the Spartans. 5. If you had viewed the city of the Spartans, you would not have thought that it had great power. 6. Socrates' friends gathered to inquire when the prison would be opened by the guard.

REVIEW EXERCISES

I. Translate:

1. τὸ ἆθλον διώκοντες, οἱ βάρβαροι ἔτυχον εἰς τὴν Ἑλλάδα πορευόμενοι. 2. βαρὺς ἐγένετο ἡμῖν ἀεὶ συνὼν ὁ κῆρυξ. 3. πρὸς θεῶν, τί ἔλαθον ὑμᾶς οἱ πολέμιοι τὰ ἡμέτερα κρυπτὰ πυθόμενοι; 4. σὺν τοῖς στρατιώταις τοῖς περὶ τὴν πόλιν ἔμεινα ἵνα πυθοίμην τίνος ἕνεκα οἱ βάρβαροι εἰς τὴν χώραν ἥκοιεν. 5. εἰ οἴκαδε πορευοίμεθα τὸν ἀγῶνα μετὰ τοῦ σοῦ ἀδελφοῦ δυναίμεθα ἂν θεωρεῖν.

II. Write in Greek:

1. This prize is so much greater that he would naturally choose it instead of that one. 2. I hear that the herald is coming with the old men, the women and the children. 3. You eluded the guards when you took the general's shield. 4. If he should proceed homeward, he would learn the bitter truth about his wife. 5. Those who were pursuing the foe fell into the hands of the barbarians.

THE FIRST AND SECOND
PERFECT ACTIVE

1. The perfect of Greek verbs is a true perfect and never has the meaning of a simple past tense as does the Latin perfect. The perfect tense denotes an action completed so shortly before the present moment that the effect of that action may be called a present state, e.g., γέγραφα ἐπιστολήν, I have written (finished) the letter; ἕστηκα, I (have taken my) stand. The pluperfect denotes an action just completed before a certain moment in the past; the future perfect, an action completed before a certain moment in the future. The perfect is also used to emphasize the completeness of an action or state, e.g., ἀπόλωλα, I am utterly ruined.

2. Most vowel stems in Greek form the perfect tense by two changes in the simple verb as found in the present stem. If the verb begins with a consonant, ε is prefixed to the consonant and then the first consonant of the verb stem is prefixed to the ε, e.g., πεπαί-δευκα. This is known as the reduplication of the verb. If the verb begins with a vowel, the usual temporal augment serves as reduplication, e.g., ἥρπακα. Then the tense sign κ is suffixed directly to the stem, and to it are added the personal endings of the perfect. Compound verbs reduplicate after the prepositional element, e.g., προπεπαίδευκα.

3. A few verbs with consonant stems form their perfect without the κ, often with a change in the stem vowel: e.g., πέμπω, second perfect πέπομφα. These are called second perfects.

4. Learn the first perfect of παιδεύω and second perfect of πέμπω and ἄγω:

πεπαίδευκα	*I have*	πέπομφα,	*I have*	ἦχα,	*I have*
πεπαίδευκας	*educated,*	πέπομφας	*sent, etc.*	ἦχας	*led, etc.*
πεπαίδευκε	*etc.*	πέπομφε		ἦχε	
πεπαιδεύκαμεν		πεπόμφαμεν		ἤχαμεν	
πεπαιδεύκατε		πεπόμφατε		ἤχατε	
πεπαιδεύκασι		πεπόμφασι		ἤχασι	

Learn the so-called second perfect of ἵστημι:

SINGULAR	PLURAL
ἕστηκα, *I am standing,*	ἕσταμεν
ἕστηκας *etc.*	ἕστατε
ἕστηκε	ἑστᾶσι

5. Learn the declension of the perfect active participle:

M	F	N
	SINGULAR	
πεπαιδευκώς	πεπαιδευκυῖα	πεπαιδευκός
πεπαιδευκότος	πεπαιδευκυίας	πεπαιδευκότος
πεπαιδευκότι	πεπαιδευκυίᾳ	πεπαιδευκότι
πεπαιδευκότα	πεπαιδευκυῖαν	πεπαιδευκός
	PLURAL	
πεπαιδευκότες	πεπαιδευκυῖαι	πεπαιδευκότα
πεπαιδευκότων	πεπαιδευκυιῶν	πεπαιδευκότων
πεπαιδευκόσι	πεπαιδευκυίαις	πεπαιδευκόσι
πεπαιδευκότας	πεπαιδευκυίας	πεπαιδευκότα

6. The perfect subjunctive and optative are usually formed by conjugating the present subjunctive and optative of the verb εἰμί with the perfect active participle. For example:

SUBJUNCTIVE		OPTATIVE	
πεπαιδευκὼς ὦ	πεπαιδευκότες ὦμεν	πεπαιδευκὼς εἴην	πεπαιδευκότες εἶμεν
πεπαιδευκὼς ᾖς	πεπαιδευκότες ἦτε	πεπαιδευκὼς εἴης	πεπαιδευκότες εἶτε
πεπαιδευκὼς ᾖ	πεπαιδευκότες ὦσι	πεπαιδευκὼς εἴη	πεπαιδευκότες εἶεν

7. The perfect active infinitive ends in -έναι; e.g., πεπαιδευκέναι, ἠχέναι, πεπομφέναι (but: ἑστάναι).

8. The pluperfect active, which like the imperfect tense has only the indicative mood, is formed by augmenting the already reduplicated form of the perfect, unless it has temporal augment, in which case nothing can be added to it. The pluperfect has its own personal

endings. Learn the following pluperfect forms of παιδεύω, πέμπω, ἄγω, and ἵστημι:

ἐπεπαιδεύκη	ἐπεπόμφη	ἤχη	εἱστήκη
ἐπεπαιδεύκης	ἐπεπόμφης	ἤχης	εἱστήκης
ἐπεπαιδεύκει(ν)	ἐπεπόμφει(ν)	ἤχει(ν)	εἱστήκει(ν)
ἐπεπαιδεύκεμεν	ἐπεπόμφεμεν	ἤχεμεν	ἕσταμεν
ἐπεπαιδεύκετε	ἐπεπόμφετε	ἤχετε	ἕστατε
ἐπεπαιδεύκεσαν	ἐπεπόμφεσαν	ἤχεσαν	ἕστασαν

9. The future perfect, which is extremely rare, will not be used in this book.

10. Reduplication. There are several exceptions to the general rules for reduplication.

(a) Verbs beginning with an aspirated mute, φ, θ, or χ, substitute the smooth mute of the same class, i.e., π, τ or κ, in reduplication, e.g., θύω, τέθυκα.

(b) Verbs beginning with two or more consonants, a double consonant, or ῥ have simply the syllabic augment, ε, in place of reduplication. ἔσταλκα, from στέλλω. Verbs in ῥ double the ρ, e.g., ἔρριφα from ῥίπτω.

(c) However, verbs beginning with a mute and a liquid usually reduplicate in the regular way, e.g., πέπνευκα.

READING

A. μὴ κρίνετε ἵνα μὴ κριθῆτε.

B. τὸ ὑπὸ πολλῶν λεγόμενον, ὡς ὅσοι Ἀθηναίων εἰσὶν ἀγαθοί, διαφερόντως εἰσὶ τοιοῦτοι, δοκεῖ ἀληθέστατα λέγεσθαι· μόνοι γὰρ ἄνευ ἀνάγκης, αὐτοφυῶς, θείᾳ μοίρᾳ, ἀληθῶς καὶ οὔ τι πλαστῶς εἰσιν ἀγαθοί. —PLATO.

C. Δύ᾽ ἡμέραι γυναικός εἰσιν ἥδισται,
ὅταν γαμῇ τις κἀκφέρῃ τεθνηκυῖαν.—HIPPONAX.

1. ἐπεὶ δὲ ἀπῆλθον οἱ πολέμιοι, τρόπαιον ἔστησαν ὡς νενικηκότες. 2. ἡ ἀταξία πολλοὺς ἤδη ἀπολώλεκεν.—XENOPHON. 3. καὶ οὐκ ἀνέλπιστόν μοι γέγονεν τὸ γεγονὸς τοῦτο, ὅτι μου κατεψηφίσασθε.—PLATO (adapted). 4. The News of Aegospotami Reaches Athens (405 B.C.). ἐν δὲ ταῖς Ἀθήναις, τῆς Παράλου ἀφικομένης, νυκτὸς ἐλέγετο ἡ συμφορά, καὶ ἡ οἰμωγὴ ἐκ τοῦ Πειραιῶς διὰ τῶν μακρῶν τειχῶν εἰς ἄστυ διῆκεν, ὁ ἕτερος τῷ ἑτέρῳ παραγγέλλων. ὥστ᾽ ἐκείνης τῆς νυκτὸς οὐδεὶς ἐκοιμήθη, οὐ μόνον τοὺς ἀπολωλότας πενθοῦντες, ἀλλὰ πολὺ μᾶλλον ἔτι αὐτοὶ

ἑαυτούς, νομίζοντες πείσεσθαι οἷα ἐποίησαν Μηλίους τε καὶ ἄλλους πολλοὺς τῶν Ἑλλήνων. τῇ δὲ ὑστεραίᾳ ἐκκλησίαν ἐποίησαν.—XENOPHON. The Character of Menon of Thessaly, One of Cyrus' Generals. Μένων δὲ ὁ Θετταλὸς δῆλος ἦν ἐπιθυμῶν μὲν πλουτεῖν, ἐπιθυμῶν δὲ ἄρχειν ὅπως πλείονα λαμβάνοι, ἐπιθυμῶν δὲ τιμᾶσθαι ἵνα πλείονα κερδαίνοι (gain). φίλος τε ἐβούλετο εἶναι τοῖς μέγιστα δυναμένοις, ἵνα ἀδικῶν μὴ διδοίη δίκην. ἐπὶ δὲ τὸ κατεργάζεσθαι (accomplish) ὧν ἐπιθυμοίη, συντομωτάτην (shortest) ᾤετο ὁδὸν εἶναι διὰ τοῦ ψεύδεσθαι καὶ ἐξαπατᾶν (deceive). τὸ δὲ ἀληθὲς τὸ αὐτὸ τῷ ἠλιθίῳ (folly) εἶναι. φιλῶν δὲ φανερὸς μὲν ἦν οὐδένα (no one, accusative), ᾧτινι δὲ λέγοι ὅτι φίλος εἴη, τούτῳ δῆλος ἐγίγνετο ἐπιβουλεύων.—XENOPHON (adapted).

Notes: 1. νενικηκότες, from νικάω. 2. ἀταξία, disorder (cf. τάττω, arrange [taxidermy]). 3. ἀνέλπιστος, unexpected (ἐλπίζω, hope, expect); γεγονός, second perfect participle of γίγνομαι; καταψηφίζομαι (+ genitive), vote to condemn. 4. Πάραλος, name of the official trireme; οἰμωγή, wailing (crying "οἴμοι"); Πειραιεύς, Piraeus, port of Athens; διῆκεν = διά + ἧκω; παραγγέλλω, report; κοιμάομαι, sleep [cemetery]; πενθέω, lament; Μήλιοι, people of the island of Melos (double accusative construction with οἷα). 5. δῆλος ἦν + participle (as φανερὸς ἦν and δῆλος ἐγίγνετο), he was manifestly (eager); τὸ αὐτό + dative, the same thing as.

VOCABULARY

ἄστυ, -εως, τό, city
τρόπαιον, -ου, τό, trophy

μακρός, -ά, -όν, long [macrocosm]
οἷος, -α, -ον, what sort of (relative); as

ἀπόλλυμι, ἀπολῶ, ἀπώλεσα (2nd aorist ἀπωλόμην), ἀπολώλεκα (2nd perfect ἀπόλωλα), destroy; perish (in middle and 2nd perfect active)
ἀφικνέομαι, ἀφίξομαι, ἀφικόμην, arrive, come
δίδωμι δίκην, pay penalty; be punished
ἐπιβουλεύω, plot against (+ dative)
ἐπιθυμέω, be eager for, strive for (+ genitive)
πάσχω, πείσομαι, ἔπαθον, πέπονθα, experience; suffer [pathetic]

ἤδη, already (of a past act); now (present); soon (future)

ENGLISH SENTENCES

1. The report about the battle was carried up to the city by messengers. 2. The Athenians feared that they would themselves pay the penalty because they had done harm to the Melians. 3. He had educated the children who were sent to him from Athens. 4. Let us inquire what sort of a city that of the Athenians is. 5. Although their

general perished, the soldiers won a complete victory. 6. Menon, although often doing wrong, never paid the penalty.

REVIEW EXERCISES

I. Translate:

1. ἡ τῶν βαρβάρων δύναμις, καίπερ μείζων φαινομένη, ἑκάστοτε ὑπὸ τῶν Ἑλλήνων ἐνικήθη. 2. ἐὰν ὑπὸ τῶν πολεμίων μὴ νικηθῶμεν, μέγα ἔσται καὶ τὸ ὄνομα καὶ τὸ κλέος ἡμῶν. 3. ἅπας κύων τὴν ἡμέραν ἔχει, ὡς ἀκούομεν. 4. φανεροὶ ἦσαν οἱ πολῖται ἀγειρόμενοι ὡς μενοῦντες ἕως ἀνοιχθείη τὸ δεσμωτήριον· οὐ μὲν γὰρ ἐγίγνωσκον εἰ ἀπέθανεν ὁ Σωκράτης, ἤκαζον δὲ ὅτι ἐγγὺς εἴη ὁ θάνατος αὐτοῦ. 5. πρὸς θεῶν, τί συμβουλεύετε ἡμῖν ποιεῖν περὶ τῶν πραγμάτων τῶνδε;

II. Write in Greek:

1. When we are ill, we do not go to the assembly. 2. He was annoyed because no one had done him a kindness. 3. On each occasion when he is in the city, he calls his friends to his house. 4. Great will be the fame of whoever shall defeat these barbarians. 5. We shall gather enough money to open the prison.

Ancient craftsmen not only built colossal statues, they also carved minute gems, which were worn on rings as seal stones. The photographs are from plaster impressions of the gems; hence the reverse direction of the signature on the first. The upper left portrait is fifth-century, and the face perhaps reflects that ability both to think and to act which Pericles praised in his countrymen. Beside him is a Greek field marshal of the Hellenistic period, when Greeks conquered the East and formed powerful warring monarchies. The lower left shows another Hellenistic personage, perhaps an Eastern nabob of more settled and easier times. The lower right shows a vigorous face, possibly one of the Romans who despoiled Greece and the East alike before bringing that universal peace which proved to be sterile in the areas where once the πόλεις had lived their intense creative existence.

THE PERFECT AND PLUPERFECT
MIDDLE AND PASSIVE
OF VOWEL STEMS.
DATIVE OF PERSONAL AGENT

1. The perfect middle and passive is formed by adding the primary middle endings directly, without any thematic vowel, to the reduplicated perfect active stem without the κ. The pluperfect is formed in an analogous fashion, with secondary endings.

2. Learn the following forms:

PERFECT	PLUPERFECT
πεπαίδευμαι	ἐπεπαιδεύμην
πεπαίδευσαι	ἐπεπαίδευσο
πεπαίδευται	ἐπεπαίδευτο
πεπαιδεύμεθα	ἐπεπαιδεύμεθα
πεπαίδευσθε	ἐπεπαίδευσθε
πεπαίδευνται	ἐπεπαίδευντο

INFINITIVE: πεπαιδεῦσθαι

3. The subjunctive and optative of this tense and voice are formed by the perfect middle-and-passive participle plus the subjunctive and optative of εἰμί. The perfect middle-and-passive participle is formed by adding -μένος to the reduplicated perfect stem. It is declined like other middle participles. But note the accent, which is peculiar to this participle, e.g., πεπαιδευμένος, πεπαιδευμένη, πεπαιδευμένον. Note also that the perfect middle infinitive is accented on the penult. Cf. Appendix 5, page 173.

4. With the perfect passive system the dative may be used without a preposition to express personal agency. This construction, which probably arose from a dative of interest, is found chiefly with verbs which are impersonal or which have a thing and not a person as their subject.

The bridge has been destroyed by Cyrus. ἡ γέφυρα λέλυται Κύρῳ.

119

READING

A. παιδὸς οὐκ ἀνδρὸς τὸ ἀμέτρως ἐπιθυμεῖν.—DEMOCRITUS.

B. ὕβριν χρὴ σβεννύναι μᾶλλον ἢ πυρκαϊήν.—HERACLITUS.

C. ἡγεῖτο γὰρ αὐτῶν ἕκαστος οὐχὶ τῷ πατρὶ καὶ τῇ μητρὶ μόνον γεγενῆσθαι, ἀλλὰ καὶ τῇ πατρίδι.—DEMOSTHENES.

1. ὅτε δὲ ἐλήφθησαν, ἐλέλυντο αἱ σπονδαί. 2. ἦλθον οἱ Ἰνδοὶ ἐκ τῶν πολεμίων οὓς ἐπεπόμφει Κῦρος ἐπὶ κατασκοπήν.—XENOPHON. 3. Ποτειδειᾶται δὲ καὶ οἱ μετὰ Ἀριστέως Πελοποννήσιοι προσδεχόμενοι τοὺς Ἀθηναίους, ἐστρατοπεδεύοντο πρὸς Ὀλύνθου ἐν τῷ ἰσθμῷ, καὶ ἀγορὰν ἔξω τῆς πόλεως ἐπεποίηντο. στρατηγὸν μὲν οὖν τοῦ πεζοῦ παντὸς οἱ σύμμαχοι ᾕρηντο Ἀριστέα, τῆς δὲ ἵππου (cavalry) Περδίκκαν. Καλλίας δ᾽ αὖ ὁ τῶν Ἀθηναίων στρατηγὸς καὶ οἱ συνάρχοντες (fellow-officers) τοὺς μὲν Μακεδόνας ἱππέας καὶ τῶν συμμάχων ὀλίγους ἐπὶ Ὀλύνθου ἀποπέμπουσιν ὅπως εἴργωσι τοὺς ἐκεῖθεν ἐπιβοηθεῖν, αὐτοὶ δὲ ἀναστήσαντες τὸ στρατόπεδον ἐχώρουν ἐπὶ τὴν Ποτείδαιαν. 4. The Revolution of Cylon, an Athenian Noble. Κύλων ἦν Ἀθηναῖος ἀνὴρ Ὀλυμπιονίκης τῶν πάλαι εὐγενής τε καὶ δυνατός (cf. δύναμαι), ἐγεγαμήκει δὲ θυγατέρα Θεαγένους Μεγαρέως (the Megarian) ἀνδρὸς ὃς κατ᾽ (at) ἐκεῖνον τὸν χρόνον ἐτυράννει Μεγάρων. χρωμένῳ δὲ τῷ Κύλωνι ἐν Δελφοῖς (Delphi) ἀνεῖλεν (replied) ὁ θεὸς ἐν τοῦ Διὸς τῇ μεγίστῃ ἑορτῇ (festival) καταλαβεῖν τὴν Ἀθηναίων ἀκρόπολιν. ὁ δὲ παρά τε τοῦ Θεαγένους δύναμιν λαβών, καὶ τοὺς φίλους ἀναπείσας, ἐπειδὴ Ὀλύμπια ἐπῆλθεν ἐν Πελοποννήσῳ, κατέλαβε τὴν ἀκρόπολιν ὡς ἐπὶ τυραννίδι (tyranny), νομίσας ἑορτήν τε τοῦ Διὸς μεγίστην εἶναι καὶ ἑαυτῷ (to himself) τι προσήκειν (was fitting), Ὀλύμπια νενικηκότι. οἱ δὲ Ἀθηναῖοι αἰσθανόμενοι ἐβοήθησάν τε πανδημεὶ (in full force) ἐκ τῶν ἀγρῶν ἐπ᾽ αὐτοὺς καὶ προσκαθεζόμενοι (taking up positions) ἐπολιόρκουν. ὁ μὲν οὖν Κύλων καὶ ὁ ἀδελφὸς αὐτοῦ ἐκδιδράσκουσιν.—THUCYDIDES (adapted).

Notes: 1. ἐλήφθησαν, from λαμβάνω; σπονδαί, truce. 2. κατασκοπή, investigation, spying [skeptic]. 3. Ποτειδειᾶται, people of Potidea; στρατοπεδεύομαι, cf. στρατόπεδον, camp; πρός + genitive, near; ἰσθμός, isthmus; Ἀριστέα, accusative of Ἀριστεύς; ἐπί + genitive, in the direction of; εἴργω, prevent; ἀνίστημι, break up. 4. Θεαγένους, of Theagenes; ἀναπείσας, winning over; Ὀλύμπια, the Olympic games; ἐπολιόρκουν, besiege; ἐκδιδράσκουσιν, historical present, run out, escape.

VOCABULARY

ἀκρόπολις, -εως, ἡ, acropolis
θυγάτηρ, -τρός, ἡ, daughter
ἱππεύς, ἱππέως, ὁ, cavalryman (cf. ἵππος)

πεζός, -οῦ, ὁ, footsoldiery
σύμμαχος, -ου, ὁ, ally
ὕβρις, -εως, ἡ, insolence, arrogant pride, violence

αἱρέω (in middle), choose, elect
αἰσθάνομαι, αἰσθήσομαι, ᾐσθόμην, perceive
βοηθέω, help, rescue (+ dative); ἐπιβοηθέω, go to help
δέχομαι, δέξομαι, ἐδεξάμην, δέδεγμαι, receive (cf. προσδέχομαι, expect)
χράομαι, χρήσομαι, ἐχρησάμην, κέχρημαι, use (+ dative); consult (an
    oracle); contracts into η, not α, in the indicative
χωρέω, go

ἀνά, preposition with dative (rare) and accusative, up, through
ἐκεῖθεν, from there (cf. ἐκεῖνος)
ἔξω, outside (adverb)
πάλαι, long ago (adverb); cf. παλαιός [paleontology]

ENGLISH SENTENCES

1. Cylon had plotted against the Athenian citizens in order that
he might become their ruler. 2. Although he and his allies fought
bravely, they perished. 3. I received the weapons in order to help
our cavalry. 4. The Athenians were not conquered by Cylon, who
with insolence attacked the acropolis. 5. Since we rescued our allies,
we received a noble prize. 6. Socrates said that what befell him was
not an evil.

REVIEW EXERCISES

I. Translate:

1. ἀπολώλεκα τὸ ἄστυ ἐν ᾧ ἐγένοντο οἱ ἐμοὶ πατέρες. 2. εἰς τὸ χωρίον
ἀφικόμενοι τρόπαιον ἐστήσαμεν καὶ σῖτον εἵλομεν ἵνα ἐσθίοιμεν. 3. πλέωμεν εἰς τὴν νῆσον ἵνα δίκην ἐπιθῶμεν (punish) τοῖς ἀνδράσιν ἐκείνοις
ἀνθ’ (in return for) ὧν ἐπάθομεν ὑπ’ αὐτῶν. 4. μακρὸς ἔσται ὁ πόλεμος·
πλείω γὰρ ἢ πέντε ἔτη μαχούμεθα. 5. δίκην δώσετε πᾶσιν ὅσοις ἐπεβου-
λεύσατε.

II. Write in Greek:

1. Now he is eager to learn what sort of women you captured
along with the men. 2. Although he is an old man, he has all his
teeth. 3. He sailed to Greece in order to see his son take the prize.
4. Let us report to the soldiers where they will find the grain. 5. May
the gods destroy all who have plotted against the city.

PERFECT MIDDLE AND PASSIVE
SYSTEM OF MUTE STEMS

In verbs with stems ending with a mute, the addition of the personal endings directly to the stem of the verb causes a number of changes for the purpose of euphony. Rules for these changes follow, with examples of the conjugation of verbs with labial, dental, and palatal stems.

(a) Before σ: A labial combines to make ψ: λέλειψαι.
   A dental is dropped: ἥρπασαι.
   A palatal combines to make ξ: πέπλεξαι.

(b) Before μ: A labial becomes μ: λέλειμμαι.
   A dental becomes σ: πέπεισμαι.
   A palatal becomes γ: πέπλεγμαι.

(c) Before τ: A labial becomes π: βέβλαπται.
   A dental becomes σ: πέπεισται.
   A palatal becomes κ: τέτακται.

(d) When σ occurs between two consonants, it is dropped: τέτριβσθε becomes τέτριφθε. (See Lesson 30 for consonant changes before θ.)

	LABIAL (λείπω, leave)	DENTAL (ἁρπάζω, seize)	PALATAL (πλέκω, twist)
		PERFECT	
	λέλειμμαι	ἥρπασμαι	πέπλεγμαι
	λέλειψαι	ἥρπασαι	πέπλεξαι
	λέλειπται	ἥρπασται	πέπλεκται
	λελείμμεθα	ἡρπάσμεθα	πεπλέγμεθα
	λέλειφθε	ἥρπασθε	πέπλεχθε
	λελειμμένοι εἰσί	ἡρπασμένοι εἰσί	πεπλεγμένοι εἰσί
INFINITIVES:	λελεῖφθαι	ἡρπάσθαι	πεπλέχθαι

ἐλελείμμην	ἡρπάσμην	ἐπεπλέγμην
ἐλέλειψο	ἥρπασο	ἐπέπλεξο
ἐλέλειπτο	ἥρπαστο	ἐπέπλεκτο
ἐλελείμμεθα	ἡρπάσμεθα	ἐπεπλέγμεθα
ἐλέλειφθε	ἥρπασθε	ἐπέπλεχθε
λελειμμένοι ἦσαν	ἡρπασμένοι ἦσαν	πεπλεγμένοι ἦσαν

In the third plural of all these verbs a periphrastic form composed of the perfect middle participle plus εἰσί in the perfect and ἦσαν in the pluperfect is used.

READING

A. οἷσιν ὁ τρόπος ἐστὶν εὔτακτος, τούτου καὶ ὁ βίος συντέτακται.— DEMOCRITUS.

B. ὁ ἀνεξέταστος βίος οὐ βιωτὸς ἀνθρώπῳ.—PLATO.

1. Solon and the Tyrant Pisistratus. Σόλων ὁ Ἐξηκεστίδου γέρων ἤδη ὢν ὑπώπτευε Πεισίστρατον τυραννίδι ἐπιθήσεσθαι, ἐπεὶ παρῆλθεν ὁ Πεισίστρατος εἰς τὴν ἐκκλησίαν τῶν Ἀθηναίων καί ᾔτει φυλακήν ὁρῶν δὲ τοὺς Ἀθηναίους τῶν μὲν αὐτοῦ λόγων ῥαθύμως ἀκούοντας, προσέχοντας δὲ τὸν νοῦν τῷ Πεισιστράτῳ, ὁ Σόλων ἔλεγεν ὅτι τῶν μὲν εἴη σοφώτερος, τῶν δὲ ἀνδρειότερος. ὁπόσοι μὲν γὰρ μὴ γιγνώσκουσιν ὅτι φυλακὴν λαβὼν περὶ τὸ σῶμα τύραννος ἔσται, τούτων ἐστὶ σοφώτερος· ὁπόσοι δὲ γιγνώσκοντες σιωπῶσι, τούτων ἀνδρειότερος.—AELIAN (adapted). 2. Problems of the Historian. καὶ ὅσα μὲν λόγῳ εἶπον ἕκαστοι, ἢ μέλλοντες πολεμήσειν ἢ ἐν αὐτῷ ἤδη ὄντες, χαλεπὸν τὴν ἀκρίβειαν (accuracy) αὐτὴν τῶν λεχθέντων διαμνημονεῦσαι ἦν ἐμοί τε ὧν αὐτὸς ἤκουσα καὶ τοῖς ἄλλοθέν ποθεν ἐμοὶ ἀπαγγέλλουσιν· ὡς δ' ἂν ἐδόκουν ἐμοὶ ἕκαστοι περὶ τῶν ἀεὶ παρόντων τὰ δέοντα μάλιστ' εἰπεῖν, ἐχομένῳ (preserving) ὅτι ἐγγύτατα τῆς ξυμπάσης γνώμης (idea) τῶν ἀληθῶς λεχθέντων, οὕτως εἴρηται. τὰ δ' ἔργα (facts) τῶν πραχθέντων ἐν τῷ πολέμῳ οὐκ ἐκ τοῦ παρατυχόντος πυνθανόμενος ἠξίωσα (I thought proper) γράφειν, οὐδ' ὡς ἐμοὶ ἐδόκει, ἀλλ' οἷς τε αὐτὸς παρῆν καὶ παρὰ τῶν ἄλλων ὅσον δυνατὸν ἀκριβείᾳ περὶ ἑκάστου ἐπεξελθών. ἐπιπόνως (with labor) δὲ ηὑρίσκετο, διότι οἱ παρόντες τοῖς ἔργοις ἑκάστοις οὐ ταὐτὰ περὶ τῶν αὐτῶν ἔλεγον, ἀλλ' ὡς ἑκατέρων τις εὐνοίας ἢ μνήμης ἔχοι . . . κτῆμά τε ἐς ἀεὶ μᾶλλον ἢ ἀγώνισμα ἐς τὸ παραχρῆμα (for the present moment) ἀκούειν ξύγκειται.—THUCYDIDES, I, 22.

Notes: 1. ἐπιτίθεμαι, aim at (+ dative); ῥαθύμως, supinely, uncritically (ῥᾴδιος, easy, + θυμός, spirit); ἀνδρεῖος (cf. ἀνήρ), brave. 2. λόγῳ, in their speeches; διαμνημονεῦσαι, carry in memory; ἄν, with the infinitive εἰπεῖν; τὰ δέοντα, the fitting remarks; εἴρηται, (my account) has been written; παρατυχόντος, i.e., a casual acquaintance; οἷς, antecedent is the events which are object of verb; ηὑρίσκετο, subject is "my conclusion"; ἑκατέρων, each side (goes with εὐνοίας, favorable feeling, i.e., bias); ξύγκειται, (my work) has been composed.

VOCABULARY

ὁπόσος, -η, -ον, how great; as great as; in plural, how many; relative form of πόσος

αἰτέω, ask (a favor); takes two accusatives

ἐξετάζω, examine (ἀν-εξέταστος)

ἐπεξέρχομαι, go through, narrate

εὑρίσκω, εὑρήσω, εὗρον, εὕρηκα, εηbυlhαrᵒ εὑρέθην, find, discover

παρατυγχάνω, happen along

πολεμέω, fight

τάττω, τάξω, ἔταξα, τέταχα, τέταγμαι, ἐτάχθην, draw up, arrange; order

ὑποπτεύω, -σω, ὑπώπτευσα, suspect (ὑπό = Latin sub; οπ- = Latin root spec-; cf. ὄψομαι from ὁράω)

αἰεί (ἀεί), always; successively, from time to time

ἄλλοθεν, from elsewhere

διότι, because

ENGLISH SENTENCES

1. As many as were present suspected that Pisistratus got a body guard in order that he might become a tyrant. 2. No one was so brave as to wish to plot against him. 3. He had been harmed by the stones that the boys threw at him. 4. When the soldiers were completely drawn up, the general ordered them to attack. 5. Although you learned how many were present, you kept silent. 6. Thucydides (ὁ Θουκυδίδης) wrote the events of the war after inquiring accurately from many who had been present.

REVIEW EXERCISES

I. Translate:

1. ἐληλαμένος τοῖς πολεμίοις εἰς τὴν ἀκρόπολιν, ὁ πεζὸς ᾔσθετο ὅτι δέοι τὸν σῖτον διαδιδόναι ἔστε βοηθοῖεν οἱ σύμμαχοι. 2. ἡ τοῦ βασιλέως θυγάτηρ μεθ' ὕβρεως τὰ τοῦ ἱππέως δῶρα ἐδέξατο. 3. τὰ τῶν φίλων πάθη ὁρῶντες, οὐκ ἠγνοεῖτε ὅτι ἐκεῖθεν οὐκ ἄνευ πόνου ἔλθτε. 4. εἶδόν που ὅτι οὐ καλῶς πράττοιεν οἱ τὰς τῶν πονηρῶν θυγατέρας γαμήσαντες. 5. χρώμεθα τοῖς τῶν φίλων ἵπποις· ἐκεῖνοι γὰρ πρὸς τὸν ποταμὸν ἐληλακότες ἔξω τῆς πόλεώς εἰσιν.

II. Write in Greek:

1. He does not see how the enemy will be able to come into his country during the night, but he is most fearful that they are planning something terrible. 2. Fear is a most terrible experience for the young. 3. Long ago he proved to be our bitterest foe. 4. We are afraid either to sit down or to lie down while so many soldiers are in the house. 5. He asked how the rulers were able to go outside the walls while the guards were there.

THE IMPERATIVE OF Ω-
AND CONTRACT VERBS

1. The endings of the second singular imperative vary and must be learned for each voice and tense, but the other forms are regular:

	ACTIVE		MIDDLE	
	SINGULAR	PLURAL	SINGULAR	PLURAL
2nd person	—	-τε	—	-σθε
3rd person	-τω	-ντων	-σθω	-σθων

2. Prohibition is expressed by μή and the present imperative or by μή and the *aorist subjunctive*.

3. Imperatives by their nature always look to the future. The present tense expresses continuous or repeated action, the aorist a single act.

4. Several important second aorist imperatives are oxytone in the second singular active: εἰπέ, ἐλθέ, ἰδέ, εὑρέ, λαβέ. But the accent is recessive when these verbs are compounded, e.g., ἄπελθε.

5. Study the following imperative forms:

PRESENT		FIRST AORIST		
ACTIVE	MIDDLE—PASSIVE	ACTIVE	MIDDLE	PASSIVE
		SINGULAR		
παίδευε	παιδεύου	παίδευσον	παίδευσαι	παιδεύθητι
παιδευέτω	παιδευέσθω	παιδευσάτω	παιδευσάσθω	παιδευθήτω
		PLURAL		
παιδεύετε	παιδεύεσθε	παιδεύσατε	παιδεύσασθε	παιδεύθητε
παιδευόντων	παιδευέσθων	παιδευσάντων	παιδευσάσθων	παιδευθέντων

SECOND AORIST

ACTIVE	MIDDLE	PASSIVE
	SINGULAR	
λίπε	λιποῦ	βλάβηθι
λιπέτω	λιπέσθω	βλαβήτω
	PLURAL	
λίπετε	λίπεσθε	βλάβητε
λιπόντων	λιπέσθων	βλαβέντων

PRESENT (Contract Verbs)

ACTIVE	M—P	ACTIVE	M—P	ACTIVE	M—P
		SINGULAR			
τίμα	τιμῶ	φίλει	φιλοῦ	δήλου	δηλοῦ
τιμάτω	τιμάσθω	φιλείτω	φιλείσθω	δηλούτω	δηλούσθω
		PLURAL			
τιμᾶτε	τιμᾶσθε	φιλεῖτε	φιλεῖσθε	δηλοῦτε	δηλοῦσθε
τιμώντων	τιμάσθων	φιλούντων	φιλείσθων	δηλούντων	δηλούσθων

READING

A. ἐν τῷ Κρανείῳ ἡλιουμένῳ αὐτῷ Ἀλέξανδρος ἐπιστάς φησι, "αἴτησόν με ὃ θέλεις." καὶ ὅς, "ἀποσκότησόν μου," ἔφη.—DIOGENES LAERTIUS.

B. νᾶφε καὶ μέμνασ' ἀπιστεῖν.—EPICHARMUS.

C. βραδέως ἐγχείρει· οὗ δ' ἂν ἄρξῃ, διαβεβαιοῦ.—BIAS.

D. νίψον ἀνόμημα μὴ μόναν ὄψιν.—A PALINDROME.

1. ἢ λέγε τι σιγῆς κρεῖττον ἢ σιγὴν ἔχε. 2. μὴ πᾶσι πίστευε.—THALES. 3. γλῶττά σου μὴ προτρεχέτω τοῦ νοῦ.—CHILON. 4. φίλων παρόντων καὶ ἀπόντων μέμνησο.—THALES. 5. νόμοις πείθου. 6. μὴ ψεύδου, ἀλλ' ἀλήθευε.—SOLON. 7. τῷ δυστυχοῦντι μὴ ἐπιγέλα.—CHILON. 8. ἀνάξιον ἄνδρα μὴ ἐπαίνει διὰ πλοῦτον.—BIAS. 9. τὸν εὐτυχεῖν δοκοῦντα μὴ ζήλου πρὶν ἂν θανόντ' ἴδῃς.—EURIPIDES.

10. ἀπορῶν τι, βούλευσαι κατὰ σαυτὸν γενόμενος.
    τὸ συμφέρον γὰρ οὐχ ὁρᾶται τῷ βοᾶν,
    ἐν τῷ πρὸς αὐτὸν δ' ἀναλογισμῷ φαίνεται.—MENANDER.

Notes: 1. ἤ . . . ἤ, either . . . or. 4. μέμνησο (2nd singular perfect middle imperative), translate as present imperative. 6. ἀληθεύω, cf. ἀληθής. 7. δυστυχέω, be ill-starred (δυσ- prefix denoting difficulty or negation + τυχ-; cf. τύχη, fate) [dyspeptic]. 9. εὐτυχέω, be fortunate; ζηλόω, envy; θανόντ', 2nd aorist participle, cf. ἀποθνήσκω, die. 10. κατὰ σαυτόν, alone, by yourself; τὸ συμφέρον, the advantageous course (cf. συμφέρω; συμφορά); βοάω, shout; ἀναλογισμός, reasoning.

127

VOCABULARY

γλῶττα, -ης, ἡ, tongue [polyglot]

ἀπορέω, be at a loss (cf. πορεύομαι)

ἐπαινέω, praise (παραινέω, exhort)

ἐπιγελάω (γελάω, laugh), laugh at

μιμνήσκω, -μνήσω, -ἔμνησα, μέμνημαι, ἐμνήσθην, recall; remind; perfect
  middle, remember + genitive [mnemonic, Mnemosyne]

πείθω, in middle, obey (+ dative)

τρέχω, δραμοῦμαι, ἔδραμον, -δεδράμηκα, run (προτρέχω, run ahead) [palin-
  drome]

φαίνω, φανῶ, ἔφηνα (aorist infinitive φῆναι), πέφηνα, ἐφάνην, reveal; usually passive = appear [fantasy, fancy, Epiphany]

ψεύδω, ψεύσω, ἔψευσα, ἔψευσμαι, ἐψεύσθην, deceive; middle, lie

ENGLISH SENTENCES

1. Do not tell everything which you know. 2. Do not obey a tyrant,
but rather the gods. 3. Appear the best to your friends and do not
deceive those who trust you. 4. Do not praise a bad man. 5. Let them
praise (imperative) if they wish to receive honor themselves. 6. Those
who are perplexed should consult (as to) what the advantageous
course is.

REVIEW EXERCISES

I. Translate:

1. τεταγμένοι ἦσαν οἱ ἱππεῖς παρὰ τῷ ποταμῷ. 2. δεδιδάγμεθα περὶ
τῆς ἐλευθερίας ὑπὸ τοῦ Σωκράτους καὶ ἐπιστάμεθα ὑπὲρ αὐτῆς μάχεσθαι
τοῖς πολεμίοις, ὁπόσοι ἂν ὦσι. 3. ὑποπτεύω αὐτοὺς ἐνθάδε παρατυχεῖν καὶ
τοῖς πολεμοῦσι βοηθῆσαι. ἀεὶ γὰρ ἀνδρεῖοί εἰσι καὶ τοῖς αἰτοῦσι πάντα
πράττουσι. 4. πότερος αὖ τῶν νέων οὐκ ἂν καλῶς ἔπραξεν εἰ ὑπὸ τοῦ
βασιλέως ἐξετάσθη; 5. οὐκοῦν ἄμεινον ἂν ἐπράττομεν εἰ μὴ πάντα τῷ
διδασκάλῳ ἐλέγομεν;

II. Write in Greek:

1. I think that it was from elsewhere that the woman learned
where her husband was, for I could not give her a complete account
of what sort of things he had been doing. 2. How many had been
educated by Socrates we could not say. 3. I did not ask him for this
because I thought that he would not be willing to do it. 4. We had
been completely arranged by the general before the enemy suspected
that we were near. 5. How many happened along as he was ex-
amining the boys he did not say.

THE IMPERATIVE OF *MI*-VERBS

Study the following imperative forms:

PERSON	PRESENT		SECOND AORIST	
	ACTIVE	M–P	ACTIVE	MIDDLE

ἵστημι

	SINGULAR		SINGULAR	
2nd	ἵστη	ἵστασο	στῆθι	L
3rd	ἱστάτω	ἱστάσθω	στήτω	A C
	PLURAL		PLURAL	K
2nd	ἵστατε	ἵστασθε	στῆτε	I N
3rd	ἱστάντων	ἱστάσθων	στάντων	G

τίθημι

	SINGULAR		SINGULAR	
2nd	τίθει	τίθεσο	θές	θοῦ
3rd	τιθέτω	τιθέσθω	θέτω	θέσθω
	PLURAL		PLURAL	
2nd	τίθετε	τίθεσθε	θέτε	θέσθε
3rd	τιθέντων	τιθέσθων	θέντων	θέσθων

δίδωμι

	SINGULAR		SINGULAR	
2nd	δίδου	δίδοσο	δός	δοῦ
3rd	διδότω	διδόσθω	δότω	δόσθω
	PLURAL		PLURAL	
2nd	δίδοτε	δίδοσθε	δότε	δόσθε
3rd	διδόντων	διδόσθων	δόντων	δόσθων

ἵημι

	SINGULAR		SINGULAR	
2nd	ἵει	ἵεσο	ἔς	οὗ
3rd	ἱέτω	ἱέσθω	ἔτω	ἔσθω
	PLURAL		PLURAL	
2nd	ἵετε	ἵεσθε	ἔτε	ἔσθε
3rd	ἱέντων	ἱέσθων	ἔντων	ἔσθων

129

READING

A. δός μοι ποῦ στῶ καὶ τὰν γᾶν κινάσω.—ARCHIMEDES.

B. ἀπόδοτε τὰ Καίσαρος Καίσαρι καὶ τὰ τοῦ θεοῦ τῷ θεῷ.—JESUS.

1. τῷ θεῷ τίθει τὰ πάντα. 2. χάριν δικαίαν καὶ δίδου καὶ λάμβανε. 3. τιμαὶ διδόσθων αἱ μέγισται τοῖς ἀγωνισαμένοις ὑπὲρ τῆς πατρίδος καὶ ζῶσι καὶ ἀποθανοῦσιν. 4. μὴ φεῦγ' ἑταῖρον ἐν κακοῖσι κείμενον. 5. Δῆλος πάλαι, ὥς φασι, νῆσος ἦν πλανωμένη· τοῦ δὲ Ποσειδῶνος φήσαντος, "στῆθι, ὦ νῆσε," εἱστήκει ἡ νῆσος. 6. μὴ λέγε τίς ἦσθα πρότερον, ἀλλὰ νῦν τίς εἶ. 7. ἄφετε τὰ παιδία ἔρχεσθαι πρός με καὶ μὴ κωλύετε αὐτά· τῶν γὰρ τοιούτων ἐστὶν ἡ βασιλεία τῶν οὐρανῶν. 8. Profitable Learning. παρ' Εὐκλείδῃ τις ἀρξάμενος γεωμετρεῖν ὡς τὸ πρῶτον θεώρημα ἔμαθεν, ἤρετο τὸν Εὐκλείδην, "τί δέ μοι πλέον ἔσται ταῦτα μανθάνοντι;" καὶ ὁ Εὐκλείδης τὸν παῖδα καλέσας, "δός," ἔφη, "αὐτῷ τριώβολον, ἐπειδὴ δεῖ αὐτῷ ἐξ ὧν μανθάνει κερδαίνειν." 9. The Lord's Prayer. Πάτερ ἡμῶν ὁ ἐν τοῖς οὐρανοῖς· ἁγιασθήτω τὸ ὄνομά σου· ἐλθέτω ἡ βασιλεία σου· γενηθήτω τὸ θέλημά σου, ὡς ἐν οὐρανῷ καὶ ἐπὶ γῆς· τὸν ἄρτον ἡμῶν ἐπιούσιον (daily) δὸς ἡμῖν σήμερον· καὶ ἄφες ἡμῖν τὰ ὀφειλήματα ἡμῶν, ὡς καὶ ἡμεῖς ἀφήκαμεν τοῖς ὀφειλέταις (debtors) ἡμῶν· καὶ μὴ εἰσενέγκῃς ἡμᾶς εἰς πειρασμόν (temptation), ἀλλὰ ῥῦσαι (save) ἡμᾶς ἀπὸ τοῦ πονηροῦ.

Notes: 4. κακοῖσι, Ionic for κακοῖς. 5. Δῆλος, Delos, island in Aegean; φασι, they say; πλανωμένη, wandering; φήσαντος, participle of φημί. 6. ἦσθα and εἶ, from εἰμί (Lesson 12). 8. Εὐκλείδῃ (dative), Euclid; γεωμετρεῖν, learn geometry; θεώρημα, theorem; παῖδα, servant. 9. ἁγιασθήτω, from ἁγιάζω, reverence; ὀφείλημα, debt (ὀφείλω, owe); ἀφήκαμεν = Attic ἀφεῖμεν; εἰσενέγκῃς, from εἰσφέρω.

VOCABULARY

ἄρτος, -ου, ὁ, bread
βασιλεία, -ας, ἡ, kingdom
θέλημα, -ματος, τό, will, wish
τριώβολον, -ου, τό, three-obol piece; a half drachma

ἀγωνίζομαι, contest, fight
ἀφίημι, allow; forgive
[ἔρομαι,] ἐρήσομαι, ἠρόμην, ask (present supplied by ἐρωτάω)
κερδαίνω, make a profit; gain
κωλύω, prevent

πρότερον, formerly, before
σήμερον (adverb), today, of this day

ENGLISH SENTENCES

1. Give bread to all whoever wish to eat. 2. Let them stand in the midst of their native land and fight for it. 3. Let him appear to his friends whenever it seems best. 4. When Poseidon (ὁ Ποσειδῶν) ordered the island of Delos to cease from wandering, the island obeyed the god. 5. Let them give in order that they may get back something also. 6. Even if (εἰ καί) one should learn geometry, he would not profit from what he learns.

REVIEW EXERCISES

I. Translate:

1. μὴ ἁμάρτανε, ἐὰν βούλῃ εἰς τὴν βασιλείαν τῶν οὐρανῶν ἐλθεῖν. 2. σπεύδετε μάχεσθαι καὶ ἀγωνίζεσθαι ὑπὲρ τῆς πατρίδος καὶ μακάριοι ἔσεσθε καὶ ζῶντες καὶ ἀποθανόντες. 3. μέχρι ἄν ἐπὶ γῆς ἦτε, εὐεργεῖτε τοὺς ἀδελφοὺς καὶ ποιεῖτε τὸ τοῦ πατρὸς θέλημα. 4. οὐ δώσω αὐτῷ τὸν ἄρτον πρὶν ἄν τριώβολον δῷ. 5. μὴ δοκεῖτε μακάριοι ἔσεσθαι ἐὰν μὴ τὰ ἁμαρτήματα ἄλλοις ἀφιῆτε.

II. Write in Greek:

1. Do not call the guests to dinner before the food is ready (ἕτοιμος). 2. So long as I hear his voice, I shall remain. 3. They turned the enemy from the city today before the allies could reach it. 4. He is making more profit than he formerly did; let us ask him how many talents he took from that ship. 5. I promise that I will guard that bridge so that I may hinder the enemy who wish to destroy it.

Looking east from the Acropolis toward Mount Hymettus, one sees the upper view, which is out of sight in Figure 4. In the foreground are the remaining columns of the temple of Olympian Zeus. Begun by the tyrant Pisistratus in the sixth century B.C., and continued by an Eastern king in the Hellenistic period, it was completed by the Roman Emperor Hadrian nearly 700 years after Pisistratus.

Beyond lies the Panathenaic stadium. This too was begun in Greek times and was finished in Pentelic marble in the second century after Christ. In the Middle Ages most of the marble was burned for lime, but when in 1896 the Olympic Games were first revived, Greek architects studied the remains and restored the whole, preserving the Greek refinement of design by which the sides were curved to give a better view for spectators sitting near the ends.

LESSON **36**

SUMMARY OF VERBS

1. The student has now studied nearly all the forms of the Greek verb. It may aid him to organize their somewhat bewildering multiplicity if we summarize the various tenses. A complete paradigm of παιδεύω will be found in Appendix 5, pp. 170–174.

2. The complete verb has six principal parts, from which can be formed all the tenses and voices and moods of the entire system. These parts and the tenses and voices formed from them are now listed. The parts are always the first person singular of the tense in question. The letters A, M, and P are used for Active, Middle, and Passive.

(a) Present Indicative $\begin{cases} \text{Present AMP} \\ \text{Imperfect AMP} \end{cases}$

(b) Future Indicative   Future AM

(c) Aorist Indicative   Aorist AM

(d) Perfect Indicative Active $\begin{cases} \text{Perfect A} \\ \text{Pluperfect A} \\ \text{(Future Perfect A)}[1] \end{cases}$

(e) Perfect Indicative Middle $\begin{cases} \text{Perfect MP} \\ \text{Pluperfect MP} \\ \text{Future Perfect MP (rare)} \end{cases}$

(f) Aorist Passive $\begin{cases} \text{Aorist P} \\ \text{Future P} \end{cases}$

[handwritten annotation: Active = I S; Middle = myself; Passive = I wash myself / I am being washed]

3. Learn the principal parts of the following verbs as types of vowel and consonant stems. It should be remembered that contract

---

[1] Only two verbs, ἵστημι and (ἀπο)θνήσκω, have a future perfect active in Attic Greek.

verbs differ from regular verbs only in the present system, μι-verbs in the present, second aorist, and (rarely) second perfect systems.

παιδεύω,	παιδεύσω,	ἐπαίδευσα,	πεπαίδευκα,	πεπαίδευμαι,	ἐπαιδεύθην
πέμπω,	πέμψω,	ἔπεμψα,	πέπομφα,	πέπεμμαι,	ἐπέμφθην
ἁρπάζω,	ἁρπάσω,	ἥρπασα,	ἥρπακα,	ἥρπασμαι,	ἡρπάσθην
πράττω,	πράξω,	ἔπραξα,	πέπραχα,	πέπραγμαι,	ἐπράχθην
			or πέπραγα,		

4. Many verbs are defective in that they lack some of the principal parts. Some are deponents. Still others have two aorists or two perfects. The principal parts of all verbs should be memorized, preferably orally, so as to be *said* as speedily and accurately as possible. Parts of the most important verbs are in the Vocabulary. See also Appendix 10, page 192.

5. Another effective means of review consists in giving synopses of verbs in different tenses. This means giving all the forms of a verb in a certain person and number of an indicated tense. As an example, a complete synopsis of λύω in the third singular follows. λύω is chosen in place of παιδεύω for the sake of brevity.

	PRESENT	IMPERFECT	FUTURE	AORIST	PERFECT	PLUPERFECT
			ACTIVE			
INDIC.	λύει	ἔλυε	λύσει	ἔλυσε	λέλυκε	ἐλελύκει
SUBJ.	λύῃ	—	—	λύσῃ	λελυκὼς ᾖ	—
OPT.	λύοι	—	λύσοι	λύσειε	λελυκὼς εἴη	—
IMP.	λυέτω	—	—	λυσάτω	λελυκὼς ἔστω	—
INF.	λύειν	—	λύσειν	λῦσαι	λελυκέναι	—
PART.	λύων		λύσων	λύσας	λελυκώς	—
			MIDDLE			
INDIC.	λύεται	ἐλύετο	λύσεται	ἐλύσατο	λέλυται	ἐλέλυτο
SUBJ.	λύηται	—	—	λύσηται	λελυμένος ᾖ	—
OPT.	λύοιτο	—	λύσοιτο	λύσαιτο	λελυμένος εἴη	—
IMP.	λυέσθω	—	—	λυσάσθω	λελύσθω	—
INF.	λύεσθαι	—	λύσεσθαι	λύσασθαι	λελύσθαι	—
PART.	λυόμενος	—	λυσόμενος	λυσάμενος	λελυμένος	—
			PASSIVE			
INDIC.	λύεται	ἐλύετο	λυθήσεται	ἐλύθη	λέλυται	ἐλέλυτο
SUBJ.	λύηται	—	—	λυθῇ	λελυμένος ᾖ	—
OPT.	λύοιτο	—	λυθήσοιτο	λυθείη	λελυμένος εἴη	—
IMP.	λυέσθω	—	—	λυθήτω	λελύσθω	—
INF.	λύεσθαι	—	λυθήσεσθαι	λυθῆναι	λελύσθαι	—
PART.	λυόμενος	—	λυθησόμενος	λυθείς	λελυμένος	—

6. Synopses follow of the second aorist of λείπω and of the second aorist passive of βλάπτω in the third person singular.

	INDICATIVE	SUBJUNCTIVE	OPTATIVE	IMPERATIVE	INFINITIVE	PARTICIPLE
ACTIVE	ἔλιπε	λίπῃ	λίποι	λιπέτω	λιπεῖν	λιπών
MIDDLE	ἐλίπετο	λίπηται	λίποιτο	λιπέσθω	λιπέσθαι	λιπόμενος
PASSIVE	ἐβλάβη	βλαβῇ	βλαβείη	βλαβήτω	βλαβῆναι	βλαβείς

READING

A. ἀλλ', ὦ φίλη παῖ, λῆγε μὲν κακῶν φρενῶν,/λῆξον δ' ὑβρίζουσ'·
οὐ γὰρ ἄλλο πλὴν ὕβρις/τάδ' ἐστί, κρείσσω δαιμόνων εἶναι θέλειν.—
EURIPIDES, *Hippolytus*.

B. τίκτει τοι κόρος ὕβριν ὅταν κακῷ ὄλβος ἔπηται
ἀνθρώπῳ καὶ ὅτῳ μὴ νόος ἄρτιος ᾖ.—THEOGNIS.

The Athenians Refuse Humiliating Spartan Terms of Peace in
404 B.C. Ἐπειδὴ αἱ νῆες αἱ ὑμέτεραι διεφθάρησαν καὶ τὰ πράγματα τὰ
ἐν τῇ πόλει ἀσθενέστερα ἐγεγένητο, οὐ πολλῷ χρόνῳ ὕστερον αἵ τε νῆες
Λακεδαιμονίων ἐπὶ τὸν Πειραιᾶ ἀφικνοῦνται καὶ ἅμα λόγοι πρὸς Λακε-
δαιμονίους περὶ τῆς εἰρήνης ἐγίγνοντο. ἐν δὲ τῷ χρόνῳ τούτῳ οἱ βουλόμενοι
νεώτερα πράγματ' (revolution) ἐν τῇ πόλει γίγνεσθαι ἐπεβούλευον, καὶ
ἡγοῦντο οὐδὲν ἄλλο σφίσιν ἐμποδὼν εἶναι ἢ τοὺς τοῦ δήμου προεστηκότας
καὶ τοὺς στρατηγοῦντας. τούτους οὖν ἐβούλοντο ἐκποδὼν ποιήσασθαι, ἵνα
ῥᾳδίως ἃ βούλοιντο διαπράττοιντο. πρῶτον μὲν οὖν Κλεοφῶντι ἐπέθεντο ἐκ
τρόπου τοιούτου. ὅτε γὰρ ἡ πρώτη ἐκκλησία περὶ τῆς εἰρήνης ἐγίγνετο καὶ
οἱ παρὰ Λακεδαιμονίων ἥκοντες ἔλεγον ἐφ' οἷς (on what terms) ἕτοιμοι
εἶεν τὴν εἰρήνην ποιεῖσθαι Λακεδαιμόνιοι, εἰ κατασκαφείη τὰ τείχη τὰ
μακρά, τόθ' ὑμεῖς τε, ὦ ἄνδρες Ἀθηναῖοι, οὐκ ἠνέσχεσθ' ἀκούσαντες περὶ
τῶν τειχῶν τῆς κατασκαφῆς, Κλεοφῶν θ' ὑπὲρ ὑμῶν πάντων ἀναστὰς
ἀντεῖπεν ὡς οὐδενὶ (no) τρόπῳ οἷόν τ' εἴη ποιεῖν ταῦτα.—LYSIAS
(adapted).

Notes: 1. νῆες, from ναῦς 2. ἀσθενέστερα, more uncertain. 3. Πειραιᾶ,
accusative of Πειραιεύς, the Piraeus, port of Athens. 6. σφίσιν, for them
(reflexive); ἐμποδών (indeclinable), in the way; προεστηκότας, those in
charge (from προΐστημι, I put in charge). 7. ἐκποδών, out of the way.
8. διαπράττομαι, accomplish; Κλεοφῶν, Cleophon, an Athenian democratic
leader; ἐκ, here = in. 11. κατασκαφείη, 2nd aorist passive of κατασκάπτω,
demolish. 14. ἀντεῖπεν, said in reply (in opposition).

VOCABULARY

πρᾶγμα, -ατος, τό, thing (πράττω); in plural, matters, situation,
trouble; νεώτερα πράγματα, revolution (cf. Latin *novae res*)

ἀσθενής, -ές, weak [neurasthenia]
ἕτοιμος, -η, -ον, ready, prepared

ἀνέχομαι, put up with; stand for (ἔχω), second aorist ἠνεσχόμην; note
  double augment in aorist
διαφθείρω, -φθερῶ, διέφθειρα (aorist passive -εφθάρην), destroy, corrupt
ἕπομαι, ἕψομαι, ἑσπόμην (imperfect εἱπόμην), follow (+ dative)
ἡγέομαι, ἡγήσομαι, ἡγησάμην, ἥγημαι, suppose, think, + accusative and
  infinitive; also lead, guide (ἡγεμών, leader [hegemony])
οἷόν τέ ἐστι, it is possible

ENGLISH SENTENCES

1. When you arrive at (into) the city, you will learn who will
lead us. 2. The Athenians were annoyed because the Lacedaemonian
messengers ordered them to make peace. 3. The city was destroyed
by the weak and wicked generals who had taken her. 4. Those who
wished revolution considered that they would be able to destroy
their enemies. 5. We shall not put up with (it) if we hear that the
city is weak. 6. Those in charge of the people plotted how they might
put them out of the way.

REVIEW EXERCISES

I. Translate:

1. μήτε ἐπαινεῖτε τοὺς ἐξ ἐκείνης τῆς χώρας εἰς τὴν Ἑλλάδα πορευο-
μένους μήτε δίδοτε αὐτοῖς τὸ ἆθλον· ἐπεγέλασαν γὰρ ἡμῖν ἀεὶ ὅτε τοὺς
ἀγῶνας τοὺς ἡμετέρους θεωροῖεν. 2. εἰς τὴν πόλιν ἥκοντες, πυνθανώμεθα
περὶ τῆς ὁδοῦ· ξένη δὴ ἡ τῶν πολιτῶν γλῶττα, Ἀθηναίους δέ τινας ἐκεῖ
εὑρήσομεν. 3. μέμνημαι ἐκείνους εἰς τὸ ἄστυ δραμεῖν καὶ πολλὰ ψεῦσαι
περὶ τῆς μάχης. οἱ δὲ πολῖται καίπερ ἀποροῦντες, οὐκ αὐτοῖς ἐπείθοντο.
4. τῆς εἰρήνης ἕνεκα οἴκαδε πλέωμεν ἵνα πάντα ἃ πρότερον εἴχομεν
σώζωμεν. 5. μὴ πειθώμεθα τοῖς τὴν πατρίδα ἀπολωλεκόσιν.

II. Write in Greek:

1. Set up your father's trophy near the house. 2. Do not obey
those who have come in order to destroy the fatherland. 3. We
thought that if they had not reported false tidings you would have
helped the cavalry. 4. While the Greeks were in that country, they
observed many marvelous things. 5. Stand there until the general
arrives.

LESSON **37**

NUMERALS

1. Learn the following cardinal numerals and their meanings:

1	εἶς, μία, ἕν (α′)	21	εἶς καὶ εἴκοσι(ν), εἴκοσι
2	δύο (β′)		καὶ εἶς, εἴκοσιν εἶς (κα′)
3	τρεῖς, τρία (γ′)	30	τριάκοντα (λ′)
4	τέτταρες, τέτταρα (δ′)	40	τετταράκοντα (μ′)
5	πέντε (ε′)	50	πεντήκοντα (ν′)
6	ἕξ (ς′)	60	ἑξήκοντα (ξ′)
7	ἑπτά (ζ′)	70	ἑβδομήκοντα (ο′)
8	ὀκτώ (η′)	80	ὀγδοήκοντα (π′)
9	ἐννέα (θ′)	90	ἐνενήκοντα (ϙ′)
10	δέκα (ι′)	100	ἑκατόν (ρ′)
11	ἕνδεκα (ια′)	200	διακόσιοι, αι, α (σ′)
12	δώδεκα (ιβ′)	300	τριακόσιοι (τ′)
13	τρεῖς καὶ δέκα (ιγ′)	400	τετρακόσιοι (υ′)
14	τέτταρες καὶ δέκα (ιδ′)	500	πεντακόσιοι (φ′)
15	πεντεκαίδεκα (ιε′)	600	ἑξακόσιοι (χ′)
16	ἑκκαίδεκα (ις′)	700	ἑπτακόσιοι (ψ′)
17	ἑπτακαίδεκα (ιζ′)	800	ὀκτακόσιοι (ω′)
18	ὀκτωκαίδεκα (ιη′)	900	ἐνακόσιοι, αι, α (ϡ′)
19	ἐννεακαίδεκα (ιθ′)	1000	χίλιοι, αι, α (͵α)
20	εἴκοσι(ν) (κ′)	10,000	μύριοι, αι, α (͵ι)

For a complete list of cardinals, ordinals, and adverbs, see Appendix 4, page 168. The symbols in parentheses were used after the fourth century B.C. in numerical notation.

2. Learn the declension of the following cardinal numerals:

	ONE			TWO	THREE		FOUR	
	M	F	N	M, F, N	M, F	N	M, F	N
N	εἶς	μία	ἕν	δύο	τρεῖς	τρία	τέτταρες	τέτταρα
G	ἑνός	μιᾶς	ἑνός	δυοῖν	τριῶν		τεττάρων	
D	ἑνί	μιᾷ	ἑνί	δυοῖν	τρισί(ν)		τέτταρσι(ν)	
A	ἕνα	μίαν	ἕν	δύο	τρεῖς	τρία	τέτταρας	τέτταρα

137

3. Note that the tens from 30 on end in -κοντα and are indeclinable, whereas the hundreds from 200 on end in -κόσιοι and are declined like the plural of ἄξιος (Lesson 4, paragraph 4).

4. An important word, οὐδείς, no one, nothing, is declined like εἷς, μία, ἕν. μηδείς, similarly declined, replaces οὐδείς in places where μή would replace οὐ.

M	F	N
οὐδείς	οὐδεμία	οὐδέν
οὐδενός	οὐδεμιᾶς	οὐδενός
οὐδενί	οὐδεμιᾷ	οὐδενί
οὐδένα	οὐδεμίαν	οὐδέν

READING

A. ζῆν οὐκ ἄξιος ὅτῳ μηδὲ εἷς ἐστι χρηστὸς φίλος.—DEMOCRITUS.

B. εἷς θεός, ἔν τε θεοῖσι καὶ ἀνθρώποισι μέγιστος,
οὔτι δέμας θνητοῖσιν ὁμοίιος οὐδὲ νόημα.—XENOPHANES.

1. ἓν ἀνδρῶν, ἓν θεῶν γένος· ἐκ μιᾶς δὲ πνέομεν μητρὸς ἀμφότεροι. —PINDAR. 2. λέαινα ὀνειδιζομένη ὑπὸ ἀλώπεκος ἐπὶ τῷ ἀεὶ ἕνα τίκτειν, "ἕνα," ἔφη, "ἀλλὰ λέοντα."—AESOP. 3. φράσω δὲ καὶ τὸ πλῆθος ἑκατέρων. συνελέγησαν γὰρ ὁπλῖται Λακεδαιμονίων μὲν εἰς ἑξακισχιλίους. Ἠλείων (of the Eleans) καὶ τῶν συμμάχων αὐτῶν ἐγγὺς τρισχίλιοι καὶ Σικυωνίων (Sicyonians) πεντακόσιοι καὶ χίλιοι, Ἐπιδαυρίων (Epidaurians) δὲ οὐκ ἐλάττους τρισχιλίων ἐγένοντο.—XENOPHON. 4. "ἐρωτᾷ σε Διονύσιος δειπνῆσαι εἰς τοὺς γάμους τῶν τέκνων ἑαυτοῦ ἐν τῇ Ἰσχυρίωνος αὔριον ἥτις ἐστὶν λ΄ ἀπὸ ὥρας θ΄."—PAPYRUS. 5. ἐνταῦθα δὴ ἀριθμὸς ἐγένετο τῶν μὲν Ἑλλήνων ἀσπὶς μυρία καὶ τετρακόσια, πελτασταὶ δὲ δισχίλιοι καὶ πεντακόσιοι, τῶν δὲ μετὰ Κύρου βαρβάρων δέκα μυριάδες καὶ ἅρματα δρεπανηφόρα ἀμφὶ τὰ εἴκοσι· τῶν δὲ πολεμίων ἐλέγοντο εἶναι ἑκατὸν καὶ εἴκοσι μυριάδες καὶ ἅρματα δρεπανηφόρα διακόσια. ἄλλοι δὲ ἦσαν ἑξακισχίλιοι ἱππεῖς, ὧν Ἀρταγέρσης ἦρχεν· οὗτοι δ' αὖ πρὸ αὐτοῦ βασιλέως τεταγμένοι ἦσαν. τοῦ δὲ βασιλέως στρατεύματος ἦσαν ἄρχοντες τέτταρες, τριάκοντα μυριάδων ἕκαστος, Ἀβροκόμας, Τισσαφέρνης, Γωβρύας, Ἀρβάκης. τούτων δὲ παρεγένοντο ἐν τῇ μάχῃ ἐνενήκοντα μυριάδες καὶ ἅρματα δρεπανηφόρα ἑκατὸν καὶ πεντήκοντα.—XENOPHON.

Notes: 1. πνέω, breathe (πνεῦμα, breath [pneumonia]). 2. λέαινα, lioness, feminine of λέων [leonine]; ἀλώπηξ, fox; τίκτω, give birth to (τέκνον). 4. τῇ Ἰσχυρίωνος, at the house of Ischyrion; ὥρας θ΄, about 3 P.M. 5. ἀσπίς (shield), an individual (shield-bearing) soldier; δρεπανηφόρα, scythe-bearing; Ἀρταγέρσης, Artagerses; Ἀβροκόμας κτλ, Abrocomas, Tissaphernes, Gobryas, Arbaces; μάχη, i.e., the Battle of Cunaxa, September 3, 401 B.C.

VOCABULARY

γάμος, -ου, ὁ, marriage [monogamy]
λέων, λέοντος, ὁ, lion [chameleon]
μυριάς, -άδος, ἡ, ten thousand (collective noun)
ὁπλίτης, -ου, ὁ, hoplite (heavy-armed infantry soldier)

ἀμφότερος, -α, -ον, singular, each; plural, both
ὅμοιος, -α, -ον (Ionic, ὁμοίιος), like [homeopathy, homogeneous]

ἀναγκάζω, compel
ὀνειδίζω, express scorn, reproach
συλλέγω (aorist passive συνελέγην), gather
φράζω (future φράσω), point out, declare (+ ὅτι); middle, consider

ἀμφί, preposition with accusative, about
εἰς (with numerals), about, almost

ENGLISH SENTENCES

1. The god said, "If you fight the king, you will destroy a mighty empire." 2. At that battle there were about one hundred thousand mercenaries, of whom Cyrus was the leader. 3. There were about four hundred hoplites and one hundred cavalrymen of the enemy who attacked us. 4. He declared that a lion could express scorn for all other wild animals. 5. There were gathered one thousand six hundred and seven hoplites, who were led to Athens.

REVIEW EXERCISES

I. Translate:

1. τὸν ἄρχοντα πονηρὸν ἡγούμενος εἶναι, συμβουλεύω σοι τὴν θυγατέρα αὐτῷ εἰς γάμον μὴ διδόναι. 2. τρεῖς λέοντας ἀποκτείνας, μέγα ἦρηκε κλέος ὁ ὁπλίτης. 3. οὐδεὶς ἄνευ δυνάμεως ἀναγκάσει ἀμφοτέρας τὰς πόλεις τὰς θύρας ἀνοιγνύναι. 4. οὐκοῦν, πρὸς θεῶν, ὀνειδίζεις τοὺς τοσαῦτα χρήματα δι' ἀδικίαν συνειλοχότας; 5. εἰς πεντακισχιλίους ὁπλίτας, ὡς εἰκάζομεν, ἑκάστοτε μετ' αὐτοῦ εἰς τὴν πόλιν ἐλαύνουσι, ἀλλ' οὔποτε φράζει τί βουλεύων αὐτοὺς ἄγει.

II. Write in Greek:

1. You have all destroyed those who were gathered in the city. 2. Having just arrived from the battle, they were eager to set up a trophy. 3. Already he is plotting against the rulers, so that he may not pay the penalty for what the army has suffered through him. 4. How many and what sort of men have perished on the long

139

journey the city will learn when she comes to the hour of trial. 5. Having been driven from the city by the young men, the philosopher must go back to his own home.

IRREGULAR SECOND AORISTS

1. A number of verbs, the most important being βαίνω, to go, have irregular second aorists active conjugated like the second aorist ἔστην. Learn the aorist ἔβην (compare with ἵστημι):

INDICA-TIVE	SUBJUNC-TIVE	OPTA-TIVE	IMPERA-TIVE	INFINI-TIVE	PARTICIPLE		
ἔβην	βῶ	βαίην		βῆναι	βάς	βᾶσα	βάν
ἔβης	βῇς	βαίης	βῆθι		βάντος	βάσης	βάντος
ἔβη	βῇ	βαίη	βήτω		βάντι	βάσῃ	βάντι
					βάντα	βᾶσαν	βάν
ἔβημεν	βῶμεν	βαῖμεν			βάντες	βᾶσαι	βάντα
ἔβητε	βῆτε	βαῖτε	βῆτε		βάντων	βασῶν	βάντων
ἔβησαν	βῶσι	βαῖεν	βάντων		βᾶσι	βάσαις	βᾶσι
					βάντας	βάσας	βάντα

2. Learn the irregular second aorist of γιγνώσκω, to know (compare with δίδωμι):

INDICA-TIVE	SUBJUNC-TIVE	OPTA-TIVE	IMPERA-TIVE	INFINI-TIVE	PARTICIPLE		
ἔγνων	γνῶ	γνοίην		γνῶναι	γνούς	γνοῦσα	γνόν
ἔγνως	γνῷς	γνοίης	γνῶθι		γνόντος	γνούσης	γνόντος
ἔγνω	γνῷ	γνοίη	γνώτω		γνόντι	γνούσῃ	γνόντι
					γνόντα	γνοῦσαν	γνόν
ἔγνωμεν	γνῶμεν	γνοῖμεν			γνόντες	γνοῦσαι	γνόντα
ἔγνωτε	γνῶτε	γνοῖτε	γνῶτε		γνόντων	γνουσῶν	γνόντων
ἔγνωσαν	γνῶσι	γνοῖεν	γνόντων		γνοῦσι	γνούσαις	γνοῦσι
					γνόντας	γνούσας	γνόντα

3. The verb δύω, to sink, has an irregular second aorist ἔδυν, conjugated as follows (compare with δείκνυμι):

INDICA-TIVE	SUBJUNC-TIVE	OPTA-TIVE	IMPERA-TIVE	INFINI-TIVE	PARTICIPLE		
ἔδυν	δύω	Not		δῦναι	δύς	δῦσα	δύν
ἔδυς	δύῃς	found	δῦθι		δύντος	δύσης	δύντος
ἔδυ	δύῃ		δύτω		δύντι	δύσῃ	δύντι
					δύντα	δῦσαν	δύν
ἔδυμεν	δύωμεν				δύντες	δῦσαι	δύντα
ἔδυτε	δύητε		δῦτε		δύντων	δυσῶν	δύντων
ἔδυσαν	δύωσι		δύντων		δῦσι	δύσαις	δῦσι
					δύντας	δύσας	δύντα

READING

A. τὸ γνῶθι σαυτὸν πᾶσίν ἐστι χρήσιμον.—MENANDER.

B. κατὰ πόλλ' ἄρ' ἐστιν οὐ καλῶς εἰρημένον
τὸ γνῶθι σαυτόν· χρησιμώτερον γὰρ ἦν
τὸ γνῶθι τοὺς ἄλλους.—MENANDER.

1. ἦλθον γὰρ ἐς 'Αθήνας καὶ οὔ τίς με ἔγνωκεν.—DEMOCRITUS.
2. δὶς ἐς τὸν αὐτὸν ποταμὸν οὐκ ἂν βαίης.—HERACLITUS. 3. πάντα ῥεῖ.
—HERACLITUS. 4. Κροῖσος "Αλυν διαβὰς μεγάλην ἀρχὴν καταλύσει.—
DELPHIC ORACLE. 5. Persian Royal Post. λέγουσι γὰρ ὡς ὅσων ἂν ἡμερῶν ᾖ ἡ πᾶσα ὁδός, τοσοῦτοι ἵπποι τε καὶ ἄνδρες διεστᾶσι, κατὰ ἡμε-
ρησίαν ὁδὸν ἑκάστην ἵππος τε καὶ ἀνὴρ τεταγμένος. τοὺς (them) οὔτε
νιφετός (snow), οὐκ ὄμβρος (rain), οὐ καῦμα (heat), οὐ νὺξ εἴργει μὴ
οὐ κατανύσαι (accomplish) τὸν προκείμενον αὐτῷ δρόμον (course) τὴν
ταχίστην.—HERODOTUS. 6. Socrates Discourses on Friendship.
ἐγὼ δ' οὖν καὶ αὐτός, ὦ 'Αντιφῶν, ὥσπερ ἄλλος τις ἢ ἵππῳ ἀγαθῷ ἢ
κυνὶ ἢ ὄρνιθι (bird) ἥδεται, οὕτω καὶ ἔτι μᾶλλον ἥδομαι φίλοις ἀγαθοῖς,
καὶ ἐάν τι ἔχω ἀγαθόν, διδάσκω καὶ ἄλλοις συνίστημι (I introduce),
παρ' ὧν ἂν ἡγῶμαι αὐτοὺς ὠφελήσεσθαί τι εἰς ἀρετήν. καὶ τοὺς θησαυροὺς
τῶν πάλαι σοφῶν ἀνδρῶν οὓς ἐκεῖνοι κατέλιπον ἐν βιβλίοις γράψαντες,
σὺν τοῖς φίλοις διέρχομαι, καὶ ἄν τι ὁρῶμεν ἀγαθόν, ἐκλεγόμεθα καὶ
μέγα νομίζομεν κέρδος, ἐὰν ἀλλήλοις ὠφέλιμοι γιγνώμεθα.—ἐμοὶ μὲν δὴ
ταῦτα ἀκούοντι ἐδόκει αὐτός τε μακάριος εἶναι καὶ τοὺς ἀκούοντας ἐπὶ
καλοκἀγαθίαν ἄγειν.—XENOPHON.

Notes: 1. ἐς = εἰς; 3. ῥεῖ from ῥέω, flow. 4. Κροῖσος, Croesus, King of Lydia,
conquered by Cyrus the Great, 546 B.C. The Halys river formed the
boundary between Lydia and Persia. 5. τὴν ταχίστην (sc. ὁδόν) adverbial
accusative, as swiftly as possible. 6. 'Αντιφῶν, Antiphon the Sophist;
μέγα, κτλ, see Lesson 18; καλοκἀγαθίαν, gentlemanliness, word applied in
fifth century B.C. to the nobles (cf. Latin optimates, French prudhommes).

142

VOCABULARY

θησαυρός, -οῦ, ὁ, treasure; treasure house

δύω, δύσω, ἔδυσα and ἔδυν, δέδυκα, δέδυμαι, ἐδύθην, cause to enter, enter; sink; put on

διέρχομαι, go through, explore

ἐκλέγομαι, select [eclectic]

ἥδομαι, take pleasure in (+ dative)

ὠφελέω, help (ὠφέλιμος)

δίς (adverb), twice

κατά, preposition + genitive and accusative, down, along; according to

ENGLISH SENTENCES

1. Croesus went to Delphi (εἰς Δελφούς) to ask whether he should attack Cyrus. 2. "I shall teach you," said Socrates, "to do good to your friends." 3. You get pleasure in those horses rather than in your noble friends. 4. Men kept (held) their books in treasure houses from which no one could steal them. 5. He would not go into the same house in which his father was. 6. There were as many horses as there were men.

REVIEW EXERCISES

I. Translate:

1. ὁ ἱππεὺς ᾔρητο τῷ βασιλεῖ ἵνα μετὰ ἑκκαίδεκα ὁπλιτῶν τὴν ἐκείνου θυγατέρα εἰς τὸν γάμον ἄγοι. 2. οἱ σύμμαχοι πάλαι ἠναγκάσθησαν μετὰ τοῦ πεζοῦ συλλεχθέντες εἰς τὴν ἀκρόπολιν χωρεῖν, ὡς τοῖς ἄρχουσι βοηθήσοντες. 3. οὐκοῦν ἤσθεσθε τὸν λέοντα ἀμφοτέρους τοὺς κύνας ἑλόντα; 4. δεχώμεθα τοὺς ξένους καὶ χρώμεθα αὐτοῖς ὡς συμμάχοις πρὸς τὴν τοῦ βασιλέως ὕβριν. 5. φράζε μοι οἵτινες ἐκεῖθεν ἔξω τῆς πόλεως ἀνὰ τὴν ὁδὸν καὶ ἀμφὶ τὸ ἱερὸν τεταγμένοι εἰσίν.

II. Write in Greek:

1. He had always been thoroughly questioned by his father after each battle, and if he was unable to tell anything, he was reproached. 2. About eleven lions were slain in the camp, but how many were found in the wood (ὕλη, -ης, ἡ) we did not learn. 3. They had been drawn up so as to fight whoever might happen along. 4. I shall ask him to tell why he suspects that the soldier is not giving a complete account of all the troubles of the army. 5. We shall choose hoplites from elsewhere because those who were sent to us are not brave.

IMPERATIVE OF εἰμί.
CONJUGATION OF εἶμι

1. Learn the present imperative of εἰμί:

	SINGULAR	PLURAL
2nd person	ἴσθι	ἔστε
3rd person	ἔστω	ἔστων

2. Learn the following active forms of εἶμι, to go; theme ἰ- (cf. Latin *ire*):

PRESENT INDICATIVE	IMPERFECT INDICATIVE	PRESENT SUBJUNC- TIVE	PRESENT OPTATIVE	PRESENT IMPERATIVE	PRESENT INFINITIVE
εἶμι	ᾖα or ᾔειν	ἴω	ἴοιμι or ἰοίην		ἰέναι
εἶ	ᾔεις or ᾔεισθα	ἴῃς	ἴοις	· ἴθι	
εἶσι(ν)	ᾔει or ᾔειν	ἴῃ	ἴοι	ἴτω	
ἴμεν	ᾖμεν	ἴωμεν	ἴοιμεν		PRESENT PARTICIPLE
ἴτε	ᾖτε	ἴητε	ἴοιτε	ἴτε	ἰών, ἰοῦσα,
ἴασι(ν)	ᾖσαν or ᾔεσαν	ἴωσι	ἴοιεν	ἰόντων	ἰόν

READING

A. ἀγεωμέτρητος μηδεὶς εἰσίτω.—EUCLID.

B. ἦθος ἀνθρώπῳ δαίμων.—HERACLITUS.

1. εὐτυχῶν μὲν μέτριος ἴσθι, ἀτυχῶν δὲ φρόνιμος. 2. χαλεπὸν τὸ ἑαυτὸν γνῶναι.—THALES. 3. γῆς ἐπέβην γυμνός, γυμνός θ' ὑπὸ γαῖαν ἄπειμι. 4. φιλόπονος ἴσθι καὶ βίον κτήσῃ καλόν. 5. ἴτω τὰ πράγματα ὅπῃ τῷ θεῷ φίλον. 6. ἔγωγε μετὰ φίλου ἑταίρου κἂν διὰ πυρὸς ἴοιμι. 7. Ἀντισθένης οἰκῶν ἐν Πειραιεῖ καθ' ἑκάστην ἡμέραν ἀνῄει εἰς ἄστυ συνεσόμενος τῷ Σωκράτει. 8. Ἡρακλῆς καὶ Θησεὺς περιῇσαν τὴν γῆν καθαροῦντες θηρίων βλαβερῶν καὶ ἀνθρώπων ἀνοσίων. 9. Κέρβερος ὁ ἐν

᾽Αιδου κύων ἥμερος μὲν ἦν, ὁπότε τις εἰσίοι, ἐξιέναι δ' οὐδένα εἴα. 10. A Definition of Education. τὴν πρὸς ἀρετὴν ἐκ παίδων παιδείαν, ποιοῦσαν ἐπιθυμητήν τε καὶ ἐραστὴν τοῦ πολίτην γενέσθαι τέλεον, ἄρχειν τε καὶ ἄρχεσθαι μετὰ δίκης ἐπιστάμενον . . . ταύτην τὴν τροφὴν ὁ λόγος βούλοιτ' ἂν μόνην παιδείαν προσαγορεύειν.—PLATO, *Laws*. 11. Accommodating The Great Man. ὡς ᾽Αλέξανδρος ἐνίκησε τοὺς Πέρσας, ἐκέλευσε τοὺς ῞Ελληνας θεὸν αὐτὸν ψηφίσασθαι. ἄλλοι μὲν οὖν ἄλλα ἐψηφίσαντο, Λακεδαιμόνιοι δ' ἐκεῖνα· "ἐπεὶ ᾽Αλέξανδρος θεὸς εἶναι βούλεται, ἔστω θεός."

Notes: 1. εὐτυχῶν, having good luck; ἀτυχῶν, having bad luck. 3. γαῖαν = γῆν. 4. φιλόπονος, fond of toil; κτήσῃ, you will get. 5. φίλον, adjective, pleasing. 6. ἔγωγε, I, at least; κἄν = καὶ ἄν (crasis). 7. ᾽Αντισθένης, Antisthenes, the Cynic philosopher; ἄστυ, i.e., Athens. 8. ῾Ηρακλῆς, Heracles; Θησεύς, Theseus; καθαροῦντες, to cleanse. 9. ῎Αιδου, (house) of Death. 10. ἐκ παίδων, from childhood; λόγος, our account.

VOCABULARY

δίκη, -ης, ἡ, justice, righteousness
ἐπιθυμητής, -οῦ, ὁ, one who is eager for
ἐραστής, -οῦ, ὁ, lover (ἐράω, ῎Ερως)

ἀνόσιος, -ον, unholy, irreligious, impious
βλαβερός, -ά, -όν, harmful
ἥμερος, -ον, gentle, tame

ἀπατάω, deceive
ἄπειμι, go away
ἐάω (imperfect εἴων), allow, permit
εἴσειμι, come to, enter
ἔξειμι, go out or away
κτάομαι, κτήσομαι, ἐκτησάμην, κέκτημαι, acquire; possess
περίειμι, go about
προσαγορεύω, call
σύνειμι, συνέσομαι, be with (+ dative)
ψηφίζομαι, vote

ὅπῃ (adverb), where, in whatever way

ENGLISH SENTENCES

1. We know that our friends will go into the city to hear the tragedies. 2. If a man goes about doing good, he will possess virtue. 3. Whoever is an eager (follower) of Socrates will learn what justice is. 4. The Athenians voted to punish the philosopher because he seemed to be harmful to the young men. 5. The dog Cerberus did not allow anyone to go into the place where he was.

We here see to the left, in the middle distance, the fields of the χώρα of Corinth; beyond the fields, the Gulf of Corinth. Mount Helicon, the legendary home of the Muses, is dim in the distance.

Seated astride the Isthmus, which connects the Peloponnesus with the rest of the Greek mainland, Corinth possessed an acropolis enormously larger and stronger than most. It was called the Acrocorinth. To hold it was to hold one of the "Fetters of Greece"; from early times down through Macedonian and Roman domination, and on through the earlier Middle Ages and the period of Venetian control, the Acrocorinth and the city beneath were important. Thus well-squared Greek blocks form much of the basis for the later walls in this picture.

The Romans considered Corinth important enough to destroy it (146 B.C.); a century later Caesar rebuilt it as the capital of all Greece (46 B.C.). About a century later still, Saint Paul lived here for some time among the early Christians, and when absent addressed Epistles to them. Medieval, i.e., Byzantine, Corinth was small and quaint; the glories of Christian Byzantine civilization mostly passed it by. But the Venetians built on the ruined walls of Acrocorinth a grand triple-gated fort. The gun emplacements which show in the photograph remind us that we have now followed the story of Greece down to the age of gunpowder, which was also the age of printing, and moreover the age when western Europe rediscovered Hellas and learned once again to read Greek. This was one stimulus that roused Europe and led to the Renaissance, the beginning of our own age.

REVIEW EXERCISES

I. Translate:

1. τρέχοντες ἐφαίνοντο οἱ παῖδες καὶ ἔβησαν εἰς τὸ ἱερὸν πρὶν τὸν ἄρχοντα γνῶναι αὐτούς. 2. τῇ γλώττῃ ἐπαινοῦσιν, ἀλλὰ τῇ ἀληθείᾳ ἐπιγελῶσιν ἡμῖν. 3. ἀπορεῖ οὐ μεμνημένος ὅπου τὸν θησαυρὸν ἔλιπε. 4. πρότερον μὲν πολλὰ εἶχον καὶ ἀεὶ ἐκέρδαινον· σήμερον δὲ οὐδὲ ἄρτον εὑρεῖν δύνανται. 5. ἀγωνιούμεθα ὑπὲρ τῆς πατρίδος ἀλλ᾽ οὐχ ὑπὲρ τῆς βασιλείας τῆς τῶν Περσῶν.

II. Write in Greek:

1. We take pleasure in helping the weak, who cannot endure the sufferings of the war. 2. Are you ready to forgive the sins of those who caused such troubles to the city by corrupting the young men who followed them? 3. They believe that by putting on that cloak he can go unseen through the enemy and choose what treasures he wishes. 4. Twice they went down the road but none of two hundred soldiers recognized them. 5. You always err when you deceive a friend.

CONJUGATION OF φημί AND οἶδα.

VERBAL ADJECTIVES.

CLAUSES OF EFFORT

1. Learn the following forms of φημί, to say (cf. Latin *fari*):

PRESENT INDICATIVE	IMPERFECT INDICATIVE	PRESENT SUBJUNC- TIVE	PRESENT OPTATIVE	PRESENT INFINITIVE	IMPERATIVE
φημί[1]	ἔφην	φῶ	φαίην	φάναι	
φῄς	ἔφης or ἔφησθα	φῇς	φαίης		φαθί or φάθι
φησί	ἔφη	φῇ	φαίη		φάτω
φαμέν	ἔφαμεν	φῶμεν	φαῖμεν		
φατέ	ἔφατε	φῆτε	φαῖτε		φάτε
φασί	ἔφασαν	φῶσι	φαῖεν		φάντων

2. Learn the following forms of οἶδα, to know:

PRESENT INDICATIVE	IMPERFECT INDICATIVE	PRESENT SUBJUNC- TIVE	PRESENT OPTATIVE	PRESENT INFINITIVE	IMPERATIVE
οἶδα	ᾔδη or ᾔδειν	εἰδῶ	εἰδείην	εἰδέναι	
οἶσθα	ᾔδησθα or ᾔδεις	εἰδῇς	εἰδείης	PARTICIPLE	ἴσθι
οἶδε	ᾔδει(ν)	εἰδῇ	εἰδείη	εἰδώς, -υῖα -ός	ἴστω
ἴσμεν	ᾖσμεν or ᾔδεμεν	εἰδῶμεν	εἰδεῖμεν or εἰδείημεν		
ἴστε	ᾖστε or ᾔδετε	εἰδῆτε	εἰδεῖτε or εἰδείητε		ἴστε
ἴσασι	ᾖσαν or ᾔδεσαν	εἰδῶσι	εἰδεῖεν or εἰδείησαν		ἴστων

This verb is really a perfect with a present sense. Do not confuse it with εἶδον, the second aorist of ὁράω.

3. Many verbs form adjectives with the termination -τέος added to the verb stem of the first aorist passive. These adjectives, like the Latin gerundive, have a passive significance and are similarly used

---

[1] φημί is enclitic in the present indicative, except in the second singular.

with the verb *to be* to denote necessity. In other words -τέος = must be, e.g., διαβατέος, must be crossed. The doer of the action is represented by a noun or pronoun in the dative case. This is called the dative of agent. Such adjectives may be used personally or impersonally. However, the impersonal verbs δεῖ and χρή are more commonly used than this construction.

We must cross the river (literally, The river must be crossed by us). ὁ ποταμὸς ἡμῖν διαβατέος ἐστί.

We must obey. ἡμῖν πειστέον ἐστί.

4. Verbs denoting effort, care, or striving may be followed by ὅπως (rarely ὡς) and the future indicative, even after a secondary tense. The negative is μή. But these verbs also admit the usual purpose construction with ἵνα, ὡς, and ὅπως, and the subjunctive or optative:

He brought it about that they should send the horses to Cyrus.
διεπράξατο ὅπως τοὺς ἵππους Κύρῳ πέμψουσιν.

READING

A. τὸ σήμερον μέλει μοι
τὸ δ᾽ αὔριον τίς οἶδεν;—ANACREONTEA.

B. ὑγιείην εὐχῇσι παρὰ θεῶν αἰτέονται ἄνθρωποι, τὴν δὲ ταύτης δύναμιν ἐν ἑαυτοῖς ἔχοντες οὐκ ἴσασιν.—DEMOCRITUS.

C. ἴδμεν ψεύδεα πολλὰ λέγειν ἐτύμοισιν ὁμοῖα,
ἴδμεν δ᾽, εὖτ᾽ ἐθέλωμεν, ἀληθέα γηρύσασθαι.—HESIOD.

D. περὶ σφυρὸν παχεῖα μισητὴ γυνή.—FRAGMENTA IAMBICA ADESPOTA.

1. οὐ τὸ ζῆν περὶ πολλοῦ ποιητέον ἀλλὰ τὸ εὖ ζῆν.—PLATO. 2. ὁ μὲν τὸ ὅλον εἰδὼς εἰδείη ἂν καὶ τὸ μέρος· οἱ δὲ μόνον τὸ μέρος εἰδότες οὐκέτι καὶ τὸ ὅλον ἴσασιν. 3. οὐδεὶς ἡμῶν οὐδὲν οἶδεν οὐδ᾽ αὐτὸ τοῦτο, πότερον οἴδαμεν (ἴσμεν) ἢ οὐκ οἴδαμεν, οὐδ᾽ αὐτὸ τὸ μὴ εἰδέναι οἴδαμεν ὅ τι ἔστιν, οὐδ᾽ ὅλως πότερον ἔστι τι ἢ οὐκ ἔστιν.—METRODORUS. 4. Ἀρίστιππος ὁ φιλόσοφος ἐρωτηθεὶς διὰ τί οἱ μὲν φιλόσοφοι ἐπὶ τὰς τῶν πλουσίων θύρας ἔρχονται, οἱ δὲ πλούσιοι ἐπὶ τὰς τῶν φιλοσόφων οὐκέτι, "ὅτι," ἔφη, "οἱ μὲν ἴσασιν ὧν δέονται, οἱ δὲ οὐκ ἴσασιν.—DIOGENES. 5. πρῶτον μὲν οὐκ ἀθυμητέον, ὦ ἄνδρες Ἀθηναῖοι, τοῖς παροῦσι πράγμασι, οὐδ᾽ εἰ πάνυ φαύλως ἔχειν δοκεῖ.—DEMOSTHENES. 6. The Fear of Death. τὸ γάρ τοι θάνατον δεδιέναι, ὦ ἄνδρες, οὐδὲν ἄλλο ἐστὶν ἢ δοκεῖν σοφὸν εἶναι, μὴ ὄντα· δοκεῖν γὰρ εἰδέναι ἐστὶν ἃ οὐκ οἶδεν. οἶδε μὲν γὰρ οὐδεὶς τὸν θάνατον οὐδ᾽ εἰ τυγχάνει τῷ ἀνθρώπῳ πάντων μέγιστον ὂν τῶν ἀγαθῶν,

δεδίασι δ' ὡς εὖ εἰδότες ὅτι μέγιστον τῶν κακῶν ἐστιν. ἐγὼ δὲ καὶ εἰ δή τῳ σοφώτερός του φαίην εἶναι, τούτῳ ἂν εἴην, ὅτι οὐκ εἰδὼς ἱκανῶς περὶ τῶν ἐν Ἅιδου, οὕτω καὶ οἴομαι οὐκ εἰδέναι.—PLATO, *Apology* (adapted).

Notes: 1. Understand ἐστίν after ποιητέον. 3. ὅλως, on the whole, generally. 5. φαύλως ἔχειν, be in bad shape; δοκεῖ, neuter plural subject takes singular verb. 6. τοι, you know (colloquial); δεδιέναι, to fear (infinitive).

VOCABULARY

θύρα, -ας, ἡ, door
μέρος, -ους, τό, part

φαῦλος, -η, -ον, mean, miserable
φρόνιμος, -η, -ον, prudent

ἀθυμέω, be disheartened
δέομαι, δεήσομαι (+ genitive), want, ask, need. Impersonal, δεῖ, it is nec-essary (+ accusative and infinitive)
μέλει, μελήσει, ἐμέλησε, it is a care (impersonal). Cf. ἐπιμελέομαι, care for (see paragraph 4), it concerns
περὶ πολλοῦ ποιεῖσθαι, consider important (more important, most import-ant, if πολλοῦ is compared)

οὐκέτι (οὐκ + ἔτι), no more, no longer, not yet
πάνυ (adverb), very; entirely (πᾶς)

ENGLISH SENTENCES

1. The rich men did not ask philosophers to come to their doors. 2. It is not necessary that a man be rich in order that he may become prudent. 3. Socrates said (ἔλεγε) that many men feared death be-cause they considered living (infinitive) of greater importance. 4. A certain wise philosopher declared that no one of us knows anything. 5. Whether this is true or not we do not know.

REVIEW EXERCISES

I. Translate:

1. οὐχ ἕτοιμοί εἰσιν οἱ πολῖται νεώτερα πράγματα βουλεύειν· ἀσθενεῖς γάρ εἰσιν, οὐδὲ ἡγοῦνται οἷόν τε εἶναι τοὺς ἄρχοντας ἀπατᾶν. 2. τῶν στρατιωτῶν πεντήκοντα αὐτῷ ἕσποντο ὡς διαφθεροῦντες τοὺς πολίτας πρὶν γνῶναι τούτους τὴν ἀλήθειαν. 3. ἥδεται ἀεὶ ὁ διδάσκαλος ἐκλεγόμενος καὶ ὠφελῶν τοὺς ἀρίστους τῶν παίδων· μετ' αὐτῶν γὰρ τοὺς τῶν φιλο-σόφων λόγους διέρχεται. 4. πονηρὸς φαίνεται καὶ ἐραστὴς ἐπιθυμητής τε τῶν ἀνοσίων καὶ βλαβερῶν πάντων. οὐ γὰρ ἔδωκεν οὔποτε τὴν δίκην τῶν

ἀδίκως πραχθέντων. 5. περιῄει τοὺς πολίτας καὶ εἰσιόντας καὶ ἐξιόντας προσαγορεύων καὶ διαπραττόμενος ὅπως ψηφιοῦνται καὶ ἐάσουσι τοὺς αὐτῷ συνιόντας τὰς ἀρχὰς λαβεῖν.

II. Write in Greek:

1. You must cross the river whenever our prudent general shall command. 2. Being miserable about the small part they had received, they besought the ruler to give them a better. But he said that it did not concern him, that he did not consider it important, and that he did not know where he could find another. 3. They have not yet opened the doors, for they are not ready to allow us to go in. 4. Did you not know that they have gathered all their friends into that house? It seems better to them to remain there until the peace is established. 5. He could not endure hearing that the long walls were being torn down.

From the copies on papyrus rolls (Figure 1), medieval monks made other copies, and so transmitted Greek literature to us. In the monkish scribal tradition, most of the features seen in our own printed books were developed: bound volumes with separate sheets for pages in place of the long one-piece papyrus rolls; small letters, few capitals; punctuation, breathings, accents. As it says, the page above is the beginning "Of Xenophon, Cyrus' Anabasis, third (book)."

NAMES MENTIONED IN THE TEXT

AELIAN. Claudius Aelianus (second century A.D.) was a Roman author and teacher who wrote in Greek a *Variae Historiae* and *de Natura Animalium.*

AESCHYLUS. Athenian tragic poet (525–456 B.C.), who wrote over seventy plays, of which seven survive.

AESOP. A writer of fables who lived about 570 B.C. He had been a slave on Samos. Socrates was said to have turned some of Aesop's fables into verse during his imprisonment.

ALCIBIADES. Athenian general and statesman (ca. 450–404 B.C.).

ANACREON. A lyric poet, born about 570 B.C.; invited to Athens by Pisistratus; honored by a statue on the Acropolis.

ANAXAGORAS. Greek philosopher born in Ionia in 500 B.C. He lived in Athens, where he was an intimate friend of Pericles and Euripides. He taught that νοῦς (Intelligence) was the cause of all things.

ANAXARCHUS. A philosopher of Abdera (Thrace), who accompanied Alexander into Asia (334 B.C.). He was of the school of Democritus, the atomist.

ANTIPHON. A Sophist and tragic poet; an opponent of Socrates.

ANTISTHENES. One of Socrates' most devoted followers; founder of the Cynic sect, which influenced the later Stoics.

APOLLODORUS. An Athenian historian and mythographer of the second century B.C. (Others date him in the first century A.D.)

ARCHIMEDES. The most famous Greek mathematician and physicist, born in Syracuse in 287 B.C. Invented engines of war for the tyrant Hiero; killed by Roman soldiers in 212 B.C.

ARIAEUS. A friend of the younger Cyrus; commanded the left wing in the battle of Cunaxa, 401 B.C.

ARISTIDES. Athenian soldier and statesman, known as "The Just"; born about 520 B.C. General at Marathon; ostracised, 480 B.C. Died a poor man.

ARISTIPPUS. Founder of the Cyrenaic school of philosophy (Hedonism), flourished about 370 B.C. Came to Athens to be a disciple of Socrates.

ARISTOTLE. Born in Stagira (Macedonia) in 384 B.C. Was a pupil of Plato in Athens; later became the tutor of Alexander (342). Returned to Athens in 335 and conducted a school (the Lyceum). Fled in 322, to Euboea where he died. His works treat of almost all the subjects of human knowledge cultivated in his time.

ARRIAN. A Greek historian and philosopher born in Nicomedia about 90 A.D.; he wrote a history of the expedition of Alexander.

BIAS. One of the Seven Sages of Greece; of Priene (Ionia); fl. 550 B.C.

CALLIMACHUS. A librarian at Alexandria, who lived from about 305 until about 240 B.C.; teacher of Apollonius of Rhodes. He was a poet, and author of eight hundred volumes.

CHILON. A Spartan ephor (556 B.C.), known as one of the Seven Sages of Greece.

CRITIAS. A pupil of Socrates; one of the Thirty Tyrants in Athens.

CROESUS. King of Lydia; proverbial for wealth. Conquered by Cyrus the Great in 546 B.C.

DARIUS I. King of Persia 521–486 B.C.

DEMOCRITUS. Greek philosopher born in Abdera (Thrace) about 460 B.C. Founder of the atomic theory. He was widely traveled and had an extensive knowledge of science and philosophy as well as of human nature.

DEMOSTHENES. An Athenian statesman and orator (384–322 B.C.), who tried to warn his countrymen against Philip of Macedon.

DIOGENES. The Cynic philosopher, born at Sinope, in Pontus, in about 412 B.C. He lived in Athens and later in Corinth, where he died at the age of nearly 90 in 323 B.C.

DIOGENES LAERTIUS. Born in Laerte in Cilicia, lived in the second century A.D. He wrote a work called *Lives of the Philosophers*.

DRACO. The author of the first written code of laws in Athens (about 621 B.C.). In his code death was the penalty for most crimes. Solon's laws superseded most of Draco's.

EPICHARMUS. Comic poet who lived most of his life in Sicily. Born about 530 B.C., died about 440.

EUCLID. The famous mathematician lived at Alexandria during the reign of Ptolemy I (304–283 B.C.). He remarked to the King that there was no "royal road" to the learning of geometry.

EURIPIDES. One of the three great Athenian tragic poets (485–406 B.C.). He was an intimate of Socrates. He is said to have represented people in his plays "not as they ought to be, but as they are."

GREEK ANTHOLOGY. A large collection of short poems of all sorts, especially epigrams, ranging in date from the seventh century B.C to the twelfth A.D. It is known also as the Palatine Anthology, from the fact that the manuscript on which it was written was preserved in the Palatine library at Heidelberg. The poems are mostly in the elegiac meter.

154

HERACLITUS. A philosopher of the Ionian school, who lived at Ephesus; fl. ca. 513 B.C. According to him everything is perpetually in a state of flux.

HERODOTUS. The "Father of History" was born in Halicarnassus in Caria (Asia Minor) in 484 B.C. Lived later in Samos and in Athens, but traveled extensively in Asia, Africa, and Europe. The subject of his work (in nine books) is mainly the wars between Greece and Persia; it is notable for its many digressions, some of them in the nature of "short stories." It is written in the Ionic dialect.

HESIOD. One of the earliest Greek poets, who lived some time later than Homer, perhaps in the eighth century. He wrote the *Works and Days* and the *Theogony*.

HIPPIAS. A tyrant at Athens, 527–510 B.C.; son of Pisistratus. He fled to Persia and tried to regain power in Athens with the help of the Persians in 490 B.C.

HIPPOCRATES. A contemporary of Socrates; founder of a school of medicine on the island of Cos.

HIPPONAX. A poet of Ephesus (fl. 540 B.C.), writer of satiric verse.

LYSIAS. One of the Attic "orators" or legal speech writers. Born in 458 B.C. Became a professional writer after his family's wealth was seized during the Tyranny of the Thirty.

MARCUS AURELIUS. Roman Emperor, 121–180 A.D. Famous also as the author of *Meditations*.

MENANDER. Born in Athens in 342 B.C., where he produced over a hundred comedies, of which only one, the *Dyscolos*, survives entire. It was discovered in 1958. There are extant many short fragments excerpted from his plays by assiduous collectors of epigrammatic material. He drowned while swimming in the harbor of Piraeus in 291.

METRODORUS OF CHIOS. An atomistic philosopher, a pupil, perhaps, of Democritus, and a complete skeptic.

MIMNERMUS. An elegiac poet, a native of Smyrna; fl. in the latter part of the seventh century B.C. He wrote plaintive and mournful poems.

PERIANDER. Tyrant of Corinth, who succeeded his father Cypselus, also tyrant of that place. He reigned until 585 B.C. A patron of letters, he is commonly called one of the Seven Sages of Greece.

PERICLES. The most famous of the Athenian statesmen. He was of a noble family and began to take part in politics in 461 B.C. as the head of the democratic party. He led armies in the field, and for the eighteen years before the outbreak of the Peloponnesian War he beautified Athens by erecting many public buildings, among them the Parthenon and Propylaea. He guided the city during only the first two years of the great war, falling victim to the plague in 429.

PHILEMON. A writer of New Comedy (lived ca. 361–262 B.C.). Wrote ninety-seven plays.

PINDAR. The greatest lyric poet of Greece (522–442 B.C.), born in Thebes. The poems which have survived were composed in commemoration of victories by various celebrated Greeks in the Olympic and other games. Alexander spared Pindar's house in Thebes when he destroyed the rest of the city.

PISISTRATUS. A tyrant of Athens who came to power in 560 B.C. as a result of the unrest which arose after Solon had left the city. Although he was expelled twice and forced his way back into power, he was a mild and beneficent ruler, a patron of literature. He died in 527.

PLATO. The Athenian philosopher lived from 427 until 347 B.C. He early became a disciple of Socrates and is the main source of our knowledge of the beliefs of his teacher. He founded the Academy, a school on the outskirts of Athens. His extant writings are in the form of dialogues. Socrates is usually the chief interlocutor.

PLUTARCH. Lived in Greece and Rome in the first century A.D., having been born in Greece. He was the author of the *Parallel Lives* of Greeks and Romans, and a collection of ethical works called *Moralia*.

POLYBIUS. Born in Arcadia in 204 B.C., he was carried as prisoner to Rome after the Macedonian wars in 168. There he wrote a history of the Roman conquest of Greece. The work began with 220 B.C. and described events through the destruction of Corinth in 146, and into 144.

PRAXITELES. One of the great Greek sculptors, who flourished in 364 B.C. He was a citizen of Athens. His most famous work is the Hermes at Olympia, the only statue extant which may be an original example of Greek sculpture by one of the six masters; the others are Roman copies.

PROMETHEUS. In mythology Prometheus is the son of the Titan Iapetus, brother of Atlas and Epimetheus. He stole fire from heaven and taught its use to men, for which crime he was punished by Zeus. The story is told in Aeschylus' *Prometheus Bound*.

PROTAGORAS. Professional Sophist, born in Abdera, Thrace, ca. 485 B.C.

PROXENUS. A Boeotian, friend of Cyrus and Xenophon; a pupil of the famous teacher Gorgias of Leontini.

SIMONIDES. Born on Ceos in 556 B.C., lived in Athens and Syracuse. He wrote many poems, employing many different forms. He is said to have been the first to make literature a profession. Died in 467 in Sicily.

SOCRATES. The Athenian philosopher (469–399 B.C.). In his youth Socrates made statues, as did his father. Later he went about the city teaching through conversation; he had no school. He conceived his task as that of awakening in the minds of his disciples moral consciousness and the impulse to gain knowledge of the meaning of life. He was accused on a political charge of "impiety" and of "corrupting the youth," and was put to death by being forced to drink poison hemlock. He established the art of dialectic and laid the foundation of formal logic. Plato recorded much of his teaching; Xenophon reported many anecdotes about him.

SOLON. The Athenian lawgiver (639–559 B.C.). One of the Seven Sages of Greece. He prompted the Athenians to go to war to recover Salamis, and recited a poem urging this course. He was chosen archon in 594 and promoted harmony between the warring factions of his city. His constitution enabled debtors to be relieved from their burdens without at the same time infringing too much on the wealthy. He extended citizenship for the Thetes, the lowest class of citizens; enlarged the usefulness of the Assembly; instituted the council of 400. After getting the people to accede to his reforms, he went away from Athens to travel for ten years.

SOPHOCLES. The tragic poet (495–406 B.C.). Only seven of his 130 plays are extant. He is said to have made the characters of his plays "not as men are but as they ought to be." He was also one of the generals in the war between Athens and Samos.

SUETONIUS. A biographer of the Roman Emperors (69–140 A.D.). Author, lawyer, secretary to the Emperor Hadrian.

THALES. One of the Seven Sages. He was born at Miletus (Asia Minor) in about 636 B.C., and died about 546. He was one of the founders of the study of philosophy and mathematics. He believed that water is the origin of all things. He once predicted an eclipse of the sun on May 28, 585 B.C.

THEMISTOCLES. An Athenian statesman (born ca. 528 B.C.). He saved his country by his foresight in building up the Athenian fleet which won the Battle of Salamis. Later, being charged with the theft of public funds, he fled, and further charges of treason being preferred against him, he went to Persia. There he gained great influence over the king, who presented him with valuable property. He died in Persia.

THEOGNIS. An elegiac and gnomic poet, born in Megara (near Athens); fl. ca. 540 B.C. He has left a large collection of maxims written in dactylic hexameter and pentameter, a combination known as elegiac verse.

THUCYDIDES. The historian (ca. 460–ca. 400 B.C.); born in Athens. Author of the great *History of the Peloponnesian War*.

XENOPHANES. A philosopher of Colophon (Asia Minor) who flourished between 540 and 500 B.C. He was also a poet. He lived much of his life in Italy, in Elea, whence he is known as an Eleatic philosopher. He is said to have been a monist.

XENOPHON. An Athenian who flourished in the end of the fifth and the beginning of the fourth centuries. He went on Cyrus' campaign against Artaxerxes (the *Anabasis*) as an observer, a kind of "war correspondent." He was also a pupil of Socrates. He lived much of his later life in a little town in Elis, in Spartan territory, writing and living the life of a country gentleman. His principal works are the *Anabasis* and the *Cyropaedia* (life of the elder Cyrus). He wrote the *Hellenica*, a continuation of Thucydides' History, the *Memorabilia* (recollections of Socrates), and numerous minor works.

APPENDIX 2

DECLENSIONS

THE DEFINITE ARTICLE

	M	F	N
		SINGULAR	
N	ὁ	ἡ	τό
G	τοῦ	τῆς	τοῦ
D	τῷ	τῇ	τῷ
A	τόν	τήν	τό
		DUAL[1]	
N, A	τώ	τώ	τώ
G, D	τοῖν	τοῖν	τοῖν
		PLURAL	
N	οἱ	αἱ	τά
G	τῶν	τῶν	τῶν
D	τοῖς	ταῖς	τοῖς
A	τούς	τάς	τά

FIRST DECLENSION

	F	F	F	F	M	M
			SINGULAR			
N	γνώμη	θάλαττα	πεῖρα	θεά	στρατιώτης	νεανίας
G	γνώμης	θαλάττης	πείρας	θεᾶς	στρατιώτου	νεανίου
D	γνώμῃ	θαλάττῃ	πείρᾳ	θεᾷ	στρατιώτῃ	νεανίᾳ
A	γνώμην	θάλατταν	πεῖραν	θεάν	στρατιώτην	νεανίαν
V	γνώμη	θάλαττα	πεῖρα	θεά	στρατιῶτα	νεανία

[1] Note the dual forms here and throughout the Appendix. In the first declension the dual endings are -α for the nominative and accusative and vocative, and -αιν for the genitive and dative: κώμα, κώμαιν. In the second declension the endings are -ω and -οιν: λόγω, λόγοιν; in the third, -ε and -οιν: ἀσπίδε, ἀσπίδοιν.

The dual occurs in verb forms, in the active voice the second and third persons dual being both -τον in primary tenses, and -τον and -την respectively in secondary tenses. The third person dual of imperatives has -των. In the passive voice -σθον is the ending for second and third persons in primary tenses, while -σθον and -σθην are second and third person secondary tense endings. The imperative third person dual here, again, has -σθων.

158

FIRST DECLENSION (Continued)

DUAL

N, A, V	γνώμα	θαλάττα	πείρα	θεά	στρατιώτα	νεανία
G, D	γνώμαιν	θαλάτταιν	πείραιν	θεαῖν	στρατιώταιν	νεανίαιν

PLURAL

N	γνῶμαι	θάλατται	πεῖραι	θεαί	στρατιῶται	νεανίαι
G	γνωμῶν	θαλαττῶν	πειρῶν	θεῶν	στρατιωτῶν	νεανιῶν
D	γνώμαις	θαλάτταις	πείραις	θεαῖς	στρατιώταις	νεανίαις
A	γνώμας	θαλάττας	πείρας	θεάς	στρατιώτας	νεανίας
V	γνῶμαι	θάλατται	πεῖραι	θεαί	στρατιῶται	νεανίαι

SECOND DECLENSION

	M		F	N

SINGULAR

	M		F	N
N	λόγος	ἄνθρωπος	ὁδός	δῶρον
G	λόγου	ἀνθρώπου	ὁδοῦ	δώρου
D	λόγῳ	ἀνθρώπῳ	ὁδῷ	δώρῳ
A	λόγον	ἄνθρωπον	ὁδόν	δῶρον
V	λόγε	ἄνθρωπε	ὁδέ	δῶρον

DUAL

	M		F	N
N, A	λόγω	ἀνθρώπω	ὁδώ	δώρω
G, D	λόγοιν	ἀνθρώποιν	ὁδοῖν	δώροιν

PLURAL

	M		F	N
N, V	λόγοι	ἄνθρωποι	ὁδοί	δῶρα
G	λόγων	ἀνθρώπων	ὁδῶν	δώρων
D	λόγοις	ἀνθρώποις	ὁδοῖς	δώροις
A	λόγους	ἀνθρώπους	ὁδούς	δῶρα

THIRD DECLENSION

	F	M	M	M	M	F

SINGULAR

	F	M	M	M	M	F
N	ἀσπίς	κλώψ	φύλαξ	δαίμων	γέρων	χάρις
G	ἀσπίδος	κλωπός	φύλακος	δαίμονος	γέροντος	χάριτος
D	ἀσπίδι	κλωπί	φύλακι	δαίμονι	γέροντι	χάριτι
A	ἀσπίδα	κλῶπα	φύλακα	δαίμονα	γέροντα	χάριν
V	ἀσπί	κλώψ	φύλαξ	δαῖμον	γέρον	χάρι

DUAL

	F	M	M	M	M	F
N, A, V	ἀσπίδε	κλῶπε	φύλακε	δαίμονε	γέροντε	χάριτε
G, D	ἀσπίδοιν	κλωποῖν	φυλάκοιν	δαιμόνοιν	γερόντοιν	χαρίτοιν

PLURAL

	F	M	M	M	M	F
N, V	ἀσπίδες	κλῶπες	φύλακες	δαίμονες	γέροντες	χάριτες
G	ἀσπίδων	κλωπῶν	φυλάκων	δαιμόνων	γερόντων	χαρίτων
D	ἀσπίσι	κλωψί	φύλαξι	δαίμοσι	γέρουσι	χάρισι
A	ἀσπίδας	κλῶπας	φύλακας	δαίμονας	γέροντας	χάριτας

THIRD DECLENSION (Continued)

	M	M	M	F	N	N
			SINGULAR			
N	πατήρ	ἀνήρ	βασιλεύς	πόλις	στράτευμα	γένος
G	πατρός	ἀνδρός	βασιλέως	πόλεως	στρατεύματος	γένους
D	πατρί	ἀνδρί	βασιλεῖ	πόλει	στρατεύματι	γένει
A	πατέρα	ἄνδρα	βασιλέα	πόλιν	στράτευμα	γένος
V	πάτερ	ἄνερ	βασιλεῦ	πόλι	στράτευμα	γένος
			DUAL			
N, A	πατέρε	ἄνδρε	βασιλῆ	πόλει	στρατεύματε	γένει
G, D	πατέροιν	ἀνδροῖν	βασιλέοιν	πολέοιν	στρατευμάτοιν	γενοῖν
			PLURAL			
N	πατέρες	ἄνδρες	βασιλεῖς	πόλεις	στρατεύματα	γένη
G	πατέρων	ἀνδρῶν	βασιλέων	πόλεων	στρατευμάτων	γενῶν
D	πατράσι	ἀνδράσι	βασιλεῦσι	πόλεσι	στρατεύμασι	γένεσι
A	πατέρας	ἄνδρας	βασιλέας	πόλεις	στρατεύματα	γένη
V	πατέρες	ἄνδρες	βασιλεῖς	πόλεις	στρατεύματα	γένη

ADJECTIVES

FIRST AND SECOND DECLENSION

	M	F	N	M	F	N
			SINGULAR			
N	ἀγαθός	ἀγαθή	ἀγαθόν	ἄξιος	ἀξία	ἄξιον
G	ἀγαθοῦ	ἀγαθῆς	ἀγαθοῦ	ἀξίου	ἀξίας	ἀξίου
D	ἀγαθῷ	ἀγαθῇ	ἀγαθῷ	ἀξίῳ	ἀξίᾳ	ἀξίῳ
A	ἀγαθόν	ἀγαθήν	ἀγαθόν	ἄξιον	ἀξίαν	ἄξιον
V	ἀγαθέ	ἀγαθή	ἀγαθόν	ἄξιε	ἀξία	ἄξιον
			DUAL			
N, A, V	ἀγαθώ	ἀγαθά	ἀγαθώ	ἀξίω	ἀξία	ἀξίω
G, D	ἀγαθοῖν	ἀγαθαῖν	ἀγαθοῖν	ἀξίοιν	ἀξίαιν	ἀξίοιν
			PLURAL			
N, V	ἀγαθοί	ἀγαθαί	ἀγαθά	ἄξιοι	ἄξιαι	ἄξια
G	ἀγαθῶν	ἀγαθῶν	ἀγαθῶν	ἀξίων	ἀξίων	ἀξίων
D	ἀγαθοῖς	ἀγαθαῖς	ἀγαθοῖς	ἀξίοις	ἀξίαις	ἀξίοις
A	ἀγαθούς	ἀγαθάς	ἀγαθά	ἀξίους	ἀξίας	ἄξια

CONTRACT ADJECTIVES OF THE FIRST AND SECOND DECLENSION

	M		F		N	
			SINGULAR			
N, V	χρυσοῦς	(χρύσεος)	χρυσῆ	(χρυσέα)	χρυσοῦν	(χρύσεον)
G	χρυσοῦ	(χρυσέου)	χρυσῆς	(χρυσέας)	χρυσοῦ	(χρυσέου)
D	χρυσῷ	(χρυσέῳ)	χρυσῇ	(χρυσέᾳ)	χρυσῷ	(χρυσέῳ)
A	χρυσοῦν	(χρύσεον)	χρυσῆν	(χρυσέαν)	χρυσοῦν	(χρύσεον)

ADJECTIVES (Continued)

DUAL

N, A, V	χρυσώ	(χρυσέω)	χρυσᾶ	(χρυσέα)	χρυσώ	(χρυσέω)
G, D	χρυσοῖν	(χρυσέοιν)	χρυσαῖν	(χρυσέαιν)	χρυσοῖν	(χρυσέοιν)

PLURAL

N, V	χρυσοῖ	(χρύσεοι)	χρυσαῖ	(χρύσεαι)	χρυσᾶ	(χρύσεα)
G	χρυσῶν	(χρυσέων)	χρυσῶν	(χρυσέων)	χρυσῶν	(χρυσέων)
D	χρυσοῖς	(χρυσέοις)	χρυσαῖς	(χρυσέαις)	χρυσοῖς	(χρυσέοις)
A	χρυσοῦς	(χρυσέους)	χρυσᾶς	(χρυσέας)	χρυσᾶ	(χρύσεα)

FIRST AND THIRD DECLENSION

	M	F	N
		SINGULAR	
N	ἡδύς	ἡδεῖα	ἡδύ
G	ἡδέος	ἡδείας	ἡδέος
D	ἡδεῖ (ἡδέ-ϊ)	ἡδείᾳ	ἡδεῖ (ἡδέ-ϊ)
A	ἡδύν	ἡδεῖαν	ἡδύ
V	ἡδύ	ἡδεῖα	ἡδύ

DUAL

N, A, V	ἡδεῖ (ἡδέ-ε)	ἡδεία	ἡδεῖ (ἡδέ-ε)
G, D	ἡδέοιν	ἡδείαιν	ἡδέοιν

PLURAL

N, V	ἡδεῖς (ἡδέ-ες)	ἡδεῖαι	ἡδέα
G	ἡδέων	ἡδειῶν	ἡδέων
D	ἡδέσι	ἡδείαις	ἡδέσι
A	ἡδεῖς	ἡδείας	ἡδέα

THIRD DECLENSION

	M, F	N	
		SINGULAR	
N	ἀληθής	ἀληθές	
G	ἀληθοῦς (ἀληθέος)	ἀληθοῦς	
D	ἀληθεῖ (ἀληθέϊ)	ἀληθεῖ	
A	ἀληθῆ (ἀληθέα)	ἀληθές	
V	ἀληθές	ἀληθές	

DUAL

N, A	ἀληθεῖ (ἀληθέε)	ἀληθεῖ	
G, D	ἀληθοῖν (ἀληθέοιν)	ἀληθοῖν	

PLURAL

N	ἀληθεῖς (ἀληθέες)	ἀληθῆ	(ἀληθέα)
G	ἀληθῶν (ἀληθέων)	ἀληθῶν	
D	ἀληθέσι	ἀληθέσι	
A	ἀληθεῖς	ἀληθῆ	(ἀληθέα)

161

ADJECTIVES (Continued)

THIRD DECLENSION COMPARATIVE

	SINGULAR			PLURAL	
	M, F	N		M, F	N
N	ἡδίων	ἥδιον	N, V	ἡδίονες, ἡδίους	ἡδίονα, ἡδίω
G	ἡδίονος	ἡδίονος	G	ἡδιόνων	ἡδιόνων
D	ἡδίονι	ἡδίονι	D	ἡδίοσι	ἡδίοσι
A	ἡδίονα, ἡδίω	ἥδιον	A	ἡδίονας, ἡδίους	ἡδίονα, ἡδίω
V	ἥδιον	ἥδιον			

DUAL

	M, F	N
N, A, V	ἡδίονε	ἡδίονε
G, D	ἡδιόνοιν	ἡδιόνοιν

IRREGULAR ADJECTIVES

	M	F	N
		SINGULAR	
N	μέγας	μεγάλη	μέγα
G	μεγάλου	μεγάλης	μεγάλου
D	μεγάλῳ	μεγάλῃ	μεγάλῳ
A	μέγαν	μεγάλην	μέγα
V	μεγάλε	μεγάλη	μέγα
		DUAL	
N, A, V	μεγάλω	μεγάλα	μεγάλω
G, D	μεγάλοιν	μεγάλαιν	μεγάλοιν
		PLURAL	
N, V	μεγάλοι	μεγάλαι	μεγάλα
G	μεγάλων	μεγάλων	μεγάλων
D	μεγάλοις	μεγάλαις	μεγάλοις
A	μεγάλους	μεγάλας	μεγάλα

	M	F	N	M	F	N
			SINGULAR			
N	πᾶς	πᾶσα	πᾶν	πολύς	πολλή	πολύ
G	παντός	πάσης	παντός	πολλοῦ	πολλῆς	πολλοῦ
D	παντί	πάσῃ	παντί	πολλῷ	πολλῇ	πολλῷ
A	πάντα	πᾶσαν	πᾶν	πολύν	πολλήν	πολύ
V	πᾶς	πᾶσα	πᾶν			
			PLURAL			
N, V	πάντες	πᾶσαι	πάντα	πολλοί	πολλαί	πολλά
G	πάντων	πασῶν	πάντων	πολλῶν	πολλῶν	πολλῶν
D	πᾶσι	πάσαις	πᾶσι	πολλοῖς	πολλαῖς	πολλοῖς
A	πάντας	πάσας	πάντα	πολλούς	πολλάς	πολλά

PARTICIPLES

<table>
<tr><td></td><td colspan="3">Present Active</td><td colspan="3">Aorist Active</td></tr>
<tr><td></td><td>M</td><td>F</td><td>N</td><td>M</td><td>F</td><td>N</td></tr>
<tr><td colspan="7" align="center">SINGULAR</td></tr>
<tr><td>N, V</td><td>λύων[2]</td><td>λύουσα</td><td>λῦον</td><td>λύσας[3]</td><td>λύσασα</td><td>λῦσαν</td></tr>
<tr><td>G</td><td>λύοντος</td><td>λυούσης</td><td>λύοντος</td><td>λύσαντος</td><td>λυσάσης</td><td>λύσαντος</td></tr>
<tr><td>D</td><td>λύοντι</td><td>λυούσῃ</td><td>λύοντι</td><td>λύσαντι</td><td>λυσάσῃ</td><td>λύσαντι</td></tr>
<tr><td>A</td><td>λύοντα</td><td>λύουσαν</td><td>λῦον</td><td>λύσαντα</td><td>λύσασαν</td><td>λῦσαν</td></tr>
<tr><td colspan="7" align="center">DUAL</td></tr>
<tr><td>N, A, V</td><td>λύοντε</td><td>λυούσα</td><td>λύοντε</td><td>λύσαντε</td><td>λυσάσα</td><td>λύσαντε</td></tr>
<tr><td>G, D</td><td>λυόντοιν</td><td>λυούσαιν</td><td>λυόντοιν</td><td>λυσάντοιν</td><td>λυσάσαιν</td><td>λυσάντοιν</td></tr>
<tr><td colspan="7" align="center">PLURAL</td></tr>
<tr><td>N, V</td><td>λύοντες</td><td>λύουσαι</td><td>λύοντα</td><td>λύσαντες</td><td>λύσασαι</td><td>λύσαντα</td></tr>
<tr><td>G</td><td>λυόντων</td><td>λυουσῶν</td><td>λυόντων</td><td>λυσάντων</td><td>λυσασῶν</td><td>λυσάντων</td></tr>
<tr><td>D</td><td>λύουσι</td><td>λυούσαις</td><td>λύουσι</td><td>λύσασι</td><td>λυσάσαις</td><td>λύσασι</td></tr>
<tr><td>A</td><td>λύοντας</td><td>λυούσας</td><td>λύοντα</td><td>λύσαντας</td><td>λυσάσας</td><td>λύσαντα</td></tr>
</table>

<table>
<tr><td></td><td colspan="3">Perfect Active</td><td colspan="3">Aorist Passive</td></tr>
<tr><td></td><td>M</td><td>F</td><td>N</td><td>M</td><td>F</td><td>N</td></tr>
<tr><td colspan="7" align="center">SINGULAR</td></tr>
<tr><td>N, V</td><td>λελυκώς</td><td>λελυκυῖα</td><td>λελυκός</td><td>λυθείς[4]</td><td>λυθεῖσα</td><td>λυθέν</td></tr>
<tr><td>G</td><td>λελυκότος</td><td>λελυκυίας</td><td>λελυκότος</td><td>λυθέντος</td><td>λυθείσης</td><td>λυθέντος</td></tr>
<tr><td>D</td><td>λελυκότι</td><td>λελυκυίᾳ</td><td>λελυκότι</td><td>λυθέντι</td><td>λυθείσῃ</td><td>λυθέντι</td></tr>
<tr><td>A</td><td>λελυκότα</td><td>λελυκυῖαν</td><td>λελυκός</td><td>λυθέντα</td><td>λυθεῖσαν</td><td>λυθέν</td></tr>
<tr><td colspan="7" align="center">DUAL</td></tr>
<tr><td>N, A, V</td><td>λελυκότε</td><td>λελυκυία</td><td>λελυκότε</td><td>λυθέντε</td><td>λυθείσα</td><td>λυθέντε</td></tr>
<tr><td>G, D</td><td>λελυκότοιν</td><td>λελυκυίαιν</td><td>λελυκότοιν</td><td>λυθέντοιν</td><td>λυθείσαιν</td><td>λυθέντοιν</td></tr>
<tr><td colspan="7" align="center">PLURAL</td></tr>
<tr><td>N, V</td><td>λελυκότες</td><td>λελυκυῖαι</td><td>λελυκότα</td><td>λυθέντες</td><td>λυθεῖσαι</td><td>λυθέντα</td></tr>
<tr><td>G</td><td>λελυκότων</td><td>λελυκυιῶν</td><td>λελυκότων</td><td>λυθέντων</td><td>λυθεισῶν</td><td>λυθέντων</td></tr>
<tr><td>D</td><td>λελυκόσι</td><td>λελυκυίαις</td><td>λελυκόσι</td><td>λυθεῖσι</td><td>λυθείσαις</td><td>λυθεῖσι</td></tr>
<tr><td>A</td><td>λελυκότας</td><td>λελυκυίας</td><td>λελυκότα</td><td>λυθέντας</td><td>λυθείσας</td><td>λυθέντα</td></tr>
</table>

[2] λιπών is declined like λύων but with oxytone accent (see page 4). διδούς and δούς have the same endings as λύων except in the nominative masculine singular, but have oxytone accent.

[3] Like λύσας in endings, but with oxytone accent (see page 4), are the present participle of ἵστημι: ἱστάς, ἱστᾶσα, ἱστάν, and the aorist participle, στάς, στᾶσα, στάν.

163

PARTICIPLES (Continued)

PARTICIPLES OF CONTRACT VERBS

	Present Active			Present Active		
	M	F	N	M	F	N
			SINGULAR			
N, V	τιμῶν	τιμῶσα	τιμῶν	ποιῶν⁵	ποιοῦσα	ποιοῦν
G	τιμῶντος	τιμώσης	τιμῶντος	ποιοῦντος	ποιούσης	ποιοῦντος
D	τιμῶντι	τιμώσῃ	τιμῶντι	ποιοῦντι	ποιούσῃ	ποιοῦντι
A	τιμῶντα	τιμῶσαν	τιμῶν	ποιοῦντα	ποιοῦσαν	ποιοῦν
			DUAL			
N, A, V	τιμῶντε	τιμώσα	τιμῶντε	ποιοῦντε	ποιούσα	ποιοῦντε
G, D	τιμώντοιν	τιμώσαιν	τιμώντοιν	ποιούντοιν	ποιούσαιν	ποιούντοιν
			PLURAL			
N, V	τιμῶντες	τιμῶσαι	τιμῶντα	ποιοῦντες	ποιοῦσαι	ποιοῦντα
G	τιμώντων	τιμωσῶν	τιμώντων	ποιούντων	ποιουσῶν	ποιούντων
D	τιμῶσι	τιμώσαις	τιμῶσι	ποιοῦσι	ποιούσαις	ποιοῦσι
A	τιμῶντας	τιμώσας	τιμῶντα	ποιοῦντας	ποιούσας	ποιοῦντα

PRONOUNS

PERSONAL AND INTENSIVE PRONOUNS

	1st	2nd	3rd		3rd	
			SINGULAR			
N	ἐγώ	σύ		αὐτός	αὐτή	αὐτό
G	ἐμοῦ, μου	σοῦ	οὗ⁶	αὐτοῦ	αὐτῆς	αὐτοῦ
D	ἐμοί, μοι	σοί	οἷ	αὐτῷ	αὐτῇ	αὐτῷ
A	ἐμέ, με	σέ	ἕ	αὐτόν	αὐτήν	αὐτό
			DUAL			
N, A	νώ	σφώ		αὐτώ	αὐτά	αὐτώ
G, D	νῷν	σφῷν		αὐτοῖν	αὐταῖν	αὐτοῖν
			PLURAL			
N	ἡμεῖς	ὑμεῖς	σφεῖς	αὐτοί	αὐταί	αὐτά
G	ἡμῶν	ὑμῶν	σφῶν	αὐτῶν	αὐτῶν	αὐτῶν
D	ἡμῖν	ὑμῖν	σφίσι	αὐτοῖς	αὐταῖς	αὐτοῖς
A	ἡμᾶς	ὑμᾶς	σφᾶς	αὐτούς	αὐτάς	αὐτά

RECIPROCAL PRONOUN

	DUAL			PLURAL		
	M,N	F		M	F	N
G			G	ἀλλήλων	ἀλλήλων	ἀλλήλων
G, D	ἀλλήλοιν	ἀλλήλαιν	D	ἀλλήλοις	ἀλλήλαις	ἀλλήλοις
A	ἀλλήλω	ἀλλήλα	A	ἀλλήλους	ἀλλήλας	ἄλληλα

⁴ Like λυθείς in endings are τιθείς and θείς.
⁵ Like ποιῶν in endings is δηλῶν, δηλοῦσα, δηλοῦν.
⁶ οὗ etc. are used as indirect reflexive pronouns in Attic Greek.

PRONOUNS (Continued)

REFLEXIVE PRONOUNS

	First Person		Second Person	
	M	F	M	F

SINGULAR

G	ἐμαυτοῦ	ἐμαυτῆς	σεαυτοῦ (σαυτοῦ)	σεαυτῆς (σαυτῆς)
D	ἐμαυτῷ	ἐμαυτῇ	σεαυτῷ (σαυτῷ)	σεαυτῇ (σαυτῇ)
A	ἐμαυτόν	ἐμαυτήν	σεαυτόν (σαυτόν)	σεαυτήν (σαυτήν)

PLURAL

G	ἡμῶν αὐτῶν	ἡμῶν αὐτῶν	ὑμῶν αὐτῶν	ὑμῶν αὐτῶν
D	ἡμῖν αὐτοῖς	ἡμῖν αὐταῖς	ὑμῖν αὐτοῖς	ὑμῖν αὐταῖς
A	ἡμᾶς αὐτούς	ἡμᾶς αὐτάς	ὑμᾶς αὐτούς	ὑμᾶς αὐτάς

Third Person

	M	F	N	M	F	N

SINGULAR

G	ἑαυτοῦ	ἑαυτῆς	ἑαυτοῦ		αὐτοῦ	αὐτῆς	αὐτοῦ
D	ἑαυτῷ	ἑαυτῇ	ἑαυτῷ	or	αὐτῷ	αὐτῇ	αὐτῷ
A	ἑαυτόν	ἑαυτήν	ἑαυτό		αὐτόν	αὐτήν	αὐτό

PLURAL

G	ἑαυτῶν	ἑαυτῶν	ἑαυτῶν		αὐτῶν	αὐτῶν	αὐτῶν
D	ἑαυτοῖς	ἑαυταῖς	ἑαυτοῖς	or	αὐτοῖς	αὐταῖς	αὐτοῖς
A	ἑαυτούς	ἑαυτάς	ἑαυτά		αὐτούς	αὐτάς	αὐτά

DEMONSTRATIVE PRONOUNS

	M	F	N	M	F	N

SINGULAR

N	οὗτος	αὕτη	τοῦτο	ὅδε	ἥδε	τόδε
G	τούτου	ταύτης	τούτου	τοῦδε	τῆσδε	τοῦδε
D	τούτῳ	ταύτῃ	τούτῳ	τῷδε	τῇδε	τῷδε
A	τοῦτον	ταύτην	τοῦτο	τόνδε	τήνδε	τόδε

DUAL

N, A	τούτω	τούτω	τούτω	τώδε	τώδε	τώδε
G, D	τούτοιν	τούτοιν	τούτοιν	τοῖνδε	τοῖνδε	τοῖνδε

PLURAL

N	οὗτοι	αὗται	ταῦτα	οἵδε	αἵδε	τάδε
G	τούτων	τούτων	τούτων	τῶνδε	τῶνδε	τῶνδε
D	τούτοις	ταύταις	τούτοις	τοῖσδε	ταῖσδε	τοῖσδε
A	τούτους	ταύτας	ταῦτα	τούσδε	τάσδε	τάδε

	M	F	N
		SINGULAR	
N	ἐκεῖνος	ἐκείνη	ἐκεῖνο
G	ἐκείνου	ἐκείνης	ἐκείνου
D	ἐκείνῳ	ἐκείνῃ	ἐκείνῳ
A	ἐκεῖνον	ἐκείνην	ἐκεῖνο
		DUAL	
N, A	ἐκείνω	ἐκείνω	ἐκείνω
G, D	ἐκείνοιν	ἐκείνοιν	ἐκείνοιν
		PLURAL	
N	ἐκεῖνοι	ἐκεῖναι	ἐκεῖνα
G	ἐκείνων	ἐκείνων	ἐκείνων
D	ἐκείνοις	ἐκείναις	ἐκείνοις
A	ἐκείνους	ἐκείνας	ἐκεῖνα

INTERROGATIVE AND INDEFINITE PRONOUNS

	M, F	N	M, F	N
		SINGULAR		
N	τίς	τί	τις	τι
G	τίνος, τοῦ	τίνος, τοῦ	τινός, του	τινός, του
D	τίνι, τῷ	τίνι, τῷ	τινί, τῳ	τινί, τῳ
A	τίνα	τί	τινά	τι
		DUAL		
N, A	τίνε	τίνε	τινέ	τινέ
G, D	τίνοιν	τίνοιν	τινοῖν	τινοῖν
		PLURAL		
N	τίνες	τίνα	τινές	τινά
G	τίνων	τίνων	τινῶν	τινῶν
D	τίσι	τίσι	τισί	τισί
A	τίνας	τίνα	τινάς	τινά

RELATIVE PRONOUNS

	M	F	N	M	F	N
			SINGULAR			
N	ὅς	ἥ	ὅ	ὅστις	ἥτις	ὅ τι
G	οὗ	ἧς	οὗ	οὗτινος, ὅτου	ἧστινος	οὗτινος, ὅτου
D	ᾧ	ᾗ	ᾧ	ᾧτινι, ὅτῳ	ᾗτινι	ᾧτινι, ὅτῳ
A	ὅν	ἥν	ὅ	ὅντινα	ἥντινα	ὅ τι
			DUAL			
N, A	ὥ	ὥ	ὥ	ὥτινε	ὥτινε	ὥτινε
G, D	οἷν	οἷν	οἷν	οἷντινοιν	οἷντινοιν	οἷντινοιν
			PLURAL			
N	οἵ	αἵ	ἅ	οἵτινες	αἵτινες	ἅτινα, ἅττα
G	ὧν	ὧν	ὧν	ὧντινων, ὅτων	ὧντινων	ὧντινων, ὅτων
D	οἷς	αἷς	οἷς	οἷστισι, ὅτοις	αἷστισι	οἷστισι, ὅτοις
A	οὕς	ἅς	ἅ	οὕστινας	ἅστινας	ἅτινα, ἅττα

PRONOUNS AND ADVERBS

PRONOUNS

INTERROGATIVE	INDEFINITE	DEMONSTRATIVE	RELATIVE	INDEFINITE RELATIVE OR INDIRECT INTERROGATIVE
τίς, who?	τις, someone	ὅδε, this οὗτος, this ἐκεῖνος, that	ὅς, who	ὅστις, whoever
πότερος, which of two?	πότερος or ποτερός, one of two	ἕτερος, the other	ὁπότερος, whichever of two	ὁπότερος, whichever of two
πόσος, how much, how many?	ποσός, of some quantity	τόσος or τοσοῦτος, so much, so many	ὅσος, as much (many) as	ὁπόσος, of whatever size or number
ποῖος, of what sort?	ποιός, of some sort	τοῖος or τοιοῦτος, such	οἷος, of what sort	ὁποῖος, of whatever sort

ADVERBS OF PLACE

ποῦ, where?	που, somewhere	ἔνθα, ἐνθάδε, or ἐνταῦθα, there ἐκεῖ, yonder	οὗ or ἔνθα, where	ὅπου, wherever
πόθεν, whence?	ποθέν, from some place	ἐνθένδε or ἐντεῦθεν or ἐκεῖθεν, thence	ὅθεν, whence	ὁπόθεν, whencesoever
ποῖ, whither?	ποι, to some place	ἐνθάδε or ἐκεῖσε, thither	οἷ, ὅποι, or ἔνθα, whither	ὅποι, whithersoever

ADVERBS OF TIME

τότε, when?	ποτέ, sometime	τότε, then	ὅτε, when ἡνίκα, when	ὁπότε, whenever

ADVERBS OF WAY

τῇ, which way, how?	πῃ, somehow	τῇδε or ταύτῃ, this way, thus	ᾗ, in which way, as	ὅπῃ, in which way, as

ADVERBS OF MANNER

ὡς, how?	πως, somehow	ὥς, ὧδε, or οὕτως, thus ἐκείνως, in that way	ὡς, as, how	ὅπως, how

CARDINAL AND ORDINAL NUMERALS.
NUMERAL ADVERBS

CARDINAL NUMBERS	ORDINAL NUMBERS	NUMERAL ADVERBS
1 εἷς, μία, ἕν, one	πρῶ-τος, η, ον, first	ἅπαξ, once
2 δύο, two	δεύ-τερος, α, ον, second	δίς, twice
3 τρεῖς, τρί-α	τρί-τος, η, ον	τρίς
4 τέτταρ-ες, τέτταρ-α	τέταρ-τος, η, ον	τετρά-κις
5 πέντε	πέμπ-τος, η, ον	πεντά-κις
6 ἕξ	ἕκ-τος, η, ον	ἑξά-κις
7 ἑπτά	ἕβδομος, η, ον	ἑπτά-κις
8 ὀκτώ	ὄγδοος, η, ον	ὀκτά-κις
9 ἐννέα	ἔνα-τος, η, ον	ἐνά-κις
10 δέκα	δέκα-τος, η, ον	δεκά-κις
11 ἕν-δεκα	ἑν-δέκα-τος, η, ον	ἑν-δεκά-κις
12 δώ-δεκα	δω-δέκα-τος, η, ον	δω-δεκά-κις
13 τρεῖς καὶ δέκα	τρί-τος καὶ δέκα-τος	τρισ-και-δεκά-κις
14 τέτταρες καὶ δέκα	τέταρ-τος καὶ δέκα-τος	τετρα-και-δεκά-κις
15 πεντε-καί-δεκα	πέμπ-τος καὶ δέκα-τος	πεντε-και-δεκά-κις
16 ἑκ-καί-δεκα	ἕκ-τος καὶ δέκα-τος	ἑκ-και-δεκά-κις
17 ἑπτα-καί-δεκα	ἕβδομος καὶ δέκα-τος	ἑπτα-και-δεκά-κις
18 ὀκτω-καί-δεκα	ὄγδοος καὶ δέκα-τος	ὀκτω-και-δεκά-κις
19 ἐννεα-καί-δεκα	ἔνα-τος καὶ δέκα-τος	ἐννεα-και-δεκά-κις
20 εἴ-κοσι(ν)	εἰ-κοσ-τός, ή, όν	εἰ-κοσά-κις
21 εἷς καὶ εἴ-κοσι(ν), εἴκοσι καὶ εἷς, εἴ-κοσιν εἷς	πρῶ-τος καὶ εἰ-κοσ-τός	ἅπαξ καὶ εἰ-κοσά-κις
30 τριά-κοντα	τρια-κοστός, ή, όν	τρια-κοντά-κις
40 τετταρά-κοντα	τετταρα-κοστός, ή, όν	τετταρα-κοντά-κις
50 πεντή-κοντα	πεντη-κοστός, ή, όν	πεντη-κοντά-κις
60 ἑξή-κοντα	ἑξη-κοστός, ή, όν	ἑξη-κοντά-κις
70 ἑβδομή-κοντα	ἑβδομη-κοστός, ή, όν	ἑβδομη-κοντά-κις
80 ὀγδοή-κοντα	ὀγδοη-κοστός, ή, όν	ὀγδοη-κοντά-κις
90 ἐνενή-κοντα	ἐνενη-κοστός, ή, όν	ἐνενη-κοντά-κις
100 ἑκατόν	ἑκατοστός, ή, όν	ἑκατοντά-κις

200	δια-κόσιοι, αι, α	δια-κοσιοστός, ή, όν	δια-κοσιά-κις
300	τρια-κόσιοι, αι, α	τρια-κοσιοστός, ή, όν	τρια-κοσιά-κις
400	τετρα-κόσιοι, αι, α	τετρα-κοσιοστός, ή, όν	τετρα-κοσιά-κις
500	πεντα-κόσιοι, αι, α	πεντα-κοσιοστός, ή, όν	πεντα-κοσιά-κις
600	ἑξα-κόσιοι, αι, α	ἑξα-κοσιοστός, ή, όν	ἑξα-κοσιά-κις
700	ἑπτα-κόσιοι, αι, α	ἑπτα-κοσιοστός, ή, όν	ἑπτα-κοσιά-κις
800	ὀκτα-κόσιοι, αι, α	ὀκτα-κοσιοστός, ή, όν	ὀκτα-κοσιά-κις
900	ἐνα-κόσιοι, αι, α	ἐνα-κοσιοστός, ή, όν	ἐνα-κοσιά-κις
1000	χίλιοι, αι, α	χιλιοστός, ή, όν	χιλιά-κις
2000	δισ-χίλιοι, αι, α	δισ-χιλιοστός, ή, όν	δισ-χιλιά-κις
3000	τρισ-χίλιοι, αι, α	τρισ-χιλιοστός, ή, όν	τρισ-χιλιά-κις
10000	μύριοι, αι, α	μυριοστός, ή, όν	μυριά-κις
11000	μύριοι καὶ χίλιοι	μυριοστὸς καὶ χιλιοστός	μυριά-κις καὶ χιλιά-κις
20000	δισ-μύριοι, αι, α	δισ-μυριοστός, ή, όν	δισ-μυριά-κις
100000	δεκα-κισ-μύριοι, αι, α	δεκα-κισ-μυριοστός, ή, όν	δεκα-κισ-μυριά-κις

COMPLETE PARADIGM OF THE VERB παιδεύω
THE PRESENT SYSTEM OF παιδεύω

	ACTIVE		MIDDLE OR PASSIVE	
	PRESENT	IMPERFECT	PRESENT	IMPERFECT
INDICATIVE	παιδεύω	ἐπαίδευον	παιδεύομαι	ἐπαιδευόμην
	παιδεύεις	ἐπαίδευες	παιδεύει	ἐπαιδεύου
	παιδεύει	ἐπαίδευε(ν)	παιδεύεται	ἐπαιδεύετο
	παιδεύετον	ἐπαιδεύετον	παιδεύεσθον	ἐπαιδεύεσθον
	παιδεύετον	ἐπαιδευέτην	παιδεύεσθον	ἐπαιδευέσθην
	παιδεύομεν	ἐπαιδεύομεν	παιδευόμεθα	ἐπαιδευόμεθα
	παιδεύετε	ἐπαιδεύετε	παιδεύεσθε	ἐπαιδεύεσθε
	παιδεύουσι(ν)	ἐπαίδευον	παιδεύονται	ἐπαιδεύοντο
SUBJUNCTIVE	παιδεύω		παιδεύωμαι	
	παιδεύῃς		παιδεύῃ	
	παιδεύῃ		παιδεύηται	
	παιδεύητον		παιδεύησθον	
	παιδεύητον		παιδεύησθον	
	παιδεύωμεν		παιδευώμεθα	
	παιδεύητε		παιδεύησθε	
	παιδεύωσι(ν)		παιδεύωνται	
OPTATIVE	παιδεύοιμι		παιδευοίμην	
	παιδεύοις		παιδεύοιο	
	παιδεύοι		παιδεύοιτο	
	παιδεύοιτον		παιδεύοισθον	
	παιδευοίτην		παιδευοίσθην	
	παιδεύοιμεν		παιδευοίμεθα	
	παιδεύοιτε		παιδεύοισθε	
	παιδεύοιεν		παιδεύοιντο	
IMPERATIVE	παίδευε		παιδεύου	
	παιδευέτω		παιδευέσθω	
	παιδεύετον		παιδεύεσθον	
	παιδευέτων		παιδευέσθων	
	παιδεύετε		παιδεύεσθε	
	παιδευόντων		παιδευέσθων	
INFINITIVE	παιδεύειν		παιδεύεσθαι	
PARTICIPLE	παιδεύων		παιδευόμενος	

THE FUTURE SYSTEM OF παιδεύω[1]

	ACTIVE	MIDDLE
	FUTURE	
INDICATIVE	παιδεύσω	παιδεύσομαι
	παιδεύσεις	παιδεύσει
	παιδεύσει	παιδεύσεται
	παιδεύσετον	παιδεύσεσθον
	παιδεύσετον	παιδεύσεσθον
	παιδεύσομεν	παιδευσόμεθα
	παιδεύσετε	παιδεύσεσθε
	παιδεύσουσι(ν)	παιδεύσονται
OPTATIVE	παιδεύσοιμι	παιδευσοίμην
	παιδεύσοις	παιδεύσοιο
	παιδεύσοι	παιδεύσοιτο
	παιδεύσοιτον	παιδεύσοισθον
	παιδευσοίτην	παιδευσοίσθην
	παιδεύσοιμεν	παιδευσοίμεθα
	παιδεύσοιτε	παιδεύσοισθε
	παιδεύσοιεν	παιδεύσοιντο
INFINITIVE	παιδεύσειν	παιδεύσεσθαι
PARTICIPLE	παιδεύσων	παιδευσόμενος

[1] The future passive will be found, with the aorist passive, on page 174.

ACTIVE   MIDDLE   ACTIVE

FIRST AORIST   PERFECT   PLUPERFECT

INDICATIVE

ἐπαίδευσα	ἐπαιδευσάμην	πεπαίδευκα	ἐπεπαιδεύκη
ἐπαίδευσας	ἐπαιδεύσω	πεπαίδευκας	ἐπεπαιδεύκης
ἐπαίδευσε(ν)	ἐπαιδεύσατο	πεπαίδευκε(ν)	ἐπεπαιδεύκει(ν)
ἐπαιδεύσατον	ἐπαιδεύσασθον	πεπαιδεύκατον	ἐπεπαιδεύκετον
ἐπαιδευσάτην	ἐπαιδευσάσθην	πεπαιδεύκατον	ἐπεπαιδευκέτην
ἐπαιδεύσαμεν	ἐπαιδευσάμεθα	πεπαιδεύκαμεν	ἐπεπαιδεύκεμεν
ἐπαιδεύσατε	ἐπαιδεύσασθε	πεπαιδεύκατε	ἐπεπαιδεύκετε
ἐπαίδευσαν	ἐπαιδεύσαντο	πεπαιδεύκασι(ν)	ἐπεπαιδεύκεσαν

SUBJUNCTIVE

παιδεύσω	παιδεύσωμαι	πεπαιδεύκω or πεπαιδευκὼς ὦ, etc.
παιδεύσῃς	παιδεύσῃ	πεπαιδεύκης
παιδεύσῃ	παιδεύσηται	πεπαιδεύκη
παιδεύσητον	παιδεύσησθον	πεπαιδεύκητον
παιδεύσητον	παιδεύσησθον	πεπαιδεύκητον
παιδεύσωμεν	παιδευσώμεθα	πεπαιδεύκωμεν
παιδεύσητε	παιδεύσησθε	πεπαιδεύκητε
παιδεύσωσι(ν)	παιδεύσωνται	πεπαιδεύκωσι(ν)

OPTATIVE

παιδεύσαιμι	παιδευσαίμην	πεπαιδεύκοιμι or πεπαιδευκὼς εἴην, etc.
παιδεύσαις, -σειας	παιδεύσαιο	πεπαιδεύκοις
παιδεύσαι, -σειε(ν)	παιδεύσαιτο	πεπαιδεύκοι
παιδεύσαιτον	παιδεύσαισθον	πεπαιδεύκοιτον
παιδευσαίτην	παιδευσαίσθην	πεπαιδευκοίτην
παιδεύσαιμεν	παιδευσαίμεθα	πεπαιδεύκοιμεν
παιδεύσαιτε	παιδεύσαισθε	πεπαιδεύκοιτε
παιδεύσαιεν, -σειαν	παιδεύσαιντο	πεπαιδεύκοιεν

IMPERATIVE

παίδευσον	παίδευσαι	πεπαιδευκὼς ἴσθι etc.
παιδευσάτω	παιδευσάσθω	
παιδεύσατον	παιδεύσασθον	
παιδευσάτων	παιδευσάσθων	
παιδεύσατε	παιδεύσασθε	
παιδευσάντων	παιδευσάσθων	

INFINITIVE

παιδεῦσαι	παιδεύσασθαι	πεπαιδευκέναι

PARTICIPLE

παιδεύσας	παιδευσάμενος	πεπαιδευκώς

172

THE PERFECT MIDDLE SYSTEM OF παιδεύω
MIDDLE OR PASSIVE

	PERFECT	PLUPERFECT	FUTURE PERFECT
INDICATIVE	πεπαίδευμαι	ἐπεπαιδεύμην	πεπαιδεύσομαι
	πεπαίδευσαι	ἐπεπαίδευσο	πεπαιδεύσει
	πεπαίδευται	ἐπεπαίδευτο	πεπαιδεύσεται
	πεπαίδευσθον	ἐπεπαίδευσθον	πεπαιδεύσεσθον
	πεπαίδευσθον	ἐπεπαιδεύσθην	πεπαιδεύσεσθον
	πεπαιδεύμεθα	ἐπεπαιδεύμεθα	πεπαιδευσόμεθα
	πεπαίδευσθε	ἐπεπαίδευσθε	πεπαιδεύσεσθε
	πεπαίδευνται	ἐπεπαίδευντο	πεπαιδεύσονται
SUBJUNCTIVE	πεπαιδευμένος ὦ		
	πεπαιδευμένος ᾖς		
	πεπαιδευμένος ᾖ		
	πεπαιδευμένω ἦτον		
	πεπαιδευμένω ἦτον		
	πεπαιδευμένοι ὦμεν		
	πεπαιδευμένοι ἦτε		
	πεπαιδευμένοι ὦσι(ν)		
OPTATIVE	πεπαιδευμένος εἴην		πεπαιδευσοίμην
	πεπαιδευμένος εἴης		πεπαιδεύσοιο
	πεπαιδευμένος εἴη		πεπαιδεύσοιτο
	πεπαιδευμένω εἴητον, εἶτον		πεπαιδεύσοισθον
	πεπαιδευμένω εἰήτην, εἴτην		πεπαιδευσοίσθην
	πεπαιδευμένοι εἴημεν, εἶμεν		πεπαιδευσοίμεθα
	πεπαιδευμένοι εἴητε, εἶτε		πεπαιδεύσοισθε
	πεπαιδευμένοι εἴησαν, εἶεν		πεπαιδεύσοιντο
IMPERATIVE	πεπαίδευσο		
	πεπαιδεύσθω		
	πεπαίδευσθον		
	πεπαιδεύσθων		
	πεπαίδευσθε		
	πεπαιδεύσθων		
INFINITIVE	πεπαιδεῦσθαι		πεπαιδεύσεσθαι
PARTICIPLE	πεπαιδευμένος		πεπαιδευσόμενος

173

THE AORIST AND FUTURE PASSIVE SYSTEM OF παιδεύω

PASSIVE

	FIRST AORIST	FIRST FUTURE
INDICATIVE	ἐπαιδεύθην	παιδευθήσομαι
	ἐπαιδεύθης	παιδευθήσει
	ἐπαιδεύθη	παιδευθήσεται
	ἐπαιδεύθητον	παιδευθήσεσθον
	ἐπαιδευθήτην	παιδευθήσεσθον
	ἐπαιδεύθημεν	παιδευθησόμεθα
	ἐπαιδεύθητε	παιδευθήσεσθε
	ἐπαιδεύθησαν	παιδευθήσονται
SUBJUNCTIVE	παιδευθῶ (παιδευθέω)	
	παιδευθῇς	
	παιδευθῇ	
	παιδευθῆτον	
	παιδευθῆτον	
	παιδευθῶμεν	
	παιδευθῆτε	
	παιδευθῶσι(ν)	
OPTATIVE	παιδευθείην	παιδευθησοίμην
	παιδευθείης	παιδευθήσοιο
	παιδευθείη	παιδευθήσοιτο
	παιδευθείητον, -θεῖτον	παιδευθήσοισθον
	παιδευθειήτην, -θείτην	παιδευθησοίσθην
	παιδευθείημεν, -θεῖμεν	παιδευθησοίμεθα
	παιδευθείητε, -θεῖτε	παιδευθήσοισθε
	παιδευθείησαν, -θεῖεν	παιδευθήσοιντο
IMPERATIVE	παιδεύθητι	
	παιδευθήτω	
	παιδεύθητον	
	παιδευθήτων	
	παιδεύθητε	
	παιδευθέντων	
INFINITIVE	παιδευθῆναι	παιδευθήσεσθαι
PARTICIPLE	παιδευθείς	παιδευθησόμενος

CONTRACT VERBS

PRESENT SYSTEM OF τιμάω, φιλέω, AND δηλόω

PRESENT ACTIVE

INDICATIVE

τιμῶ	(τιμάω)	φιλῶ	(φιλέω)	δηλῶ	(δηλόω)
τιμᾷς	(τιμάεις)	φιλεῖς	(φιλέεις)	δηλοῖς	(δηλόεις)
τιμᾷ	(τιμάει)	φιλεῖ	(φιλέει)	δηλοῖ	(δηλόει)
τιμᾶτον	(τιμάετον)	φιλεῖτον	(φιλέετον)	δηλοῦτον	(δηλόετον)
τιμᾶτον	(τιμάετον)	φιλεῖτον	(φιλέετον)	δηλοῦτον	(δηλόετον)
τιμῶμεν	(τιμάομεν)	φιλοῦμεν	(φιλέομεν)	δηλοῦμεν	(δηλόομεν)
τιμᾶτε	(τιμάετε)	φιλεῖτε	(φιλέετε)	δηλοῦτε	(δηλόετε)
τιμῶσι	(τιμάουσι)	φιλοῦσι	(φιλέουσι)	δηλοῦσι	(δηλόουσι)

SUBJUNCTIVE

τιμῶ	(τιμάω)	φιλῶ	(φιλέω)	δηλῶ	(δηλόω)
τιμᾷς	(τιμάῃς)	φιλῇς	(φιλέῃς)	δηλοῖς	(δηλόῃς)
τιμᾷ	(τιμάῃ)	φιλῇ	(φιλέῃ)	δηλοῖ	(δηλόῃ)
τιμᾶτον	(τιμάητον)	φιλῆτον	(φιλέητον)	δηλῶτον	(δηλόητον)
τιμᾶτον	(τιμάητον)	φιλῆτον	(φιλέητον)	δηλῶτον	(δηλόητον)
τιμῶμεν	(τιμάωμεν)	φιλῶμεν	(φιλέωμεν)	δηλῶμεν	(δηλόωμεν)
τιμᾶτε	(τιμάητε)	φιλῆτε	(φιλέητε)	δηλῶτε	(δηλόητε)
τιμῶσι	(τιμάωσι)	φιλῶσι	(φιλέωσι)	δηλῶσι	(δηλόωσι)

OPTATIVE

τιμῴην	(τιμαοίην)	φιλοίην	(φιλεοίην)	δηλοίην	(δηλοοίην)
τιμῴης	(τιμαοίης)	φιλοίης	(φιλεοίης)	δηλοίης	(δηλοοίης)
τιμῴη	(τιμαοίη)	φιλοίη	(φιλεοίη)	δηλοίη	(δηλοοίη)
[τιμῴητον	(τιμαοίητον)	[φιλοίητον	(φιλεοίητον)	[δηλοίητον	(δηλοοίητον)
τιμῳήτην	(τιμαοιήτην)	φιλοιήτην	(φιλεοιήτην)	δηλοιήτην	(δηλοοιήτην)
τιμῴημεν	(τιμαοίημεν)	φιλοίημεν	(φιλεοίημεν)	δηλοίημεν	(δηλοοίημεν)
τιμῴητε	(τιμαοίητε)	φιλοίητε	(φιλεοίητε)	δηλοίητε	(δηλοοίητε)
τιμῴησαν][1]	(τιμαοίησαν)	φιλοίησαν]	(φιλεοίησαν)	δηλοίησαν]	(δηλοοίησαν)

ALTERNATE OPTATIVE

[τιμῷμι	(τιμάοιμι)	[φιλοῖμι	(φιλέοιμι)	[δηλοῖμι	(δηλόοιμι)
τιμῷς	(τιμάοις)	φιλοῖς	(φιλέοις)	δηλοῖς	(δηλόοις)
τιμῷ]	(τιμάοι)	φιλοῖ]	(φιλέοι)	δηλοῖ]	(δηλόοι)
τιμῷτον	(τιμάοιτον)	φιλοῖτον	(φιλέοιτον)	δηλοῖτον	(δηλόοιτον)
τιμῴτην	(τιμαοίτην)	φιλοίτην	(φιλεοίτην)	δηλοίτην	(δηλοοίτην)
τιμῷμεν	(τιμάοιμεν)	φιλοῖμεν	(φιλέοιμεν)	δηλοῖμεν	(δηλόοιμεν)
τιμῷτε	(τιμάοιτε)	φιλοῖτε	(φιλέοιτε)	δηλοῖτε	(δηλόοιτε)
τιμῷεν	(τιμάοιεν)	φιλοῖεν	(φιλέοιεν)	δηλοῖεν	(δηλόοιεν)

IMPERATIVE

τίμα	(τίμαε)	φίλει	(φίλεε)	δήλου	(δήλοε)
τιμάτω	(τιμαέτω)	φιλείτω	(φιλεέτω)	δηλούτω	(δηλοέτω)
τιμᾶτον	(τιμάετον)	φιλεῖτον	(φιλέετον)	δηλοῦτον	(δηλόετον)
τιμάτων	(τιμαέτων)	φιλείτων	(φιλεέτων)	δηλούτων	(δηλοέτων)
τιμᾶτε	(τιμάετε)	φιλεῖτε	(φιλέετε)	δηλοῦτε	(δηλόετε)
τιμώντων	(τιμαόντων)	φιλούντων	(φιλεόντων)	δηλούντων	(δηλοόντων)

INFINITIVE

τιμᾶν	(τιμάειν)	φιλεῖν	(φιλέειν)	δηλοῦν	(δηλόειν)

PARTICIPLE

τιμῶν	(τιμάων)	φιλῶν	(φιλέων)	δηλῶν	(δηλόων)

IMPERFECT ACTIVE

ἐτίμων	(ἐτίμαον)	ἐφίλουν	(ἐφίλεον)	ἐδήλουν	(ἐδήλοον)
ἐτίμας	(ἐτίμαες)	ἐφίλεις	(ἐφίλεες)	ἐδήλους	(ἐδήλοες)
ἐτίμα	(ἐτίμαε)	ἐφίλει	(ἐφίλεε)	ἐδήλου	(ἐδήλοε)
ἐτιμᾶτον	(ἐτιμάετον)	ἐφιλεῖτον	(ἐφιλέετον)	ἐδηλοῦτον	(ἐδηλόετον)
ἐτιμάτην	(ἐτιμαέτην)	ἐφιλείτην	(ἐφιλεέτην)	ἐδηλούτην	(ἐδηλοέτην)
ἐτιμῶμεν	(ἐτιμάομεν)	ἐφιλοῦμεν	(ἐφιλέομεν)	ἐδηλοῦμεν	(ἐδηλόομεν)
ἐτιμᾶτε	(ἐτιμάετε)	ἐφιλεῖτε	(ἐφιλέετε)	ἐδηλοῦτε	(ἐδηλόετε)
ἐτίμων	(ἐτίμαον)	ἐφίλουν	(ἐφίλεον)	ἐδήλουν	(ἐδήλοον)

PRESENT MIDDLE AND PASSIVE

INDICATIVE

τιμῶμαι	(τιμάομαι)	φιλοῦμαι	(φιλέομαι)	δηλοῦμαι	(δηλόομαι)
τιμᾷ	(τιμάῃ,-άει)	φιλῇ, φιλεῖ	(φιλέῃ,-έει)	δηλοῖ	(δηλόῃ,-όει)
τιμᾶται	(τιμάεται)	φιλεῖται	(φιλέεται)	δηλοῦται	(δηλόεται)
τιμᾶσθον	(τιμάεσθον)	φιλεῖσθον	(φιλέεσθον)	δηλοῦσθον	(δηλόεσθον)
τιμᾶσθον	(τιμάεσθον)	φιλεῖσθον	(φιλέεσθον)	δηλοῦσθον	(δηλόεσθον)
τιμώμεθα	(τιμαόμεθα)	φιλούμεθα	(φιλεόμεθα)	δηλούμεθα	(δηλοόμεθα)
τιμᾶσθε	(τιμάεσθε)	φιλεῖσθε	(φιλέεσθε)	δηλοῦσθε	(δηλόεσθε)
τιμῶνται	(τιμάονται)	φιλοῦνται	(φιλέονται)	δηλοῦνται	(δηλόονται)

¹ Bracketed forms of the optative are not in good usage.

176

τιμῶμαι	(τιμάωμαι)	φιλῶμαι	(φιλέωμαι)	δηλῶμαι	(δηλόωμαι)
τιμᾷ	(τιμάῃ)	φιλῇ	(φιλέῃ)	δηλοῖ	(δηλόῃ)
τιμᾶται	(τιμάηται)	φιλῆται	(φιλέηται)	δηλῶται	(δηλόηται)
τιμᾶσθον	(τιμάησθον)	φιλῆσθον	(φιλέησθον)	δηλῶσθον	(δηλόησθον)
τιμᾶσθον	(τιμάησθον)	φιλῆσθον	(φιλέησθον)	δηλῶσθον	(δηλόησθον)
τιμώμεθα	(τιμαώμεθα)	φιλώμεθα	(φιλεώμεθα)	δηλώμεθα	(δηλοώμεθα)
τιμᾶσθε	(τιμάησθε)	φιλῆσθε	(φιλέησθε)	δηλῶσθε	(δηλόησθε)
τιμῶνται	(τιμάωνται)	φιλῶνται	(φιλέωνται)	δηλῶνται	(δηλόωνται)

τιμῴμην	(τιμαοίμην)	φιλοίμην	(φιλεοίμην)	δηλοίμην	(δηλοοίμην)
τιμῷο	(τιμάοιο)	φιλοῖο	(φιλέοιο)	δηλοῖο	(δηλόοιο)
τιμῷτο	(τιμάοιτο)	φιλοῖτο	(φιλέοιτο)	δηλοῖτο	(δηλόοιτο)
τιμῷσθον	(τιμάοισθον)	φιλοῖσθον	(φιλέοισθον	δηλοῖσθον	(δηλόοισθον)
τιμῴσθην	(τιμαοίσθην)	φιλοίσθην	(φιλεοίσθην)	δηλοίσθην	(δηλοοίσθην)
τιμῴμεθα	(τιμαοίμεθα)	φιλοίμεθα	(φιλεοίμεθα)	δηλοίμεθα	(δηλοοίμεθα)
τιμῷσθε	(τιμάοισθε)	φιλοῖσθε	(φιλέοισθε)	δηλοῖσθε	(δηλόοισθε)
τιμῷντο	(τιμάοιντο)	φιλοῖντο	(φιλέοιντο)	δηλοῖντο	(δηλόοιντο)

τιμῶ	(τιμάου)	φιλοῦ	(φιλέου)	δηλοῦ	(δηλόου)
τιμάσθω	(τιμαέσθω)	φιλείσθω	(φιλεέσθω)	δηλούσθω	(δηλοέσθω)
τιμᾶσθον	(τιμάεσθον)	φιλεῖσθον	(φιλέεσθον)	δηλοῦσθον	(δηλόεσθον)
τιμάσθων	(τιμαέσθων)	φιλείσθων	(φιλεέσθων)	δηλούσθων	(δηλοέσθων)
τιμᾶσθε	(τιμάεσθε)	φιλεῖσθε	(φιλέεσθε)	δηλοῦσθε	(δηλόεσθε)
τιμάσθων	(τιμαέσθων)	φιλείσθων	(φιλεέσθων)	δηλούσθων	(δηλοέσθων)

τιμᾶσθαι	(τιμάεσθαι)	φιλεῖσθαι	(φιλέεσθαι)	δηλοῦσθαι	(δηλόεσθαι)

τιμώμενος	(τιμαόμενος)	φιλούμενος	(φιλεόμενος)	δηλούμενος	(δηλοόμενος)

Imperfect Middle and Passive

ἐτιμώμην	(ἐτιμαόμην)	ἐφιλούμην	(ἐφιλεόμην)	ἐδηλούμην	(ἐδηλοόμην)
ἐτιμῶ	(ἐτιμάου)	ἐφιλοῦ	(ἐφιλέου)	ἐδηλοῦ	(ἐδηλόου)
ἐτιμᾶτο	(ἐτιμάετο)	ἐφιλεῖτο	(ἐφιλέετο)	ἐδηλοῦτο	(ἐδηλόετο)
ἐτιμᾶσθον	(ἐτιμάεσθον)	ἐφιλεῖσθον	(ἐφιλέεσθον)	ἐδηλοῦσθον	(ἐδηλόεσθον)
ἐτιμάσθην	(ἐτιμαέσθην)	ἐφιλείσθην	(ἐφιλεέσθην)	ἐδηλούσθην	(ἐδηλοέσθην)
ἐτιμώμεθα	(ἐτιμαόμεθα)	ἐφιλούμεθα	(ἐφιλεόμεθα)	ἐδηλούμεθα	(ἐδηλοόμεθα)
ἐτιμᾶσθε	(ἐτιμάεσθε)	ἐφιλεῖσθε	(ἐφιλέεσθε)	ἐδηλοῦσθε	(ἐδηλόεσθε)
ἐτιμῶντο	(ἐτιμάοντο)	ἐφιλοῦντο	(ἐφιλέοντο)	ἐδηλοῦντο	(ἐδηλόοντο)

177

MI-VERBS

PRESENT SYSTEM OF τίθημι

	ACTIVE		MIDDLE AND PASSIVE	
	PRESENT	IMPERFECT	PRESENT	IMPERFECT
INDICATIVE	τίθημι	ἐτίθην	τίθεμαι	ἐτιθέμην
	τίθης	ἐτίθεις	τίθεσαι	ἐτίθεσο
	τίθησι	ἐτίθει	τίθεται	ἐτίθετο
	τίθετον	ἐτίθετον	τίθεσθον	ἐτίθεσθον
	τίθετον	ἐτιθέτην	τίθεσθον	ἐτιθέσθην
	τίθεμεν	ἐτίθεμεν	τιθέμεθα	ἐτιθέμεθα
	τίθετε	ἐτίθετε	τίθεσθε	ἐτίθεσθε
	τιθέασι	ἐτίθεσαν	τίθενται	ἐτίθεντο

	PRESENT		PRESENT	
SUBJUNCTIVE	τιθῶ		τιθῶμαι	
	τιθῇς		τιθῇ	
	τιθῇ		τιθῆται	
	τιθῆτον		τιθῆσθον	
	τιθῆτον		τιθῆσθον	
	τιθῶμεν		τιθώμεθα	
	τιθῆτε		τιθῆσθε	
	τιθῶσι		τιθῶνται	
OPTATIVE	τιθείην		τιθείμην	
	τιθείης		τιθεῖο	
	τιθείη		τιθεῖτο	
	τιθεῖτον or τιθείητον		τιθεῖσθον	
	τιθείτην τιθειήτην		τιθείσθην	
	τιθεῖμεν τιθείημεν		τιθείμεθα	
	τιθεῖτε τιθείητε		τιθεῖσθε	
	τιθεῖεν τιθείησαν		τιθεῖντο	
IMPERATIVE	τίθει		τίθεσο	
	τιθέτω		τιθέσθω	
	τίθετον		τίθεσθον	
	τιθέτων		τιθέσθων	
	τίθετε		τίθεσθε	
	τιθέντων		τιθέσθων	
INFINITIVE	τιθέναι		τίθεσθαι	
PARTICIPLE	τιθείς, -εῖσα, -έν		τιθέμενος, -η, -ον	

PRESENT SYSTEM OF δίδωμι

	ACTIVE		MIDDLE AND PASSIVE	
	PRESENT	IMPERFECT	PRESENT	IMPERFECT
INDICATIVE	δίδωμι	ἐδίδουν	δίδομαι	ἐδιδόμην
	δίδως	ἐδίδους	δίδοσαι	ἐδίδοσο
	δίδωσι	ἐδίδου	δίδοται	ἐδίδοτο
	δίδοτον	ἐδίδοτον	δίδοσθον	ἐδίδοσθον
	δίδοτον	ἐδιδότην	δίδοσθον	ἐδιδόσθην
	δίδομεν	ἐδίδομεν	διδόμεθα	ἐδιδόμεθα
	δίδοτε	ἐδίδοτε	δίδοσθε	ἐδίδοσθε
	διδόασι	ἐδίδοσαν	δίδονται	ἐδίδοντο

	PRESENT		PRESENT
SUBJUNCTIVE	διδῶ		διδῶμαι
	διδῷς		διδῷ
	διδῷ		διδῶται
	διδῶτον		διδῶσθον
	διδῶτον		διδῶσθον
	διδῶμεν		διδώμεθα
	διδῶτε		διδῶσθε
	διδῶσι		διδῶνται

OPTATIVE	διδοίην		διδοίμην
	διδοίης		διδοῖο
	διδοίη		διδοῖτο
	διδοῖτον or	διδοίητον	διδοῖσθον
	διδοίτην	διδοιήτην	διδοίσθην
	διδοῖμεν	διδοίημεν	διδοίμεθα
	διδοῖτε	διδοίητε	διδοῖσθε
	διδοῖεν	διδοίησαν	διδοῖντο

IMPERATIVE	δίδου		δίδοσο
	διδότω		διδόσθω
	δίδοτον		δίδοσθον
	διδότων		διδόσθων
	δίδοτε		δίδοσθε
	διδόντων		διδόσθων
INFINITIVE	διδόναι		δίδοσθαι
PARTICIPLE	διδούς, -οῦσα, -όν		διδόμενος, -η, -ον

SECOND AORIST SYSTEM OF τίθημι AND δίδωμι

	ACTIVE	MIDDLE	ACTIVE	MIDDLE
INDICATIVE	[ἔθηκα	ἐθέμην	[ἔδωκα	ἐδόμην
	ἔθηκας	ἔθου	ἔδωκας	ἔδου
	ἔθηκε]	ἔθετο	ἔδωκε]	ἔδοτο
	ἔθετον	ἔθεσθον	ἔδοτον	ἔδοσθον
	ἐθέτην	ἐθέσθην	ἐδότην	ἐδόσθην
	ἔθεμεν	ἐθέμεθα	ἔδομεν	ἐδόμεθα
	ἔθετε	ἔθεσθε	ἔδοτε	ἔδοσθε
	ἔθεσαν	ἔθεντο	ἔδοσαν	ἔδοντο
SUBJUNCTIVE	θῶ	θῶμαι	δῶ	δῶμαι
	θῇς	θῇ	δῷς	δῷ
	θῇ	θῆται	δῷ	δῶται
	θῆτον	θῆσθον	δῶτον	δῶσθον
	θῆτον	θῆσθον	δῶτον	δῶσθον
	θῶμεν	θώμεθα	δῶμεν	δώμεθα
	θῆτε	θῆσθε	δῶτε	δῶσθε
	θῶσι	θῶνται	δῶσι	δῶνται

	ACTIVE		MIDDLE	ACTIVE		MIDDLE
OPTATIVE	θείην		θείμην	δοίην		δοίμην
	θείης		θεῖο	δοίης		δοῖο
	θείη		θεῖτο	δοίη		δοῖτο
	θεῖτον	θείητον	θεῖσθον	δοῖτον	δοίητον	δοῖσθον
	θείτην	θειήτην	θείσθην	δοίτην	δοιήτην	δοίσθην
	θεῖμεν	θείημεν	θείμεθα	δοῖμεν	δοίημεν	δοίμεθα
	θεῖτε	θείητε	θεῖσθε	δοῖτε	δοίητε	δοῖσθε
	θεῖεν	θείησαν	θεῖντο	δοῖεν	δοίησαν	δοῖντο

	ACTIVE	MIDDLE	ACTIVE	MIDDLE
IMPERATIVE	θές	θοῦ	δός	δοῦ
	θέτω	θέσθω	δότω	δόσθω
	θέτον	θέσθον	δότον	δόσθον
	θέτων	θέσθων	δότων	δόσθων
	θέτε	θέσθε	δότε	δόσθε
	θέντων	θέσθων	δόντων	δόσθων
INFINITIVE	θεῖναι	θέσθαι	δοῦναι	δόσθαι
PARTICIPLE	θείς, θεῖσα, θέν	θέμενος, -η, -ον	δούς, δοῦσα, δόν	δόμενος, -η, -ον

PRESENT SYSTEM OF ἵστημι

	ACTIVE		MIDDLE AND PASSIVE	
	PRESENT	IMPERFECT	PRESENT	IMPERFECT
INDICATIVE	ἵστημι	ἵστην	ἵσταμαι	ἱστάμην
	ἵστης	ἵστης	ἵστασαι	ἵστασο
	ἵστησι	ἵστη	ἵσταται	ἵστατο
	ἵστατον	ἵστατον	ἵστασθον	ἵστασθον
	ἵστατον	ἱστάτην	ἵστασθον	ἱστάσθην
	ἵσταμεν	ἵσταμεν	ἱστάμεθα	ἱστάμεθα
	ἵστατε	ἵστατε	ἵστασθε	ἵστασθε
	ἱστᾶσι	ἵστασαν	ἵστανται	ἵσταντο

	PRESENT	PRESENT
SUBJUNCTIVE	ἱστῶ	ἱστῶμαι
	ἱστῇς	ἱστῇ
	ἱστῇ	ἱστῆται
	ἱστῆτον	ἱστῆσθον
	ἱστῆτον	ἱστῆσθον
	ἱστῶμεν	ἱστώμεθα
	ἱστῆτε	ἱστῆσθε
	ἱστῶσι	ἱστῶνται
OPTATIVE	ἱσταίην	ἱσταίμην
	ἱσταίης	ἱσταῖο
	ἱσταίη	ἱσταῖτο
	ἱσταῖτον or ἱσταίητον	ἱσταῖσθον
	ἱσταίτην ἱσταιήτην	ἱσταίσθην
	ἱσταῖμεν ἱσταίημεν	ἱσταίμεθα
	ἱσταῖτε ἱσταίητε	ἱσταῖσθε
	ἱσταῖεν ἱσταίησαν	ἱσταῖντο
IMPERATIVE	ἵστη	ἵστασο
	ἱστάτω	ἱστάσθω
	ἵστατον	ἵστασθον
	ἱστάτων	ἱστάσθων
	ἵστατε	ἵστασθε
	ἱστάντων	ἱστάσθων
INFINITIVE	ἱστάναι	ἵστασθαι
PARTICIPLE	ἱστάς, -ᾶσα, -άν	ἱστάμενος, -η, -ον

ἵστημι

	ACTIVE		ACTIVE	
			SECOND PERFECT	SECOND PLUPERFECT
	SECOND AORIST			
INDICATIVE	ἔστην		[ἔστηκα	[εἱστήκη
	ἔστης		ἔστηκας	εἱστήκης
	ἔστη		ἔστηκε]	εἱστήκει]
	ἔστητον		ἔστατον	ἔστατον
	ἐστήτην		ἔστατον	ἐστάτην
	ἔστημεν		ἔσταμεν	ἔσταμεν
	ἔστητε		ἔστατε	ἔστατε
	ἔστησαν		ἑστᾶσι	ἔστασαν

		SECOND PERFECT
SUBJUNCTIVE	στῶ	ἑστῶ
	στῇς	ἑστῇς
	στῇ	ἑστῇ
	στῆτον	ἑστῆτον
	στῆτον	ἑστῆτον
	στῶμεν	ἑστῶμεν
	στῆτε	ἑστῆτε
	στῶσι	ἑστῶσι
OPTATIVE	σταίην	ἑσταίην
	σταίης	ἑσταίης
	σταίη	ἑσταίη
	σταῖτον or σταίητον	ἑσταῖτον or ἑσταίητον
	σταίτην σταιήτην	ἑσταίτην ἑσταιήτην
	σταῖμεν σταίημεν	ἑσταῖμεν ἑσταίημεν
	σταῖτε σταίητε	ἑσταῖτε ἑσταίητε
	σταῖεν σταίησαν	ἑσταῖεν ἑσταίησαν
IMPERATIVE	στῆθι	ἔσταθι
	στήτω	ἑστάτω
	στῆτον	ἔστατον
	στήτων	ἑστάτων
	στῆτε	ἔστατε
	στάντων	ἑστάντων
INFINITIVE	στῆναι	ἑστάναι
PARTICIPLE	στάς, στᾶσα, στάν	ἑστώς, ἑστῶσα, ἑστός

PRESENT SYSTEM OF δείκνυμι

	ACTIVE		MIDDLE AND PASSIVE	
	PRESENT	IMPERFECT	PRESENT	IMPERFECT
INDICATIVE	δείκνυμι	ἐδείκνυν	δείκνυμαι	ἐδεικνύμην
	δείκνυς	ἐδείκνυς	δείκνυσαι	ἐδείκνυσο
	δείκνυσι	ἐδείκνυ	δείκνυται	ἐδείκνυτο
	δείκνυτον	ἐδείκνυτον	δείκνυσθον	ἐδείκνυσθον
	δείκνυτον	ἐδεικνύτην	δείκνυσθον	ἐδεικνύσθην
	δείκνυμεν	ἐδείκνυμεν	δεικνύμεθα	ἐδεικνύμεθα
	δείκνυτε	ἐδείκνυτε	δείκνυσθε	ἐδείκνυσθε
	δεικνύασι	ἐδείκνυσαν	δείκνυνται	ἐδείκνυντο

	PRESENT	PRESENT
SUBJUNCTIVE	δεικνύω	δεικνύωμαι
	δεικνύῃς	δεικνύῃ
	δεικνύῃ	δεικνύηται
	δεικνύητον	δεικνύησθον
	δεικνύητον	δεικνύησθον
	δεικνύωμεν	δεικνυώμεθα
	δεικνύητε	δεικνύησθε
	δεικνύωσι	δεικνύωνται
OPTATIVE	δεικνύοιμι	δεικνυοίμην
	δεικνύοις	δεικνύοιο
	δεικνύοι	δεικνύοιτο
	δεικνύοιτον	δεικνύοισθον
	δεικνυοίτην	δεικνυοίσθην
	δεικνύοιμεν	δεικνυοίμεθα
	δεικνύοιτε	δεικνύοισθε
	δεικνύοιεν	δεικνύοιντο
IMPERATIVE	δείκνυ	δείκνυσο
	δεικνύτω	δεικνύσθω
	δείκνυτον	δείκνυσθον
	δεικνύτων	δεικνύσθων
	δείκνυτε	δείκνυσθε
	δεικνύντων	δεικνύσθων
INFINITIVE	δεικνύναι	δείκνυσθαι
PARTICIPLE	δεικνύς, -ῦσα, -ύν	δεικνύμενος, -η, -ον

PRESENT SYSTEM OF ἵημι

	ACTIVE		MIDDLE AND PASSIVE		ACTIVE	MIDDLE
	PRESENT	IMPERFECT	PRESENT	IMPERFECT	SECOND AORIST¹	

INDICATIVE

ACTIVE PRESENT	ACTIVE IMPERFECT	MID. & PASS. PRESENT	MID. & PASS. IMPERFECT	ACTIVE SECOND AORIST	MIDDLE
ἵημι	ἵην	ἵεμαι	ἱέμην	[ἧκα	εἵμην
ἵης, ἱεῖς	ἵεις	ἵεσαι	ἵεσο	ἧκας	εἷσο
ἵησι	ἵει	ἵεται	ἵετο	ἧκε]	εἷτο
ἵετον	ἵετον	ἵεσθον	ἵεσθον	εἷτον	εἷσθον
ἵετον	ἱέτην	ἵεσθον	ἱέσθην	εἵτην	εἵσθην
ἵεμεν	ἵεμεν	ἱέμεθα	ἱέμεθα	εἷμεν	εἵμεθα
ἵετε	ἵετε	ἵεσθε	ἵεσθε	εἷτε	εἷσθε
ἱᾶσι	ἵεσαν	ἵενται	ἵεντο	εἷσαν	εἷντο

SUBJUNCTIVE

PRESENT (Active)	PRESENT (Mid. & Pass.)	Active Aorist	Middle
ἱῶ	ἱῶμαι	ὦ	ὦμαι
ἱῇς	ἱῇ	ᾖς	ᾖ
ἱῇ	ἱῆται	ᾖ	ᾖται
ἱῆτον	ἱῆσθον	ἦτον	ἦσθον
ἱῆτον	ἱῆσθον	ἦτον	ἦσθον
ἱῶμεν	ἱώμεθα	ὦμεν	ὤμεθα
ἱῆτε	ἱῆσθε	ἦτε	ἦσθε
ἱῶσι	ἱῶνται	ὦσι	ὦνται

OPTATIVE

Active Present	Mid. & Pass. Present	Active Aorist	Middle
ἱείην	ἱείμην	εἴην	εἵμην
ἱείης	ἱεῖο	εἴης	εἷο
ἱείη	ἱεῖτο	εἴη	εἷτο
ἱεῖτον or ἱείητον	ἱεῖσθον	εἷτον or εἴητον	εἷσθον
ἱείτην ἱειήτην	ἱέσθην	εἴτην εἰήτην	εἵσθην
ἱεῖμεν ἱείημεν	ἱείμεθα	εἷμεν εἴημεν	εἵμεθα
ἱεῖτε ἱείητε	ἱεῖσθε	εἷτε εἴητε	εἷσθε
ἱεῖεν ἱείησαν	ἱεῖντο	εἷεν εἴησαν	εἷντο

IMPERATIVE

Active Present	Mid. & Pass. Present	Active Aorist	Middle
ἵει	ἵεσο	ἕς	οὗ
ἱέτω	ἱέσθω	ἔτω	ἔσθω
ἵετον	ἵεσθον	ἔτον	ἔσθον
ἱέτων	ἱέσθων	ἔτων	ἔσθων
ἵετε	ἵεσθε	ἔτε	ἔσθε
ἱέντων	ἱέσθων	ἔντων	ἔσθων

INFINITIVE

Active Present	Mid. & Pass. Present	Active Aorist	Middle
ἱέναι	ἵεσθαι	εἷναι	ἕσθαι

PARTICIPLE

Active Present	Mid. & Pass. Present	Active Aorist	Middle
ἱείς, ἱεῖσα, ἱέν	ἱέμενος	εἵς, εἷσα, ἕν	ἕμενος

¹ ἵημι in the second aorist is rarely found except in compounds.

184

PRESENT SYSTEM OF οἶδα AND φημί

	ACTIVE		ACTIVE	
	SECOND PERFECT	SECOND PLUPERFECT	PRESENT	IMPERFECT
INDICATIVE	οἶδα	ᾔδη or ᾔδειν	φημί	ἔφην
	οἶσθα	ᾔδησθα or ᾔδεις	φής	ἔφησθα or ἔφης
	οἶδε	ᾔδει or ᾔδειν	φησί	ἔφη
	ἴστον	ᾖστον	φατόν	ἔφατον
	ἴστον	ᾖστην	φατόν	ἐφάτην
	ἴσμεν	ᾖσμεν or ᾔδεμεν	φαμέν	ἔφαμεν
	ἴστε	ᾖστε or ᾔδετε	φατέ	ἔφατε
	ἴσασι	ᾖσαν or ᾔδεσαν	φασί	ἔφασαν

	SECOND PERFECT	PRESENT
SUBJUNCTIVE	εἰδῶ	φῶ
	εἰδῇς	φῇς
	εἰδῇ	φῇ
	εἰδῆτον	φῆτον
	εἰδῆτον	φῆτον
	εἰδῶμεν	φῶμεν
	εἰδῆτε	φῆτε
	εἰδῶσι	φῶσι

OPTATIVE	εἰδείην	φαίην
	εἰδείης	φαίης
	εἰδείη	φαίη
	εἰδεῖτον	φαῖτον or φαίητον
	εἰδείτην	φαίτην φαιήτην
	εἰδεῖμεν or εἰδείημεν	φαῖμεν φαίημεν
	εἰδεῖτε εἰδείητε	φαῖτε φαίητε
	εἰδεῖεν εἰδείησαν	φαῖεν φαίησαν

IMPERATIVE	ἴσθι	φαθί or φάθι
	ἴστω	φάτω
	ἴστον	φάτον
	ἴστων	φάτων
	ἴστε	φάτε
	ἴστων	φάντων

INFINITIVE	εἰδέναι	φάναι
PARTICIPLE	εἰδώς, εἰδυῖα, εἰδός, gen. εἰδότος, etc.	

PRESENT SYSTEM OF εἰμί AND εἶμι

	ACTIVE			ACTIVE		
	PRESENT	IMPERFECT		PRESENT	IMPERFECT	
INDICATIVE	εἰμί	ἦ or ἦν		εἶμι	ᾖα or ᾔειν	
	εἶ	ἦσθα		εἶ	ᾔεις ᾔεισθα	
	ἐστί	ἦν		εἶσι	ᾔει ᾔειν	
	ἐστόν	ἦστον or ἦτον		ἴτον	ᾔτον	
	ἐστόν	ἤστην ἤτην		ἴτον	ᾔτην	
	ἐσμέν	ἦμεν		ἴμεν	ᾖμεν	
	ἐστέ	ἦστε ἦτε		ἴτε	ᾖτε	
	εἰσί	ἦσαν		ἴασι	ᾖσαν or ᾔεσαν	

	PRESENT	PRESENT
SUBJUNCTIVE	ὦ	ἴω
	ᾖς	ἴῃς
	ᾖ	ἴῃ
	ἦτον	ἴητον
	ἦτον	ἴητον
	ὦμεν	ἴωμεν
	ἦτε	ἴητε
	ὦσι	ἴωσι

OPTATIVE	εἴην			ἰοιμι or ἰοίην	
	εἴης			ἴοις	
	εἴη			ἴοι	
	εἶτον or εἴητον			ἴοιτον	
	εἴτην εἰήτην			ἰοίτην	
	εἶμεν εἴημεν			ἴοιμεν	
	εἶτε εἴητε			ἴοιτε	
	εἶεν εἴησαν			ἴοιεν	

IMPERATIVE	ἴσθι	ἴθι
	ἔστω	ἴτω
	ἔστον	ἴτον
	ἔστων	ἴτων
	ἔστε	ἴτε
	ἔστων	ἰόντων

INFINITIVE	εἶναι	ἰέναι
PARTICIPLE	ὤν, οὖσα, ὄν, gen. ὄντος, etc.	ἰών, ἰοῦσα, ἰόν, gen. ἰόντος, etc.

A SUMMARY OF GREEK SYNTAX

THE NOUN

1. Nominative Case
   Subject of a finite verb, p. 6
   Predicate nominative, p. 7

2. Genitive Case
   Possession, p. 6, 7, 42, 58, 99
   Absolute, p. 74
   Partitive, p. 42
   Personal agent, with ὑπό, p. 32, 110
   Source, p. 50n
   Place from which (usually with prepositions), p. 190–191
   Time within which, p. 22
   Comparison (when ἤ is omitted), p. 30
   Separation, p. 6, 61n

3. Dative Case
   Indirect object, p. 6
   Place where (usually with prepositions), p. 6, 190
   Time when, p. 22
   Possession, p. 22
   Interest, p. 119
   Degree of difference, p. 30
   Agent (with perfect passive system and with verbals), p. 119, 149
   Means or instrument, p. 6, 110
   Specification, p. 39

4. Accusative Case
   Direct object, p. 6
   Subject of infinitive or participle in indirect discourse, p. 15, 75
   Subject of the infinitive in other constructions, p. 95
   Duration of time or extent of space, p. 21
   Specification, p. 39
   Place to which (with prepositions), p. 190

5. Vocative Case
   Direct address, p. 6

1. Purpose is expressed by: ἵνα, ὡς, or ὅπως with the subjunctive in primary sequence, with the optative in secondary sequence, p. 83

   ὡς with the future participle (ὡς may be omitted), p. 74

   A relative clause with the future indicative

   ὅπως and the future indicative after verbs of striving or effort, p. 149

   The genitive of the articular infinitive, p. 54n

   The infinitive (rarely)

   The negative for all purpose constructions is μή.

2. Result is expressed by: ὥστε plus the indicative for actual result, negative οὐ, p. 19
   ὥστε plus the infinitive for natural result, negative μή, p. 19

3. Indirect Discourse

   Most verbs of mental action and some of saying are followed by the infinitive with subject accusative, p. 15

   Most verbs of saying are followed by ὅτι or ὡς with the mood of the verb unchanged in primary sequence, whereas it *may* be changed to the corresponding tense of the optative in secondary sequence, p. 87

   Verbs of sense perception usually take the participle with subject accusative, though many also take the ὅτι construction, p. 75

   Indirect questions follow the rule for the ὅτι construction, p. 88

   Subordinate clauses in all types of indirect discourse remain unchanged in mood in primary sequence. In secondary sequence, primary tenses of the indicative and any verbs in the subjunctive *may* be changed to the optative, with ἄν dropping out, but secondary tenses of the indicative remain unchanged, p. 87

4. Conditions

	PROTASIS (Negative μή)	APODOSIS (Negative usually οὐ)
SIMPLE	εἰ + Indicative	Indicative
FUTURE MORE VIVID	ἐάν + Subjunctive	Future Indicative or equivalent, p. 78
FUTURE LESS VIVID	εἰ + Optative	Optative + ἄν, p. 86, 88
PRESENT GENERAL	ἐάν + Subjunctive	Present Indicative, p. 78
PAST GENERAL	εἰ + Optative	Imperfect Indicative, p. 86
PRESENT CONTRARY TO FACT	εἰ + Imperfect Indicative	Imperfect Indicative + ἄν, p. 99
PAST CONTRARY TO FACT	εἰ + Aorist Indicative	Aorist Indicative + ἄν, p. 99
FUTURE MOST VIVID (MINATORY, MONITORY)	εἰ + Future Indicative	Future Indicative

5. A relative pronoun or adverb (whenever, whoever) may introduce a condition, p. 78, 86

188

6. Temporal clauses, p. 95

πρίν following an affirmative clause means *before* and takes the infinitive with subject accusative.

πρίν meaning *until*, after a negative clause, and ἕως, ἔστε, and μέχρι, which always means *until* or *while*, take the following construction:

1. To denote a definite past act they take the indicative, usually aorist. The same is true of ἐπεί and ἐπειδή, *when* or *after* or *since*.

2. When they denote an anticipated, a future, or a repeated act, they take the subjunctive with ἄν in primary sequence, the optative without ἄν in secondary sequence.

7. Verbs of fearing are followed by clauses beginning with μή for an affirmative, μὴ οὐ for a negative fear, with the subjunctive in primary, the optative in secondary sequence, p. 92

8. Commands are expressed by the imperative, negative μή. Negative command may also be expressed by μή plus the aorist subjunctive, p. 126

9. The subjunctive may be used independently to express exhortation, in the first person plural. The negative is μή, p. 103

10. Wishes

Future wishes may be expressed by the optative, with or without εἴθε or εἰ γάρ, p. 83

Impossible wishes are expressed by εἴθε or εἰ γάρ with the imperfect indicative for present time, the aorist indicative for past time. They may also be expressed by the various persons of ὤφελον with the present or aorist infinitive, p. 83

The negative in all wishes is μή.

THE PREPOSITIONS, WITH THEIR
COMMONEST MEANINGS

ἀμφί + acc., about

ἀνά + acc., up along, up

ἀντί + gen., instead of, for

ἀπό + gen., from

διά + gen., through

    + acc., through, on account of

εἰς + acc., into, up to, until, for, against

ἐν + dat., in, among

ἐκ, ἐξ + gen., out of, from

ἐπί, upon; + gen., on (superposition)

          + dat., on, near, next to (proximity)

          + acc., on, against

κατά, down; + gen., down from, against

            + acc., down, during, by (distributive), according to

μετά, + gen., with

      + acc., after

παρά, beside; + gen., from the side of, from

          + dat., at the side of, at

          + acc., to the side of, throughout (of time), compared with

περί,[1] about; + gen., about, concerning

         + acc., about, near

πρό[1] + gen., before

πρός, at, by; + gen., toward, from (the side or point of view of)

         + dat., at, near, in addition to

         + acc., to, towards, with reference to, according to, against

σύν + dat., with, by aid of

ὑπέρ, over; + gen., above, in behalf of

         + acc., over, exceeding

ὑπό, under, by; + gen., under, by (personal agent), through (cause)

          + dat., under (of rest)

          + acc., under (of motion), toward (of time), during

---

[1] περί and πρό never elide.

ἄνευ + gen., without

ἄχρι + gen., until

ἐγγύς + gen., near

εἴσω + gen., within

ἐκτός + gen., outside

ἔμπροσθεν + gen., in front of

ἐναντίον + gen., against, opposite, before

ἕνεκα or ἕνεκεν + gen., for the sake of

ἐντός + gen., within

ἔξω + gen., outside, beyond

εὐθύ + gen., straight to

μεταξύ + gen., between

μέχρι + gen., as far as

ὄπισθεν + gen., behind

πλήν + gen., except

πλησίον + gen., near

χωρίς + gen., separate from

ὡς + acc., to (with persons)

SEVENTY-FIVE OF THE COMMONEST IRREGULAR VERBS, WITH THEIR PRINCIPAL PARTS

A hyphen (-) before a form indicates that it is found only in compounds. Forms are given as in H. W. Smyth's *Greek Grammar*, as revised by G. M. Messing, Harvard University Press, Cambridge, 1956.

ἀγγέλλω, ἀγγελῶ, ἤγγειλα, ἤγγελκα, ἤγγελμαι, ἠγγέλθην, announce
ἄγω, ἄξω, ἤγαγον, ἦχα, ἦγμαι, ἤχθην, lead
αἱρέω, αἱρήσω, εἶλον, ᾕρηκα, ᾕρημαι, ᾑρέθην, take; mid., choose
αἴρω, ἀρῶ, ἦρα, ἦρκα, ἦρμαι, ἤρθην, raise
αἰσθάνομαι, αἰσθήσομαι, ᾐσθόμην, ᾔσθημαι, perceive
ἀκούω, ἀκούσομαι, ἤκουσα, ἀκήκοα, —, ἠκούσθην, hear
ἁλίσκομαι, ἁλώσομαι, ἑάλων or ἥλων, ἑάλωκα or ἥλωκα, be captured
ἀποθνῄσκω, ἀποθανοῦμαι, ἀπέθανον, τέθνηκα, die
ἀποκτείνω, ἀποκτενῶ, ἀπέκτεινα, ἀπέκτονα, kill
ἀπόλλυμι, ἀπολῶ, ἀπώλεσα and ἀπωλόμην, ἀπολώλεκα and ἀπόλωλα, destroy;
     mid. and 2nd perf., perish
ἁρπάζω, ἁρπάσομαι, ἥρπασα, ἥρπακα, ἥρπασμαι, ἡρπάσθην, seize
ἄρχω, ἄρξω, ἦρξα, ἦρχα, ἦργμαι, ἤρχθην, rule, begin
ἀφικνέομαι, ἀφίξομαι, ἀφικόμην, ἀφῖγμαι, arrive
βαίνω, βήσομαι, ἔβην, βέβηκα, go
βάλλω, βαλῶ, ἔβαλον, βέβληκα, βέβλημαι, ἐβλήθην, throw; pelt
βλάπτω, βλάψω, ἔβλαψα, βέβλαφα, βέβλαμμαι, ἐβλάφθην and ἐβλάβην, harm
βούλομαι, βουλήσομαι, —, —, βεβούλημαι, ἐβουλήθην, wish
γαμέω, γαμῶ, ἔγημα, γεγάμηκα, wed
γίγνομαι, γενήσομαι, ἐγενόμην, γέγονα, γεγένημαι, become, be
γιγνώσκω, γνώσομαι, ἔγνων, ἔγνωκα, ἔγνωσμαι, ἐγνώσθην, know
γράφω, γράψω, ἔγραψα, γέγραφα, γέγραμμαι, ἐγράφην, write
δείκνυμι, δείξω, ἔδειξα, δέδειχα, δέδειγμαι, ἐδείχθην, show
δίδωμι, δώσω, ἔδωκα, δέδωκα, δέδομαι, ἐδόθην, give
δοκέω, δόξω, ἔδοξα, —, δέδογμαι, —, seem, think; impersonal, seem best
δύω, -δύσω, -ἔδυσα and ἔδυν, -δέδυκα, -δέδυμαι, -ἐδύθην, enter, go down,
     sink, cause to enter

εἰμί, ἔσομαι, be (missing tenses supplied from γίγνομαι)
εἶμι, go
ἐλαύνω, ἐλῶ, ἤλασα, -ἐλήλακα, ἐλήλαμαι, ἠλάθην, drive, march
ἕπομαι, ἕψομαι, ἑσπόμην, —, follow
ἔρχομαι, ἐλεύσομαι, ἦλθον, ἐλήλυθα, come, go
ἐσθίω, ἔδομαι, ἔφαγον, ἐδήδοκα, —, —, eat
εὑρίσκω, εὑρήσω, ηὗρον or εὗρον, ηὕρηκα or εὕρηκα, εὕρημαι, εὑρέθην, find
ἔχω, ἕξω or σχήσω, ἔσχον, ἔσχηκα, —, —, have, hold
ἵημι, ἥσω, ἧκα, εἷκα, εἷμαι, εἵθην, send, throw
ἵστημι, στήσω, ἔστησα and ἔστην, ἔστηκα, ἔσταμαι, ἐστάθην, stand
καίω or κάω, καύσω, ἔκαυσα, κέκαυκα, κέκαυμαι, ἐκαύθην, burn
καλέω, καλῶ, ἐκάλεσα, κέκληκα, κέκλημαι, ἐκλήθην, call
κόπτω, κόψω, ἔκοψα, -κέκοφα, κέκομμαι, ἐκόπην, cut
λαμβάνω, λήψομαι, ἔλαβον, εἴληφα, εἴλημμαι, ἐλήφθην, take
λανθάνω, λήσω, ἔλαθον, λέληθα, —, —, escape notice; mid., forget
λέγω, λέξω, ἔλεξα, εἴρηκα, λέλεγμαι, ἐλέχθην, say
λέγω, -λέξω, -ἔλεξα, -εἴλοχα, -εἴλεγμαι and -λέλεγμαι, -ἐλέχθην and -ἐλέγην,
    collect
λείπω, λείψω, ἔλιπον, λέλοιπα, λέλειμμαι, ἐλείφθην, leave
μανθάνω, μαθήσομαι, ἔμαθον, μεμάθηκα, learn
μάχομαι, μαχοῦμαι, ἐμαχεσάμην, μεμάχημαι, fight
μέλει, μελήσει, ἐμέλησε, μεμέληκε, concern (impersonal)
μέλλω, μελλήσω, ἐμέλλησα, —, intend, be about to
μένω, μενῶ, ἔμεινα, μεμένηκα, remain
μιμνήσκω, -μνήσω, -ἔμνησα, —, μέμνημαι, ἐμνήσθην, remind; mid., remember
νομίζω, νομιῶ, ἐνόμισα, νενόμικα, νενόμισμαι, ἐνομίσθην, believe, think
οἴομαι or οἶμαι, οἰήσομαι, ᾠήθην, think
ὁράω, ὄψομαι, εἶδον, ἑόρακα and ἑώρακα, ἑώραμαι and ὦμμαι, ὤφθην, see
πάσχω, πείσομαι, ἔπαθον, πέπονθα, suffer
πείθω, πείσω, ἔπεισα, πέπεικα and πέποιθα, πέπεισμαι, ἐπείσθην, persuade;
    2nd perfect, trust; mid., believe, obey
πέμπω, πέμψω, ἔπεμψα, πέπομφα, πέπεμμαι, ἐπέμφθην, send
πίνω, πίομαι or πιοῦμαι, ἔπιον, πέπωκα, -πέπομαι, ἐπόθην, drink
πίπτω, πεσοῦμαι, ἔπεσον, πέπτωκα, fall
πλέω, πλεύσομαι or πλευσοῦμαι, ἔπλευσα, πέπλευκα, πέπλευσμαι, ἐπλεύσθην,
    sail
πράττω, πράξω, ἔπραξα, πέπραχα and πέπραγα, πέπραγμαι, ἐπράχθην, do
πυνθάνομαι, πεύσομαι, ἐπυθόμην, πέπυσμαι, learn, inquire
σκεδάννυμι, σκεδῶ, ἐσκέδασα, ἐσκέδασμαι, ἐσκεδάσθην, scatter
στρέφω, στρέψω, ἔστρεψα, —, ἔστραμμαι, ἐστρέφθην and ἐστράφην, turn
τάττω, τάξω, ἔταξα, τέταχα, τέταγμαι, ἐτάχθην, arrange, draw up (of troops)
τέμνω, τεμῶ, ἔτεμον, -τέτμηκα, τέτμημαι, ἐτμήθην, cut
τίθημι, θήσω, ἔθηκα, τέθηκα, τέθειμαι, ἐτέθην, place, put
τίκτω, τέξομαι, ἔτεκον, τέτοκα, beget, bring forth
τρέπω, τρέψω, ἔτρεψα, τέτροφα, τέτραμμαι, ἐτρέφθην and ἐτράπην, turn;
    mid., flee

193

τρέφω, θρέψω, ἔθρεψα, τέτροφα, τέθραμμαι, ἐθρέφθην and ἐτράφην, support,
    nourish
τρέχω, δραμοῦμαι, ἔδραμον, -δεδράμηκα, run
τυγχάνω, τεύξομαι, ἔτυχον, τετύχηκα, hit, happen, obtain
ὑπισχνέομαι, ὑποσχήσομαι, ὑπεσχόμην, ὑπέσχημαι, promise
φαίνω, φανῶ, ἔφηνα, πέφαγκα and πέφηνα, πέφασμαι, ἐφάνθην and ἐφάνην,
    show; mid. and 2nd perf. and 2nd aor. pass., appear
φέρω, οἴσω, ἤνεγκα and ἤνεγκον, ἐνήνοχα, ἐνήνεγμαι, ἠνέχθην, bear, carry
φεύγω, φεύξομαι or φευξοῦμαι, ἔφυγον, πέφευγα, flee
φημί, φήσω, ἔφησα, —, say

GREEK-ENGLISH VOCABULARY

A

ἁ, Doric for Attic ἡ
Ἀβρόκομας, -ου, ὁ, Abrocomas
ἀγαθός, -ή, -όν, good, noble, brave
ἄγαν, too much, in excess
ἀγγέλλω, ἀγγελῶ, ἤγγειλα, ἤγγελκα, ἤγγελμαι, ἠγγέλθην, announce
ἄγγελος, -ου, ὁ, messenger
ἀγείρω, collect
ἀγεωμέτρητος, -ον, ignorant of geometry
ἁγιάζω, reverence
ἄγκυρα, -ας, ἡ, anchor
ἀγνοέω, not to know
ἀγνώμων, -ον (-ονος), senseless, thoughtless
ἀγορά, -ᾶς, ἡ, market place
ἀγοράζω, buy
ἀγράμματος, -ον, unlettered, illiterate
ἄγροικος, -ου, ὁ, rustic
ἀγρός, -οῦ, ὁ, field
ἄγω, ἄξω, ἤγαγον, ἦχα, ἦγμαι, ἤχθην, drive, lead, manage
ἀγών, -ῶνος, ὁ, contest, struggle
ἀγωνίζομαι, v, contest, struggle
ἀγώνισμα, -τος, τό, prize essay
Ἀδείμαντος, -ου, ὁ, Adeimantus (Plato's brother)
ἀδελφός, -οῦ, ὁ, brother
ἄδηλος, -ον, unknown, unseen
ἀδικέω, be unjust, do wrong
ἀδικία, -ας, ἡ, injustice
ἄδικος, -ον, unjust
ἀδίκως, unjustly
ἀεί (αἰεί), always, ever; from time to time; successive, successively; eternity
ἀθάνατος, -ον, deathless, immortal
Ἀθῆναι, -ῶν, Athens
Ἀθηναῖος, -α, -ον, Athenian

ἆθλον, -ου, τό, prize, reward
ἀθροίζω, -σω, ἤθροισα, gather
ἀθυμέω, be dispirited
ἀθυμητέος, -α, -ον (verbal adj.), not to despair, not to be despaired of
Αἰγοσποταμοί, -ῶν, οἱ, Aegospotami (river)
Αἴγυπτος, -ου, ἡ, Egypt
Ἅιδης, -ου, ὁ, Hades; the underworld or its god
αἰθήρ, -έρος, ὁ, ether, upper air
αἴνιγμα, -ατος, τό, riddle, enigma
αἱρέω, αἱρήσω, εἶλον, ᾕρηκα, ᾕρημαι, ᾑρέθην, take; middle, choose
αἰσθάνομαι, αἰσθήσομαι, ᾐσθόμην, perceive
αἰσχρός, -ά, -όν, disgraceful
αἰτέω, ask (a favor)
αἰχμάλωτος, -ου, ὁ, captive
ἀκούω, ἀκούσομαι, ἤκουσα, ἀκήκοα, ἠκούσθην, hear; listen to (+ genitive)
ἀκρίβεια, -ας, ἡ, accuracy
ἀκριβῶς, accurately
ἀκρόπολις, -εως, ἡ, acropolis
ἀλεκτρυών, -όνος, ὁ, cock
Ἀλέξανδρος, -ου, ὁ, Alexander
ἀλήθεια, -ας, ἡ, truth
ἀληθεύω, speak truth, be true
ἀληθής, -ές (οῦς), true
ἀληθῶς, truly, actually
Ἀλκιβιάδης, -ου, ὁ, Alcibiades
ἀλλά, but, well (English colloquial)
ἀλλάττω, ἀλλάξω, ἤλλαξα, alter, change
ἀλλήλων, each other
ἄλλοθεν, from elsewhere
ἄλλος, -η, -ο, another, else, other
ἄλλοτε, at another time
ἀλλότριος, -α, -ον, another's
Ἅλυς, -υος, ὁ, the Halys River

ἀλώπηξ, -εκος, ἡ, fox
ἅμα, at once; together with (+ dative); at the same time with
ἁμαρτάνω, err, go wrong; miss mark; sin
ἀμείνων, -ον (-ονος), better
ἀμέτρως, without restraint, without measure
ἀμφί, around, concerning (+ accusative)
ἀμφότερος, -α, -ον, sing. each; pl. both
ἄν, untranslatable particle
ἄν = ἐάν, if
ἀνά, up (+ accusative)
ἀναβαίνω, go up
ἀναγκάζω, -σω, ἠνάγκασα, compel
ἀνάγκη, -ης, ἡ, necessity; fate; (it is) necessary
ἀναιρέω, reply (of an oracle)
ἀναλογισμός, -οῦ, ὁ, calculation, reasoning
ἀναμένω, wait for
ἀνάξιος, -ον, unworthy
ἀναπείθω, persuade
ἀνατίθημι, set up, dedicate (ἀνέθηκαν = ἀνέθεσαν)
ἀνδρεία, -ας, ἡ, manliness, bravery
ἀνδρεῖος, -α, -ον, manly, brave
ἀνεῖλον (aorist of ἀναιρέω), gave a response (of an oracle)
ἄνειμι, go up
ἀνελπιστός, -όν, unhoped for, unlooked for
ἄνεμος, -ου, ὁ, wind
ἀνεξέταστος, -ον, without inquiry, unexamined
ἄνευ, without (+ genitive)
ἀνέχομαι (ἔχω), ἀνέξομαι, ἠνεσχόμην, put up with, endure
ἀνήρ, ἀνδρός, ὁ, man, male, husband
ἄνθρωπος, -ου, ὁ, human being; man
ἀνίστημι (ἵστημι), stand up, raise up, break camp
ἀνόητος, -ον, foolish, senseless
ἀνοίγνυμι and ἀνοίγω, ἀνοίξω, ἀνέῳξα, ἀνέῳχα, ἀνέῳγμαι, ἀνεῴχθην, open
ἀνόμημα, -ατος, τό, sin
ἀνόσιος, -α, -ον, unholy, irreligious, impious

ἀντεῖπον (λέγω), said in reply
ἀντί, in place of, for (+ genitive)
'Αντισθένης, -ους, ὁ, Antisthenes
'Αντιφῶν, 'Αντιφῶντος, ὁ, Antiphon
ἀντιποιέομαι, lay claim to; contend with someone (dat.) for something (gen.)
ἄξιος, -α, -ον, worthy
ἀξιόω, ἀξιώσω, ἠξίωσα, demand, ask; think proper, expect
ἀξίως, worthily
ἀξυνεσίη, -ης, ἡ (Ionic), stupidity
ἀπαγγέλλω, report back
ἀπάγω, lead back
ἅπας, ἅπασα, ἅπαν (πᾶς), all
ἀπατάω, deceive
ἄπειμι, be absent (εἰμί)
ἄπειμι, go away (εἶμι)
ἄπειρος, -ον, inexperienced
ἀπέρχομαι, go away
ἀπιστέω, disbelieve, distrust; disobey
ἀπιστία, -ας, ἡ, distrust, disbelief
ἀπό from (+ genitive)
ἀποβάλλω, throw away
ἀποδίδωμι, give back; pay back
ἀποθνήσκω, ἀποθανοῦμαι, ἀπέθανον, τέθνηκα, die, be killed
ἀποκτείνω, ἀποκτενῶ, ἀπέκτεινα (ἀπέκτανον), ἀπέκτονα, kill
ἀπόλλυμι, ἀπολῶ, ἀπώλεσα (ἀπωλόμην), ἀπολώλεκα (ἀπόλωλα), destroy; lose, perish
ἀπομιμέομαι, imitate
ἀποπέμπω, send away
ἀπορέω, be at a loss
ἀπορίπτω, cast away
ἀποσκοτίζω, aorist ἀπεσκότησα, get out of one's light
ἀποτρέπω (τρέπω, τρέψω, ἔτρεψα, τέτροφα, τέτραμμαι, ἐτρέφθην or ἐτράπην), turn away, divert
ἄρα, therefore, after all
'Αρβάκης, -ου, ὁ, Arbaces
ἀργυροῦς, -ᾶ, -οῦν, silver (adjective)
ἀρέσκω, be pleasing to (+ dative), please (+ accusative)
ἀρετή, -ῆς, ἡ, virtue, goodness, excellence
'Αριαῖος, -ου, ὁ, Ariaeus

ἀριθμός, -οῦ, ὁ, number, enumeration
'Αριστείδης, -ους, ὁ, Aristides
'Αριστεύς, -έως, ὁ, Aristeus
'Αρίστιππος, -ου, ὁ, Aristippus
ἄριστον, -ου, τό, breakfast, lunch
ἄριστος, -η, -ον, noblest, best
"Αρκαδες, -ων, οἱ, Arcadians
ἅρμα, -ατος, τό, chariot
ἁρπάζω, ἁρπάσομαι, ἥρπασα, ἥρπακα,
ἥρπασμαι, ἡρπάσθην, seize, snatch
'Αρταγέρσης, -ου, ὁ, Artagerses
'Αρταξέρξης, -ου, ὁ, Artaxerxes
ἄρτιος, -α, -ον, complete, fitted
ἄρτος, -ου, ὁ, bread
ἀρχαῖος, -α, -ον, ancient, old
ἀρχή, -ῆς, ἡ, beginning; province;
empire; rule; office
ἄρχω, ἄρξω, ἦρξα, ἦρχα, ἦργμαι,
ἤρχθην, command, rule; middle,
begin
ἄρχων, -οντος, ὁ, ruler; archon;
commander
'Ασία, -ας, ἡ, Asia
ἀσθενής, -ές (οῦς), weak
ἀσπίς, -ίδος, ἡ, shield
ἄστυ, -εως, τό, city
ἀσφαλής, -ές (οῦς), safe
ἀσφαλῶς, adv. safely
ἀταξία, -ας, ἡ, disorder, lack of
discipline
ἀτερπέστατος, -η, -ον, most unpleasant
ἀτυχέω, be unlucky
αὖ, on the other hand; again; in
turn
αὔριον, tomorrow (adverb)
αὖτις, again
αὐτομολέω, desert
αὐτόμολος, -ου, ὁ, deserter
αὐτός, -ή, -ό, self; same; he, she, it,
they (pronoun)
αὐτοῦ, -ῆς, -οῦ, of himself (reflexive)
αὐτοῦ, there (adverb)
αὐτοφυῶς, naturally, spontaneously
ἀφαιρέω, take away
ἀφίημι, allow; forgive
ἀφικνέομαι, ἀφίξομαι, ἀφικόμην, ἀφῖγμαι, come, arrive
ἀφίστημι (ἵστημι), stand off; revolt

ἄφρων, -ον (-ονος), senseless
'Αχιλλεύς, -έως, ὁ, Achilles

B

βαίνω, βήσομαι, ἔβην, βέβηκα, go
βάλλω, βαλῶ, ἔβαλον, βέβληκα, βέβλημαι, ἐβλήθην, throw, hurl, pelt
βάρβαρος, -ον, foreign; βάρβαροι, οἱ
(substantive), Persians, foreigners
βαρύς, -εῖα, -ύ, heavy; grievous; annoying
βασιλεία, -ας, ἡ, kingdom
βασιλεύς, -έως, ὁ, king
βασιλεύω, be king, rule
βατός, -ή, -όν, passable
βέβαιος, -α, -ον, firm, secure
βελτίων, -ον (-ονος), better
βέλτιστος, -η, -ον, best
βιβλίον, -ου, τό, book
βίος, -ου, ὁ, life, livelihood
βιωτός, -ή, -όν, worth living
βλαβερός, -ά, -όν, harmful
βλάπτω, βλάψω, ἔβλαψα, βέβλαφα,
βέβλαμμαι, 2nd aorist passive
ἐβλάβην, harm
βοάω, βοήσομαι, ἐβόησα, shout
βοηθέω (ἐπιβοηθέω), go to help
Βορέας, -ου, ὁ, Boreas, the North
Wind
βουλεύω, plan, advise; middle, get
advice, take counsel with
βουλή, -ῆς, ἡ, plan; counsel; Council
of 500
βουλιμιάω, be as hungry as an ox,
have "boulimy"
βούλομαι, βουλήσομαι, βεβούλημαι,
ἐβουλήθην, will, wish
βραδύς, -εῖα, -ύ, slow
βραδέως, slowly
βραχύς, -εῖα, -ύ, short
Βρισηίς, -ίδος, ἡ, Briseis
βροτός, -οῦ, ὁ, mortal man
βρωτός, -ή, -όν, edible

Γ

γᾶ, Doric for γῆ
γαῖα = γῆ, earth
γαμέω, γαμῶ, ἔγημα, γεγάμηκα,
marry

197

γάμος, -ου, ό, marriage
γάρ, for, indeed (postpositive)
γαστήρ, -τέρος, ή, belly
γε, at least; of course (enclitic)
γέγονα, from γίγνομαι
γενναῖος, -α, -ον, noble
γένος, -ους, τό, race, kind
γέρας, γέρως, τό, prize, reward
γέρων, -οντος, ό, old man
γέφυρα, -ας, ή, bridge
γεωμετρέω, learn geometry
γεωργός, -οῦ, ό, farmer
γῆ, γῆς, ή, earth, land
γηρύομαι, utter
γίγνομαι, γενήσομαι, ἐγενόμην, γέγ-
    ονα, γεγένημαι, become, be; be
    born, arise, develop
γιγνώσκω, γνώσομαι, ἔγνων, ἔγνωκα,
    ἔγνωσμαι, ἐγνώσθην, know
γίνομαι, late form of γίγνομαι
γλυκύς, -εῖα, -ύ, sweet, pleasant
γλῶττα, -ης, ή, tongue
γνώμη, -ης, ή, judgment, opinion,
    idea
γονεύς, γονέως, ό, parent
γόνος, -ου, ό or ή, offspring
γόνυ, γόνατος, τό, knee
Γοργώ, -όνος, ή, Gorgon
γράφω, γράψω, ἔγραψα, γέγραφα,
    γέγραμμαι, ἐγράφην, write
γυμνάζω, exercise
γυμνικός, -ή, -όν, gymnastic
γυμνός, -ή, -όν, naked
γυνή, γυναικός, ή, woman; wife
Γωβρύας, ό, Gobryas
γωνία, -ας, ή, angle; corner

Δ

δαίμων, -ονος, ό, divinity, fate
Δαρεῖος, -ου, ό, Darius (Persian
    king)
δέ, and, but on the other hand
    (postpositive)
-δε, suffix indicating place to which
δέδοικα, see δείδω, fear
δεῖ, it is necessary
δείδω, ἔδεισα, δέδοικα, 2nd perfect
    δέδια, fear
δείκνυμι, δείξω, ἔδειξα, δέδειχα,
    δέδειγμαι, ἐδείχθην, show

δειλός, -ή, -όν, cowardly, wretched;
    idle
δεινός, -ή, -όν, terrible, fearful
δειπνέω, eat dinner
δεῖπνον, -ου, τό, dinner, meal
δέκα, ten
Δελφοί, -ῶν, οἱ, Delphi
δέμας, τό, form; body
δέομαι (δέω), want, ask; need
    (+ genitive)
δεσμός, -οῦ, ό, bond
δεσμωτήριον, -ου, τό, prison
δεύτερος, -α, -ον, second
δέχομαι, δέξομαι, ἐδεξάμην, receive
δέω, δεήσω, ἐδέησα, need, lack
δή, surely, indeed
δῆλος, -η, -ον, evident
Δῆλος, -ου, ή, Delos (the island)
δηλόω, make clear, reveal
δημοκρατία, -ας, ή, democracy; rule
    of the demos
δῆμος, -ου, ό, the people
διά, through (+ genitive), on ac-
    count of (+ accusative)
διαβαίνω, cross
διαβατέος, -α, -ον, must be crossed
διαβεβαιόομαι, be positive, carry
    thru
διαδίδωμι, give in turn, distribute
διακόσιοι, -αι, -α, two hundred
διαμείβομαι, exchange
διαμνημονεύω, call to mind
διανοέομαι, think, have in mind
διαπράττομαι, accomplish, bring a-
    bout
διατίθημι, arrange, dispose
διαφερόντως, exceptionally
διαφέρω, bear about, differ
διαφθείρω, destroy
διδάσκαλος, -ου, ό, teacher
διδάσκω, διδάξω, ἐδίδαξα, teach,
    instruct
διδράσκω, —, ἔδραν, run away
δίδωμι, δώσω, ἔδωκα, δέδωκα, δέδο-
    μαι, ἐδόθην, give
δίδωμι δίκην, pay the penalty
διέρχομαι, go through, relate
διήκω, pass through
διίστημι (ἵστημι), stand apart or at
    intervals

198

δίκαιος, -α, -ον, just, deserving
δικαιοσύνη, -ης, ἡ, justice, righteousness
δικαίως, justly
δικαστής, -οῦ, ὁ, juryman
δίκη, -ης, ἡ, justice, righteousness; penalty; δίκην ἐπιτίθημι, inflict punishment
Διονύσιος, -ου, ὁ, Dionysius
Διός, see Ζεύς
διότι, because
διπλάσιος, -α, -ον, double
δίπους, -ουν, two-footed
δίς, twice (adverb)
δισχίλιοι, -αι, -α, two thousand
διώκω, διώξω, ἐδίωξα, δεδίωχα, ἐδιώχθην, pursue
δοκέω, seem, think; as impersonal, seem, seem best
δόξα, -ης, ἡ, opinion, reputation
δουλεία, -ας, ἡ, slavery
δουλεύω, be a slave
δοῦλος, -ου, ὁ, slave
δράκων, -οντος, ὁ, serpent, dragon
Δράκων, -οντος, ὁ, Draco
δρεπανηφόρος, -ον, scythe-bearing
δρόμος, -ου, ὁ, race course, running
δύναμαι, δυνήσομαι, δεδύνημαι, ἐδυνήθην, be able, be powerful
δύναμις, -εως, ἡ, power; force (troops)
δυνατός, ή, -όν, able, powerful
δύο, two
δυστυχέω, be ill-starred
δυστυχής, -ές, unfortunate
δύω, δύσω, ἔδυσα and ἔδυν, δέδυκα, δέδυμαι, ἐδύθην, enter, cause to enter, sink, set
δῶρον, -ου, τό, gift

E

ἐάν (εἰ + ἄν), if
ἑαυτοῦ, -ῆς, -οῦ, of himself (reflexive)
ἐάω, ἐάσω, εἴασα, allow, permit
ἐγγράφω, write in or on
ἐγγύς, near, nearly (adverb; preposition + genitive)
ἐγείρω, arouse, waken (transitive or intransitive)

ἐγχειρέω (χείρ), take in hand, undertake
ἐγώ, I (pronoun)
ἔγωγε, I at least
ἔδαφος, -ους, τό, ground, floor
ἐθέλω, ἐθελήσω, ἠθέλησα, ἠθέληκα, be willing, wish
εἰ, if
εἰδέναι, from οἶδα
εἶδον, from ὁράω
εἴδωλον, -ου, τό, image, likeness
εἴθε, Oh that (+ optative)
εἰκάζω, εἰκάσω, ἤκασα, liken; conjecture, imagine
εἰκός, (it is) likely
εἴκοσι, twenty
εἴκω, εἴξω, εἶξα, yield, give in to
εἷλον, see αἱρέω
εἶμι, go (with future sense)
εἰμί, ἔσομαι, be
εἶναι, see εἰμί
εἶξαι, see εἴκω
εἶπον (λέγω), I said
εἴργω, εἴρξω, εἶρξα, shut in or out, prevent from
εἴρημαι, perfect M-P of λέγω
εἰρήνη, -ης, ἡ, peace
εἰς, into; about (with numerals); at (of time); to, against (+ accusative)
εἷς, μία, ἕν, one
εἴσειμι, go in, enter
εἰσπλέω, sail into
εἰσφέρω, bring in, lead
εἶχον, from ἔχω (imperfect)
ἐκ (ἐξ), out of (+ genitive)
ἕκαστος, -η, -ον, each
ἑκάστοτε, at each time, on each occasion
Ἑκαταῖος, -ου, ὁ, Hecataeus
ἑκάτερος, -α, -ον, each of two, pl. both
ἑκατόν, one hundred
ἐκβάλλω, cast out, exile
ἐκδιδράσκω, run out, escape
ἐκδύω, cause to put off, put off
ἐκεῖθεν, from there
ἐκεῖνος, -η, -ο, that, that one, the former
ἐκκαίδεκα, sixteen

ἐκκλησία, -ας, ἡ, assembly; meeting
ἐκλέγομαι, select
ἐκποδών, out of the way (adverb)
ἐκπορεύομαι, go out
ἐκφέρω, carry out (for burial)
ἔκφορα, -ων, τά, produce, crop
ἐλάττων, -ον (-ονος), less, fewer
ἐλαύνω, ἐλῶ, ἤλασα, ἐλήλακα, ἐλή-
    λαμαι, ἠλάθην, ride; drive, charge,
    march
ἐλευθερία, -ας, ἡ, freedom
ἐλεύθερος, -α, -ον, free
ἐλήφθην, see λαμβάνω
Ἑλλάς, -άδος, ἡ, Greece
Ἕλλην, Ἕλληνος, ὁ, a Greek
Ἑλληνικός, -ή, -όν, Greek
ἐλπίς, -ίδος, ἡ, hope
ἔλθω, see ἔρχομαι
ἕλω, see αἱρέω
ἐμαυτοῦ, -ῆς, of myself (reflexive)
ἐμός, -ή, -όν, my, mine
ἔμπεδος, -ον, fixed firm, secure
ἐμποδών, in the way, under foot
ἔμπροσθεν, before, in front (+ geni-
    tive)
ἐν, in, among (proclitic; + dative)
ἕν, one (neuter)
ἐναρόω, plough in
ἐνδείκνυμι, show, reveal
ἔνδοθεν, within
ἔνειμι, be in
ἕνεκα, on account of (postpositive;
    + genitive)
ἐνενήκοντα, ninety
ἔνθα, there, where
ἐνθάδε, thither, there, here
ἐνθουσιασμός, -οῦ, ὁ, enthusiasm
ἐνί (ἐν), in (poetic)
ἐννέα, nine
ἐνταῦθα, here, there
ἐντεῦθεν, from here, from there
ἐντίθημι (τίθημι), place in
ἐντός, within (+ genitive)
ἔντοσθε(ν), from within, within
ἕξ, six
ἐξ, out of (+ genitive)
ἐξαγγέλλω, announce
ἐξάγω, lead out
ἐξακισχίλιοι, -αι, -α, six thousand
ἐξαπατάω, deceive thoroughly

ἔξειμι, go from, go out
ἐξέρχομαι, come out, go out
ἔξεστι(ν), it is possible
ἐξετάζω (cf. ἀνεξέταστος), examine
ἐξῆγον, imperfect of ἐξάγω
Ἐξηκεστίδης, -ου, ὁ (son of Execes-
    tes), Solon
ἑξηκοντούτης, -ες, sixty years of age
ἐξουσία, -ας, ἡ, power, means;
    ability, opportunity
ἔξω, outside (+ genitive)
ἔξωθεν, from outside, outside
ἑορτή, -ῆς, ἡ, festival; holiday
ἐπαινέω, approve, praise
ἐπεί, when, since, after (conjunc-
    tion)
ἐπειδάν (ἐπειδή + ἄν), when, since
ἐπειδή, when, since
ἔπειτα, thereupon, then, future
ἐπέρχομαι, come toward, come on
    (of events)
ἐπεξέρχομαι, go through, narrate
ἐπί, on, near, against (Appendix 9)
ἐπιβαίνω, go toward, or against
ἐπιβοηθέω, go to help
ἐπιβουλεύω, plot against (+ dative)
ἐπιγελάω, laugh at
Ἐπιδάμνιοι, οἱ, people of Epidamnus
Ἐπιδαύριοι, οἱ, Epidaurians
ἐπιδείκνυμι, point out
ἐπιθυμέω, desire eagerly
ἐπιθυμητής, -οῦ, ὁ, eager follower,
    one desirous of something
ἐπιθυμία, -ας, ἡ, desire
ἐπιούσιος, -α, -ον, daily
ἐπιπόνως, laboriously
ἐπίσταμαι, know, know how to
ἐπιστολή, -ῆς, ἡ, letter
ἐπιτερπέστατος, -η, -ον, most delight-
    ful
ἐπιτίθημι (τίθημι), add, place on;
    middle, attack, make an attempt
    on or for (+ dative)
ἕπομαι, ἕψομαι, ἑσπόμην (imperfect
    εἱπόμην), follow
ἑπτά, seven
ἐραστής, -οῦ, ὁ, lover
ἔργον, -ου, τό, work, deed, act, fact
ἐρημόω, make desert, desolate
ἐρίζω, contest, dispute

200

ἔρχομαι, ἐλεύσομαι, ἦλθον, ἐλήλυθα, come, go

ἔρομαι, ask (found usually only in imperfect εἰρόμην and second aorist ἠρόμην)

ἐρωτάω, ἐρωτήσω, ἠρώτησα and ἠρόμην, ask (a question), (rarely) invite

ἐς, like εἰς, into

ἐσθ' = ἐστί (before rough breathing)

ἐσθίω, ἔδομαι, ἔφαγον, ἐδήδοκα, eat

ἐσθλός, -ή, -όν, noble, good

ἐσθλῶς, nobly

ἐστί(ν), from εἰμί

ἔστι, it exists; it is possible

ἔστε, until

ἕστηκα (participle ἑστώς), see ἵστημι

ἔστω, from εἰμί

ἔσχον, from ἔχω (2nd aorist)

ἑταῖρος, -ου, ὁ, comrade

ἕτερος, -α, -ον, other, another, opponent (of two persons or groups)

ἕτερος . . . ἕτερος, the one . . . the other

ἔτι, still, yet

ἕτοιμος, -η, -ον, ready

ἔτος, -ους, τό, year

ἔτυμος, -η, -ον, true

εὖ, well (adverb)

εὐγενής, -ές, of good birth

εὐδαιμονίζω, congratulate; think happy

εὐεργετέω, do good; do good to

εὐθύς, at once, immediately

Εὐκλείδης, -ου, ὁ, Euclid (the geometrician)

εὔλογος, -ον, reasonable

εὔνοια, -ας, ἡ, favorable feeling

εὔνους, -ουν, well-disposed

Εὐριπίδης, -ου, ὁ, Euripides

εὑρίσκω, εὑρήσω, εὗρον, εὕρηκα, εὕρημαι, εὑρέθην, find

Εὐρώπη, -ης, ἡ, Europe

εὐσέβεια, -ας, ἡ, reverence

εὔτακτος, -ον, well-disciplined

εὖτε, when

εὐτυχέω, have good fortune

εὐτυχής, -ές, fortunate

εὐφραίνω, delight

Εὐφράτης, -ου, ὁ, Euphrates

εὐφυής, -ές, of good disposition, well born

εὐχή, -ῆς, ἡ, prayer; εὐχῇσι, Ionic dative plural

ἔφαγον, aorist of ἐσθίω, eat

ἔφασαν, from φημί

ἔφη, from φημί

'Εφιάλτης, -ου, ὁ, Ephialtes

ἐφίημι, command

ἐφίστημι, stop; middle, halt, stand over

ἔχθρα, -ας, ἡ, enmity

ἔχω, ἕξω (σχήσω), ἔσχον, ἔσχηκα (imperfect εἶχον), have, hold, keep

ἕως, until

Z

ζάω, ζήσω (imperfect ἔζων), live

Ζεύς, Διός, ὁ, Zeus

ζηλόω, envy

ζημία, -ας, ἡ, penalty, fine

ζητέω, seek

ζῷον, -ου, τό, animal

H

ἤ, or, than; ἤ . . . ἤ, either . . . or

ἡγέομαι, lead, guide; consider, think

ἡδέως, happily, gladly

ἤδη, already; now; presently

ἥδιστος, -η, -ον, sweetest, pleasantest

ἡδίων, -ον (-ονος), sweeter, pleasanter

ἥδομαι, be pleased, enjoy oneself

ἡδονή, -ῆς, ἡ, pleasure, happiness

ἡδύς, -εῖα, -ύ, sweet, pleasant

ἦθος, -ους, τό, character

ἥκω, ἥξω, have come, be present, come

'Ηλεῖοι, -ων, οἱ, Eleans (of Elis)

ἦλθον, aorist of ἔρχομαι, came

ἠλίθιος, -α, -ον, foolish

ἥλιος, -ου, ὁ, sun

ἡλιόομαι, sun oneself

ἡμεῖς, nominative plural of ἐγώ

ἡμέρα, -ας, ἡ, day

ἡμερήσιος, -α, -ον, of a day

ἥμερος, -ον, tame, gentle

ἡμέτερος, -α, -ον, our

ἦν, from εἰμί

ἦν, I said, from ἠμί
Ἡρακλῆς, -έους, ὁ, Heracles
ἦσαν, from εἰμί
Ἡσίοδος, -ου, ὁ, Hesiod
ἡσυχία, -ας, ἡ, quiet, calmness
ἡσυχίαν ἄγω, be quiet
ἥσυχος, -ον, calm, quiet
ἤτοι, truly; you know
ἤτοι . . . ἤ, either . . . or
ἡττάομαι, be defeated

Θ

θ', symbol for 9
θάλαττα, -ης, ἡ, sea
θάλλω, flourish
θάνατος, -ου, ὁ, death
θανών, see ἀποθνῄσκω
θαρσέω, take courage
θάττων, -ον (-ονος), swifter
θαυμάζω, θαυμάσομαι, ἐθαύμασα,
   marvel, marvel at
θαυμαστός, -ή, -όν, marvelous
θεά, -ᾶς, ἡ, goddess
Θεαγένης, ὁ, Theagenes
θεάομαι, watch, observe
θεῖος, -α, -ον, divine
θέλημα, -ατος, τό, will, wish
θέλω, see ἐθέλω
Θεμιστοκλῆς, -έους, ὁ, Themistocles
-θεν, suffix denoting place from
   which
θεός, -οῦ, ὁ, god; ἡ, goddess; πρὸς
   θεῶν, in the name of the gods
θεραπεύω, heal
Θερμοπύλαι, -ῶν, αἱ, Thermopylae
θερμός, -ή, -όν, warm
Θετταλός, -ή, -όν, Thessalian
θεωρέω, look at; consider
θεώρημα, -ατος, τό, theorem
Θηβαῖος, -α, -ον, Theban
θηρεύω (θηράω), hunt
θηρίον, -ου, -τό, wild animal
θησαυρός, -οῦ, ὁ, treasure; treasury
Θησεύς, -έως, ὁ, Thesus
θνητός, -ή, -όν, mortal
Θρᾷξ, Θρᾳκός, ὁ, Thracian
θρίξ, τριχός, ἡ, hair
θυγάτηρ, θυγατρός, ἡ, daughter
θύρα, -ας, ἡ, door
θύω, sacrifice

202

I

ἰάομαι, heal, cure
ἰατρός, -οῦ, ὁ, physician
ἴδιος, -α, -ον, private, one's own
ἴδμεν = ἴσμεν
ἰδών, see ὁράω
ἱερός, -ά, -όν, sacred, holy; τὰ ἱερά,
   temples
ἵημι, ἥσω, ἧκα (-εἷμεν), -εἷκα, -εἷμαι,
   -εἵθην, send, hurl; middle, rush
ἱκανός, -ή, -όν, sufficient, capable
ἱκανῶς, sufficiently (adverb)
ἱμάτιον, -ου, τό, cloak
ἵνα, in order that (conjunction)
Ἰνδοί, -ῶν, οἱ, Indians
ἱππεύς, -έως, ὁ, horseman; pl.
   cavalry
ἱππικός, -ή, -όν, cavalry (adjective)
ἵππος, -ου, ὁ, horse; ἡ, mare;
   cavalry
ἰσθμός, -οῦ, ὁ, isthmus
ἴσος, -η, -ον, equal
ἵστημι, στήσω, ἔστησα (ἔστην), ἔστηκα, ἔσταμαι, ἐστάθην, place;
   stand (2nd aorist and perfect
   are intransitive)
ἱστορία, -ας, ἡ, investigation, history
Ἰσχυρίων, -ονος, ὁ, Ischyrion
ἰσχυρός, -ά, -όν, strong
ἰσχύω, avail, be powerful
ἴσχω, hold, control
ἴσως, perhaps

K

κα, Doric for Attic ἄν
καθαίρω, καθαρῶ, ἐκάθηρα, —, κεκά-
   θαρμαι, ἐκαθάρθην, cleanse, purify
κάθημαι, sit down
καί, and, also, even, merely; καί . . .
   καί, both . . . and; καὶ δὴ καί,
   furthermore
καίπερ, although, and yet
καιρός, -οῦ, ὁ, critical time, opportunity
Καῖσαρ, Καίσαρος, ὁ, Caesar
κἀκφέρῃ = καὶ ἐκφέρῃ
κακός, -ή, -όν, bad, cowardly
κακῶς, badly, ill
κακῶς ἔχω, be badly off

κακῶς ποιέω, harm
καλέω, καλῶ, ἐκάλεσα, κέκληκα, κέκλημαι, ἐκλήθην, summon, call
Καλλίας, -ου, ὁ, Callias
κάλλιστος, -η, -ον, fairest
καλλίων, -ον (-ονος), more beautiful
κάλλος, -ους, τό, beauty
καλοκἀγαθία, -ας, ἡ, gentlemanliness
καλός, -ή, -όν, good, beautiful, noble
καλύπτω, καλύψω, hide
καλῶς, well
κάμνω, καμοῦμαι, ἔκαμον, κέκμηκα,
toil, suffer
κἄν for καὶ ἐν; κἄν, for καὶ ἄν
καρδία, -ας, ἡ, heart
καρπός, -οῦ, ὁ, fruit
κάρτα, very
κατά, down, down from, against;
during, by (with numerals and
times), according to (Appendix 9)
καταβαΰζω, bark at
κατακαίω (-κάω), burn up
κατάκειμαι (κεῖμαι), lie down
καταλαμβάνω, overtake, seize
καταλείπω, leave behind, abandon
καταλύω, destroy
κατανύω, accomplish
καταπλήττω, astonish
κατὰ σαυτόν, by yourself
κατασκάπτω, κατασκάψω, κατέσκαψα,
κατέσκαφα, κατέσκαμμαι, κατε-
σκάφην, tear down, demolish
κατασκαφή, -ῆς, ἡ, demolition
κατασκευάζω, prepare, arrange
κατασκευή, -ῆς, ἡ, preparation,
equipment
κατασκοπή, -ῆς, ἡ, spying
κατάστασις, -εως, ἡ, establishment
κατατίθημι (τίθημι), put down, deposit
καταφυγή, -ῆς, ἡ, refuge
καταψηφίζομαι, vote against, find
guilty, condemn
κατ᾽ ἐμὸν νόον, according to my mind
κατεργάζομαι, accomplish
καῦμα, -ατος, τό, heat, burning
κεῖμαι, lie
κεῖνος = ἐκεῖνος
κελεύω, κελεύσω, ἐκέλευσα, κεκέλευ-
κα, κεκέλευσμαι, ἐκελεύσθην, order

κέρας, κέρως, τό, horn, wing of army
Κέρβερος, -ου, ὁ, Cerberus
κερδαίνω, κερδανῶ, ἐκέρδανα, gain,
profit
κέρδος, -ους, τό, gain, advantage
κεφαλή, -ῆς, ἡ, head
κῆρυξ, -υκος, ὁ, herald
Κῆτω, -οῦς, ἡ, Ceto
κινδυνεύω, run a risk, seem likely
κινέω, future κινήσω, move; Doric
future κινάσω
κλέος, -ους, τό, report; fame
Κλεοφῶν, -ῶντος, ὁ, Cleophon
κλώψ, κλωπός, ὁ, thief
Κνίδος, -ου, ἡ, Cnidus
κοιμάω, put to sleep; middle, sleep
κοινός, -ή, -όν, common
κολάζω, punish
κομίζω, bring, accompany
Κορίνθιος, -α, -ον, Corinthian
Κόρινθος, -ου, ὁ, Corinth
κόρος, -ου, ὁ, satiety
κόσμος, -ου, ὁ, order, adornment;
universe, world
κότινος, -ου, ὁ, wild olive
Κρανεῖον, -ου, τό, Craneion
κρατέω, be powerful, conquer
κρατήρ, -ῆρος, ὁ, mixing bowl
κράτιστος, -η, -ον, strongest, best
κρείττων, -ον (-ονος), stronger, better
κρεμάννυμι, hang
Κρής, Κρητός, ὁ, a Cretan
κρίνω, κρινῶ, ἔκρινα, κέκρικα, κέκρι-
μαι, ἐκρίθην, judge
κρίσις, -εως, ἡ, judgment, decision,
trial
κριτής, -οῦ, ὁ, judge
Κροῖσος, -ου, ὁ, Croesus
κρυπτός, -ή, -όν, hidden
κτάομαι, κτήσομαι, κέκτημαι, get
possession of, possess
κτῆμα, -ατος, τό, possession
κυβερνήτης, -ου, ὁ, pilot
Κύλων, -ος, ὁ, Cylon
Κύπρις, -ιδος, ἡ, Aphrodite (the
Cyprian goddess because she was
born on Cyprus)
Κῦρος, -ου, ὁ, Cyrus
κύων, κυνός, ὁ, ἡ, dog
κωλύω, prevent

Λ

Λ', symbol for 30

Λακεδαιμόνιος, -α, -ον, Spartan

λαμβάνω, λήψομαι, ἔλαβον, εἴληφα, εἴλημμαι, ἐλήφθην, take, seize

λαμπρός, -ά, -όν, bright

λανθάνω, λήσω, ἔλαθον, escape notice, deceive

λέαινα, -ης, ἡ, lioness

λέγω, λέξω (ἐρῶ) ἔλεξα (εἶπον), εἴρηκα, λέλεγμαι and εἴρημαι, ἐλέχθην, say, call, tell, talk

λείπω, λείψω, ἔλιπον, λέλοιπα, λέλειμμαι, ἐλείφθην, leave

λεπτός, -ή, -όν, fine, light

λεχθήσεται, from λέγω

λέων, -οντος, ὁ, lion

Λεωνίδας, -ου, ὁ, Leonidas

λήγω, λήξω, cease

λίαν, too, over (adverb)

λίθος, -ου, ὁ, stone

λογισμός, -οῦ, ὁ, reasoning

λόγος, -ου, ὁ, saying, speech; word, account, comment, diplomatic conversation

λοιπός, -ή, -όν, remaining

λοχαγός, -οῦ, ὁ, captain

λυπέω, annoy, be pained

λύπη, -ης, ἡ, pain, grief

Λύσανδρος, -ου, ὁ, Lysander

λύω, λύσω, ἔλυσα, λέλυκα, λέλυμαι, ἐλύθην, loose, destroy, break

M

μάθημα, -τος, τό, knowledge

μαίνομαι, be mad, rave

μακάριος, -α, -ον, blessed, happy

Μακεδών, -όνος, ὁ, Macedonian

μακρός, -ά, -όν, long

μάλιστα, most, most of all, especially

μᾶλλον, more, rather

μανθάνω, μαθήσομαι, ἔμαθον, learn, understand, know

Μαραθών, -ῶνος, ὁ, Marathon

μάτην, in vain (adverb)

Μαχάων, -ονος, ὁ, Machaon

μάχη, -ης, ἡ, battle

μάχομαι, μαχοῦμαι, ἐμαχεσάμην, fight (+ dative)

Μέγαρα, -ων, τά, Megara

Μεγαρεύς, -έως, ὁ, a Megarian

μέγας, μεγάλη, μέγα, large, great

μέγιστος, -η, -ον, largest, greatest

μεθίστημι, change

μείζων, -ον (-ονος), larger

μέλει, it is a care, it concerns (impersonal)

μελέτη, -ης, ἡ, practice

μέλλω, μελλήσω, ἐμέλλησα, to be about to (+ infinitive), to delay; τὸ μέλλον, the future

μέμνασ' = μέμνησο, remember (imperative)

μέμνημαι, perfect middle from μιμνήσκω, to remember; cf. Latin memini

μέν, on the one hand (often not translated)

Μένανδρος, -ου, ὁ, Menander

Μενέλαος, -ου, ὁ, Menelaus

μένω, μενῶ, ἔμεινα, μεμένηκα, remain, wait for

Μένων, -ωνος, ὁ, Menon

μέρος, -ους, τό, part

μέσος, -η, -ον, middle

μεστός, -ή, -όν, full (of)

μετά, with + gen.; after + acc.

μεταδίδωμι (δίδωμι), give a share

μετανοέω, think after; repent

μεταπέμπομαι, summon

μέτριος, -α, -ον, measured; according to the "mean" (τὸ μέτριον), moderate

μέτρον, -ου, τό, measure; "mean"

μέχρι, until (+ genitive)

μή, not, that not, lest (negative adverb and conjunction)

μηδέ, not even, not . . . either

μηδείς, μηδεμία, μηδέν, no one, nothing

Μηδικός, -ή, -όν, Median

Μῆδος, -ου, ὁ, Mede

μῆκος, -ους, τό, length

Μήλιος, -α, -ον, Melian

μηνιάω, be angry

μήτε . . . μήτε, neither . . . nor

μήτηρ, -τρός, ἡ, mother

μικρός, -ά, -όν, small

Μίλητος, -ου, ἡ, Miletus

μιμνήσκω, μνήσω, ἔμνησα, μέμνημαι, ἐμνήσθην, remind; middle, remember

Μίνως, Μίνω, ὁ, Minos

μισητός, -ή, -όν, hateful

μνήμη, -ης, ἡ, recollection, remembrance

μοῖρα, -ας, ἡ, fate, destiny

μόναν, Doric for μόνην

μόνον, only (adverb)

μόνος, -η, -ον, sole, only

Μοῦσα, -ης, ἡ, Muse

μυριάς, -άδος, ἡ, group of ten thousand, myriad

μύριοι, -αι, -α, ten thousand

μωρία, -ας, ἡ, folly

N

ναῦς, νεώς, ἡ, ship

ναύτης, -ου, ὁ, a sailor

νάφω, see νήφω

νεανίας, -ου, ὁ, young man

Νεῖλος, -ου, ὁ, Nile

νενικηκώς, -κότος, from νικάω

νέος, -α, -ον, new, young

νεότης, -τητος, ἡ, youth

νῆσος, -ου, ἡ, island

νήφω, be sober (Doric νάφω)

νίζω, νίψομαι, ἔνιψα, wash

νικάω, νικήσω, ἐνίκησα, win victory, conquer

νίπτω, wash

νιφετός, -ή, -όν, snowy

νοέω, (-νοοῦμαι), think

νόημα, -ατος, τό, thought

νομίζω, νομιῶ, ἐνόμισα, think

νομοθέτης, -ου, ὁ, lawgiver

νόμος, -ου, ὁ, custom; law

νόος, Ionic for νοῦς

νοσέω, be ill

νόσος, -ου, ἡ, sickness, disease

νοῦς (νόος), νοῦ, ὁ, mind, intelligence

νῦν, now

νύξ, νυκτός, ἡ, night

Ξ

ξανθός, -ή, -όν, yellow

ξεῖνος = ξένος

ξένος, -ου, ὁ, stranger, friend, guest, mercenary (soldier)

ξένος, -η, -ον, foreign (adjective)

Ξενοφάνης, -εως, ὁ, Xenophanes

Ξενοφῶν, -ῶντος, ὁ, Xenophon

Ξέρξης, -ου, ὁ, Xerxes

ξύγκειται, has been composed, lies before you

ξύμπας (πᾶς), entirely all, whole

ξύνεσις, -εως, ἡ, understanding (Ionic)

O

ὁ, ἡ, τό, the (definite article)

ὁ δέ, and he, but he; the other (with ὁ μέν)

ὅδε, ἥδε, τόδε, this, the following

ὁδός, -οῦ, ἡ, road, way, journey

ὀδούς, ὀδόντος, ὁ, tooth

οἶδα, know

οἴκαδε, homeward

οἰκέω, dwell, live

οἰκία, -ας, ἡ, house

οἴκοθεν, from home

οἶκος, -ου, ὁ, house

οἶμαι (οἴομαι), οἰήσομαι, ᾠήθην, think

οἰμωγή, -ῆς, ἡ, lamenting

οἷος, οἵα, οἷον, what sort of, such

οἷός τέ εἰμι, I am able; οἷόν τέ ἐστι, it is possible

ὀκτώ, eight

ὄλβος, -ου, ὁ, happiness, wealth

ὀλίγος, -η, -ον, little, few

ὅλος, -η, -ον, whole

Ὀλύμπια, τά, Olympic games

Ὀλυμπιονίκης, -ου, ὁ, Olympic victor

Ὀλύμπιος, -α, -ον, Olympic, Olympian

Ὄλυνθος, ου, ὁ, Olynthus

ὅλως, entirely, altogether

ὁ μέν (with ὁ δέ) the one

ὄμβρος, -ου, ὁ, thunderstorm

Ὅμηρος, -ου, ὁ, Homer

ὄμμα, -ατος, τό, eye

ὅμοιος, -α, -ον (epic, ὁμοίϊος), like

ὁμολογέω, admit; agree

ὁμονοέω, think with, agree

ὄναρ, τό, dream

205

ὀνειδίζω, scorn, reproach
ὄνομα, -ατος, τό, name
ὀνομάζω, call by name, name
ὅπη, wherever, where, in whatever way
ὄπισθεν, from behind, behind (+ genitive)
ὁπλίτης, -ου, ὁ, hoplite
ὅπλον, -ου, τό, weapon; plural, arms
ὁπόσος, -η, -ον, as large as; as many as
ὁπόταν, when, whenever
ὁπότε, when, whenever
ὁπότερος, -α, -ον, which of two
ὅπου, where
ὅπως, in order that (conjunction)
ὁράω, ὄψομαι, εἶδον, ἑώρακα, ἑώραμαι, ὤφθην (imperfect ἑώρων), see
ὀργή, -ῆς, ἡ, anger, temperament
ὀργίζομαι, be angry
ὀρθῶς, correctly (adverb)
ὅρκος, -ου, ὁ, oath
ὄρνις, ὄρνιθος, ἡ, bird
'Ορόντας, -ου, ὁ, Orontas
ὅς, ἥ, ὅ, who, which, what (relative); he
ὅσος, -η, -ον, how large, how great, what; plural, how many; as much as, as many as
ὅσπερ, ἥπερ, ὅπερ, the very one who
"Οσσα, -ης, ἡ, Ossa
ὅστις, ἥτις, ὅ τι, whoever, whatever
ὄστρακον, -ου, τό, sherd
ὅταν (ὅτε + ἄν), when, whenever
ὅτε, when, whenever
ὅτι, that, because; with superlative, as . . . as possible
οὐ (οὐκ, οὐχ), not (negative adverb)
οὐδέ, not even; not . . . either
οὐδείς, οὐδεμία, οὐδέν, no one, nothing
οὐκέτι, no longer, not yet, never
οὐκοῦν, therefore (particle expecting affirmative reply; cf. Latin nonne)
οὖν, therefore; now (English colloquial)
οὔποτε, never
οὐρανός, -οῦ, ὁ, heaven

οὖς, ὠτός, τό, ear
οὐσία, -ας, ἡ, property; substance
οὔτε, neither
οὗτος, αὕτη, τοῦτο, this
οὕτω(ς), thus (adverb)
οὐχί = οὐ
ὀφειλέτης, -ου, ὁ, debtor
ὀφείλημα, -ατος, τό, debt
ὀφθαλμός, -οῦ, ὁ, eye
ὄψις, -εως, ἡ, sight, seeing, face, appearance

Π

πάθος, -ους, τό, experience; suffering, matter, trouble
παιδεία, -ας, ἡ, education
παίδευσις, -εως, ἡ, education
παιδεύω, παιδεύσω, ἐπαίδευσα, πεπαίδευκα, πεπαίδευμαι, ἐπαιδεύθην, educate
παιδίον, -ου, τό, child
παῖς, παιδός, ὁ, ἡ, child, boy, slave
πάλαι, long ago, formerly
παλαιός, -ά, -όν, ancient
Πάν, Πανός, ὁ, Pan
πανδημεί, with all the force (adverb)
πανταχοῦ, everywhere
παντοδαπός, -ή, -όν, of every kind
πάντως, wholly
πάνυ, very, entirely
παρά + gen., from the side of; + dat., at the side of, with, at the court of; + acc., to the side of
παραγγέλλω, pass the word along, order
παράγγελμα, -τος, τό, precept, order
παραγίγνομαι, be present, arrive
παράδεισος, -ου, ὁ, park
παραδίδωμι, give over
παράδοξος, -ον, contrary to expectation
Πάραλος, -ου, ἡ, Paralus (the state despatch boat of Athens)
τὸ παράπαν, at all, entirely
παρατυγχάνω, happen along
παραυτίκα (αὐτίκα), at once, for the moment

παραχρῆμα, immediately, the present moment
πάρειμι (εἰμί), to be at hand, be present
παρέρχομαι, go forward, go past
παρίστημι, middle, stand by, help
πάροδος, -ου, ἡ, passage, entrance
παρόντα, -ων, τά, present circumstances
παρρησία, -ας, ἡ, freedom of speech
Παρυσάτις, -άτιδος, ἡ, Parysatis
πᾶς, πᾶσα, πᾶν, all, every
πάσχω, πείσομαι, ἔπαθον, πέπονθα, experience, suffer; εὖ πάσχω, be well treated; κακῶς πάσχω, be ill treated
πατήρ, πατρός, ὁ, father
πατρίς, -ίδος, ἡ, native land, country
παχύς, -εῖα, -ύ, thick
πεδίον, -ου, τό, plain
πεζός, -οῦ, ὁ, footsoldier; infantry
πείθω, πείσω, ἔπεισα, πέπεικα (πέποιθα) πέπεισμαι, ἐπείσθην, persuade; πείθομαι (passive), obey (+ dative); second perfect, trust
πεινάω, be hungry
πεῖρα, -ας, ἡ, trial, attempt
πειρασμός, -οῦ, ὁ, trial, temptation
Πειραιεύς, -έως, ὁ, the Piraeus, port of Athens
πειράω, try; generally passive, attempt
πείσεσθαι, see πάσχω
Πεισίστρατος, -ου, ὁ, Peisistratus
Πελοπόννησος, -ου, ἡ, the Peloponnesus, πελοποννήσιος, -α, -ον, adj.
πελταστής, -οῦ, ὁ, a peltast (a light-armed soldier)
πέμπω, πέμψω, ἔπεμψα, πέπομφα, πέπεμμαι, ἐπέμφθην, send
πένης, -ητος, ὁ, poor man
πενθέω, lament, mourn for
πένομαι, be poor, toil
πεντακισχίλιοι, -αι, -α, five thousand
πεντακόσιοι, -αι, -α, five hundred
πέντε, five
πεντήκοντα, fifty
-περ, a suffix which adds the emphatic notion of "the very"; added to relative pronouns, adjectives, or adverbs
Περδίκκας, ὁ, Perdiccas
περί, about, concerning, near (Appendix 9)
περὶ πολλοῦ ποιέομαι, consider important; make much of
περίειμι, go around
Περικλῆς, -έους, ὁ, Pericles
περιμένω, wait around for
περίπατος, -ου, ὁ, a walking around, stroll
περισπείρω, wreathe around
περιτίθημι (τίθημι), place around
Πέρσαι, -ῶν, οἱ, Persians
πέτρα, -ας, ἡ, rock
Πήλιον, -ου, τό, Pelion
πήρα, -ας, ἡ, bag, sack
πικρός, -ά, -όν, bitter, sharp
πίνω, πίομαι or πιοῦμαι, ἔπιον, πέπωκα, drink
πίπτω, πεσοῦμαι, ἔπεσον, πέπτωκα, fall
πιστεύω, trust (+ dative)
πιστός, -ή, -όν, trusted
πλανάω, wander
πλαστῶς, falsely, artificially
Πλάτων, -ωνος, ὁ, Plato
πλεῖστος, -η, -ον, most
πλείων or πλέων, -ον (-ονος), more
πλέκω, weave, contrive
πλευρά, -ᾶς, ἡ, side, rib
πλέω, πλεύσομαι, ἔπλευσα, sail
πλῆθος, -ους, τό, number, crowd, quantity
πλήν, except (+ genitive)
πλησίον, near (+ genitive)
πλησίος, -α, -ον, near
πλοῖον, -ου, τό, boat
πλοῦς, -οῦ, ὁ, sailing, voyage
πλούσιος, -α, -ον, rich
πλουτέω, be rich
πλοῦτος, -ου, ὁ, wealth
πνεῦμα, -τος, τό, breath, inspiration
πνέω, breathe; blow
ποθέν, from somewhere (adverb)
ποιέω, ποιήσω, ἐποίησα, πεποίηκα, πεποίημαι, ἐποιήθην, do, make, hold (a meeting)

ποιητέος, -α, -ον (verbal adjective) to be done, to be considered (with περὶ πολλοῦ)

ποιητής, -οῦ, ὁ, poet

ποῖος, -α, -ον, of what sort?

πολεμέω, fight (+ dative)

πολέμιοι, -ων, οἱ, enemy

πόλεμος, -ου, ὁ, war

πολιορκέω, besiege

πόλις, -εως, ἡ, city

πολιτεία, -ας, ἡ, government

πολίτης, -ου, ὁ, citizen

πολιτικός, -ή, -όν, political, of a πόλις

πολλάκις, often

πολυμαθίη, -ης, ἡ (Ionic) much knowledge

πολύς, πολλή, πολύ, much, many

πονηρός, -ά, -όν, wretched, evil

πόνος, -ου, ὁ, toil, suffering

πορεύομαι, go, advance

Ποσειδῶν, -ῶνος, ὁ, Poseidon

ποταμός, -οῦ, ὁ, river

πότε, when?

ποτέ, once, at some time

Ποτείδαια, -ας, ἡ, Potideia

Ποτειδειάτης, -ου, ὁ, citizen of Potideia

πότερον (πότερα), whether?

πότερον . . . ἤ, whether . . . or

πότερος, -α, -ον, which of two?

ποῦ, where?

πού, somewhere, anywhere; of course

πρᾶγμα, -ατος, τό, thing, affair; trouble (plural); πράγματα νεώτερα, revolution

πρᾶξις, -εως, ἡ, a doing, affair, work

Πραξιτέλης, -ου, ὁ, Praxiteles

πράττω, πράξω, ἔπραξα, πέπραχα, πέπραγα, πέπραγμαι, ἐπράχθην, do

πράττω κακῶς, fare ill

πράττω καλῶς, fare well, be well off

πρέσβυς, -εως, ὁ, old man, ambassador

πρεσβύτερος, -α, -ον, older

πρίν, before; until (adverb or conjunction)

πρό, before, in front of (+ genitive)

προδίδωμι (δίδωμι), betray

προέρχομαι, advance, pass (of time)

πρόθυμος, -ον, eager

προΐστημι (from ἵστημι), stand before, be in charge of

πρόκειμαι, lie before

προμαχέω, fight for

Προμηθεύς, -έως, ὁ, Prometheus

προνοέω, think ahead

Πρόξενος, -ου, ὁ, Proxenus

πρός, + genitive, near by; + dative, near; + accus., toward, against

πρὸς θεῶν, by the gods, in the name of the gods

προσαγορεύω, address

προσδέχομαι, receive, await

προσδοκάω, expect

πρόσειμι, belong to

προσέρχομαι, approach

προσέχω (τὸν νοῦν + dative), attend to, heed

προσήκω, come toward, be fitting

προσκαθέζομαι, take up position against

πρότερον, before

προτρέχω, run forward

προφέρω, carry ahead, bring forth

προφύλαξ, -ακος, ὁ, outer guard

πρῶτον, adv., first, in the first place

πρῶτος, -η, -ον, first

πτέρυξ, -υγος, ἡ, wing

Πυθαγόρης, -ου, ὁ (Ionic), Pythagoras

πυνθάνομαι, πεύσομαι, ἐπυθόμην, inquire

πῦρ, πυρός, τό, fire

Πύρρων, -ωνος, ὁ, Pyrrho

πυρκαϊή, -ῆς, ἡ (Ionic), fire, pyre

πῶς, how?

πως, somehow (enclitic)

Ρ

ῥᾴδιος, -α, -ον, easy

ῥᾳδίως, easily

ῥᾳθύμως, lightheartedly, easily

ῥέω, flow

ῥῆμα, -τος, τό, word, command

Ῥόδιος, -α, -ον, Rhodian, of Rhodes

ῥώμη, -ης, ἡ, strength

Σ

σαλπιγκτής, -οῦ, ὁ, trumpeter

σάλπιγξ, σάλπιγγος, ἡ, trumpet

σατράπης, -ου, ὁ, provincial governor
σβέννυμι, σβέσω, ἔσβεσα, extinguish
σεαυτοῦ, -ῆς, -οῦ, of yourself (reflexive)
σελήνη, -ης, ἡ, moon
σήμερον, today (adverb)
σιγή, -ῆς, ἡ, silence
Σικυώνιος, -α, -ον, Sicyonian
σῖτος, -ου, ὁ, grain, food
σιωπάω, be silent
σκηνή, -ῆς, ἡ, tent; stage building, stage
σκιά, -ᾶς, ἡ, shadow
σκότος, -ου, ὁ, darkness
Σόλων, -ωνος, ὁ, Solon
σός, -ή, -όν, your (singular)
Σοφοκλῆς, -έους, ὁ, Sophocles
σοφός, -ή, -όν, wise, prudent
Σπαρτιάτης, -ου, ὁ, Spartan
σπέρμα, -τος, τό, seed
σπεύδω, hasten, be eager
σπονδή, -ῆς, ἡ, drink offering
σπονδαί, -ῶν, αἱ, truce
στέλλω, send, aorist ἔστειλα
στέφανος, -ου, ὁ, crown
στορέννυμι, στορῶ, ἐστόρεσα, level, lay low
στράτευμα, -ατος, τό, army
στρατεύω, make war, be in an army
στρατεύομαι, go on a campaign
στρατηγέω, be general (+ genitive of persons)
στρατηγός, -οῦ, ὁ, general
στρατιά, -ᾶς, ἡ, army
στρατιώτης, -ου, ὁ, soldier
στρατοπεδεύομαι, encamp
στρατόπεδον, -ου, τό, camp
σύ, you (singular pronoun)
συλλαμβάνω, arrest
συλλέγω, συλλέξω, συνέλεξα, συνείλοχα, συνείλεγμαι, συνελέγην, collect
συμβουλεύω, advise, counsel
συμβουλεύομαι, seek advice
σύμμαχος, -ου, ὁ, ally
συμφέρον, -οντος, τό, expedient
συμφορά, -ᾶς, ἡ, chance, calamity
σύν, with (+ dative)
συναγείρω, συνήγειρα, collect
συνακολουθέω, follow

συνάπτω, συνάψω, συνῆψα, fasten together, attach; middle, lend a hand
συνάρχων, -οντος, ὁ, fellow-magistrate
σύνειμι (εἰμί), be with; (εἶμι) go with
συνίστημι, introduce
συντάττω, put in order
σύντομος, -ον, concise, brief
συσπεύδω, eagerly help
σφεῖς, indirect reflexive, third person plural
Σφίγξ, Σφιγγός, ἡ, Sphinx
σφυρόν, -οῦ, τό, ankle
σώζω, save
Σωκράτης, -ους, ὁ, Socrates
σῶμα, -ατος, τό, body, person
Σῶσος, -ου, ὁ, Sosus
Σωσώ, -ῶτος, ἡ, Soso
σωτήρ, -ῆρος, ὁ, savior
σωφροσύνη, -ης, ἡ, moderation, discretion
σώφρων, -ον (-ονος), discreet, prudent

T

τάλαντον, -ου, τό, a talent ($1100)
τάν, Doric for Attic τήν
τἄνδοθεν, crasis for τὰ ἔνδοθεν
Ταρσεύς, -έως, ὁ (a man) of Tarsus
τάττω, τάξω, ἔταξα, τέταχα, τέταγμαι, ἐτάχθην, draw up, arrange, assign, appoint
ταῦρος, -ου, ὁ, bull
τάφρος, -ου, ἡ, ditch
ταχύς, -εῖα, -ύ, swift
τε, and (postpositive)
τεθνάναι, see ἀποθνήσκω
τέθνηκα, see ἀποθνήσκω
τείνω, τενῶ, ἔτεινα, stretch
τεῖχος, -ους, τό, wall
τέκνον, -ου, τό, child
τέλεος, -α, -ον, complete
τελευτάω, bring to an end, die
τελευτή, -ῆς, ἡ, end
τέλος, -ους, τό, end, purpose; accusative used adverbially, finally
τέρπω, τέρψω, ἔτερψα, amuse, enjoy
τέρψις, -εως, ἡ, enjoyment
τετρακόσιοι, -αι, -α, four hundred
τετράπους, ὁ, ἡ, four-footed
τετταράκοντα, forty

209

τέτταρες, -α, four
τῇδε, here, in this direction
Τίγρης, -ητος, ὁ, Tigris
τίθημι, θήσω, ἔθηκα (ἔθεμεν), τέθηκα, τέθειμαι (κεῖμαι), ἐτέθην, put, place; give (laws)
τίκτω, τέξομαι, ἔτεκον, bring forth
τιμάω, τιμήσω, ἐτίμησα, honor
τιμή, -ῆς, ἡ, honor, respect; office
Τιμοκρέων, -οντος, ὁ, Timocreon
τίς, τί (τίνος), who, what?
τις, τι (τινός), anyone, anything; someone, something; τι (accusative used adverbially), at all
Τισσαφέρνης, -ου, ὁ, Tissaphernes
τοι, you know (enclitic)
τοιοῦτος, τοιαύτη, τοιοῦτον, such
τοσοῦτος, τοσαύτη, τοσοῦτο, so great
τότε, then; οἱ τότε, the men of that time
τραῦμα, -ατος, τό, wound
τραχύς, -εῖα, -ύ, harsh, rough
τρεῖς, τρία, three
τρέπω, τρέψω, ἔτρεψα, τέτροφα, τέτραμμαι, ἐτρέφθην or ἐτράπην, turn
τρέφω, θρέψω, ἔθρεψα, τέτροφα, τέθραμμαι, ἐτράφην (ἐθρέφθην), nourish
τρέχω, δραμοῦμαι, ἔδραμον, δεδράμηκα, run
τριάκοντα, thirty
τρίβω, rub
τρίγωνον, -ου, τό, triangle
τρίπους, -ουν, three-footed
τρισχίλιοι, -αι, -α, three thousand
τρίτος, -η, -ον, third
τριώβολον, -ου, τό, three-obol piece
τρόπαιον, -ου, τό, trophy, victory
τρόπος, -ου, ὁ, character, manner
τροφή, -ῆς, ἡ, upbringing
Τρῶες, οἱ, Trojans
τυγχάνω, τεύξομαι, ἔτυχον, τετύχηκα, hit; happen; happen to (+ participle); happen upon, obtain (+ genitive)
τυραννέω, be a tyrant, rule
τυραννίς, -ίδος, ἡ, tyranny
τύραννος, -ου, ὁ, ruler, tyrant
τυφλός, -ή, -όν, blind
τύχη, -ης, ἡ, fate, luck

210

Υ

ὑβρίζω, be insolent, act proudly
ὕβρις, -εως, ἡ, insolence, overbearing pride
ὑγίεια, -ας, ἡ, health (Ionic, ὑγιείη)
Ὑδάρνης, -ου, ὁ, Hydarnes
ὕδωρ, -ατος, τό, water
ὕλη, -ης, ἡ, wood
υἱός, -οῦ, ὁ, son
ὑμεῖς, nominative plural of σύ
ὑμέτερος, -α, -ον, your (plural)
ὑπακούω, attend to, heed, obey (+ dative)
ὑπέρ, over; in behalf of (+ genitive); exceeding (+ accusative)
ὑπερβάλλω, exceed
ὑπισχνέομαι, ὑποσχήσομαι, ὑπεσχόμην, ὑπέσχημαι, promise
ὕπνος, -ου, ὁ, sleep
ὑπό, under, by, during, toward (of time) (Appendix 9)
ὑποπτεύω, suspect
ὑποτείνω, ὑποτενῶ, ὑπέτεινα, ὑποτέτακα, ὑποτέταμαι, ὑπετάθην, stretch under; subtend
ὑστεραῖος, -α, -ον, of the next day, ἡ ὑστεραία, next day
ὕστερος, -α, -ον, later

Φ

φάγοι, φαγών, see ἐσθίω
φαίνω, φανῶ, ἔφηνα, πέφηνα, πέφασμαι, ἐφάνην, make appear, show; middle, appear, seem
φανερός, -ά, -όν, open, visible
φάρμακον, -ου, τό, drug, medicine
φαῦλος, -η, -ον, mean, miserable
φαύλως, miserably
φέρω, οἴσω, ἤνεγκα (ἤνεγκον), ἐνήνοχα, ἐνήνεγμαι, ἠνέχθην, bear, carry
φεῦ, alas
φεύγω, φεύξομαι, ἔφυγον, πέφευγα, flee
φημί, φήσω, ἔφησα, say
φθάνω, φθήσομαι, ἔφθην, anticipate (+ participle)
φθονέω, be envious, envy

φθόνος, -ου, ὁ, envy, grudge
φιλέω, love; greet, welcome
φιλία, -ας, ἡ, love, friendship
φίλιος, -α, -ον, friendly
φιλόπονος, -ον, fond of toil
φίλος, -ου, ὁ, friend
φίλος, -η, -ον, dear, pleasing
φιλοσοφέω, love wisdom, seek knowledge
φιλόσοφος, -ου, ὁ, philosopher
φοβέομαι, φοβήσομαι, πεφόβημαι, ἐφοβήθην, fear
φοβερός, -ά, -όν, fearful
φόβος, -ου, ὁ, fear
φορητός, -ή, -όν, bearable
Φόρκυς, -υος, ὁ, Phorcys
φράζω, φράσω, ἔφρασα, show, declare; middle, ponder, consider
φρήν, φρενός, ἡ, mind, understanding
φρονέω, be wise
φρόνιμος, -ον, discreet, prudent, sensible
φρονίμως, sensibly, prudently
φροντίς, -ίδος, ἡ, thought
φυλακή, -ῆς, ἡ, guard, garrison
φύλαξ, -ακος, ὁ, also ἡ, guard
φυλάττω, φυλάξω, ἐφύλαξα, πεφύλαχα, πεφύλαγμαι, ἐφυλάχθην, guard
φύσις, -εως, ἡ, nature
φωνή, -ῆς, ἡ, sound, voice
φῶς, φωτός, τό, light

X

χαλεπός, -ή, -όν, difficult, hard, harsh, χαλεπῶς φέρω, be annoyed
χαλκός, -οῦ, ὁ, metal, bronze
χαλκοῦς, ῆ, -οῦν, of copper, bronze
χάρις, -ιτος, ἡ, favor, grace, thanks; χάριν (+ genitive) (= ἕνεκα), for the sake of
χείρ, χειρός, ἡ, hand
χείρων, -ον (-ονος), worse
χίλιοι, -αι, -α, thousand
Χίλων, -ωνος, ὁ, Chilon
χιών, -όνος, ἡ, snow, winter storm

χράομαι, χρήσομαι, ἐχρησάμην, κέχρημαι, use, consult an oracle (+ dative)
χρή, it is necessary
χρῆμα, -ατος, τό, thing; plural, money
χρήσιμος, -η, -ον, useful
χρηστός, -ή, -όν, useful, good
χρόνος, -ου, ὁ, time
χρυσός, -οῦ, ὁ, gold
χρυσοῦς, -ῆ, -οῦν, of gold, golden
χρυσοφόρος, -ον, wearing gold
χώ, crasis for καὶ ὁ
χώρα, -ας, ἡ, country
χωρέω, go
χωρίζω, separate, divide
χωρίον, -ου, τό, place in the country, spot
χωρίς, separately, apart from (adverb; + genitive)

Ψ

ψευδής, -ές, false
ψεῦδος, -ους, τό, the false
ψεύδω, ψεύσω, ἔψευσα, ἔψευσμαι, ἐψεύσθην, deceive; middle, lie
ψηφίζομαι, vote
ψυχή, -ῆς, ἡ, soul

Ω

ὦ, O (used with vocative)
ὤν, οὖσα, ὄν, participle of εἰμί
ὥρα, -ας, ἡ, season, hour, time
ὡραῖος, -η, -ον (Ionic), timely
ὡς, as
ὡς (adverb), how
ὡς, as . . . as possible (superlative); that (in indirect discourse); how (conjunction); on the ground that (+ participle); because; in order that; when, since
ὥσπερ, just as
ὥστε, and so; so that
Ὦτος, -ου, ὁ, Otus, a giant
ὠφελέω, help
ὠφέλιμος, -ον, helpful

ENGLISH–GREEK VOCABULARY

Students should check the principal parts of verbs in the
Greek–English Vocabulary

A

able, be, δύναμαι
about, περί + gen.; εἰς + acc. (with numbers)
about to be, μέλλω
account: give — of, διεξέρχομαι; on — of, διά + acc.
accurately, μετ' ἀκριβείας
acropolis, ἀκρόπολις, -εως, ἡ
act, ἄγω, ποιέω
addition: in — to, πρός + dat.
advantageous course, συμφέρον, -οντος, τό
advise, συμβουλεύω
afraid, be, φοβέομαι
after, μετά + acc.
afterwards, ἔπειτα
against, πρός + acc.; εἰς + acc.
agora, ἀγορά, -ᾶς, ἡ
all, πᾶς, πᾶσα, πᾶν; ἅπας, ἅπασα, ἅπαν
allow, ἐάω, ἀφίημι
ally, σύμμαχος, -ου, ὁ
almost, εἰς + acc.
also, καί
although, καίπερ + participle
always, ἀεί
among, ἐν + dative
ancient, παλαιός, -ά, -όν
and, καί, τε
and so, ὥστε + indicative
anger, ὀργή, -ῆς, ἡ
animal, wild, θηρίον, -ου, τό
annoyed, be, χαλεπῶς φέρω
another, ἄλλος, -η, -ο
anyone, anything, τις, τι (τινός)
appear, φαίνομαι
apply, προστίθημι
Aristides, Ἀριστείδης, -ου, ὁ

arm (weapon), ὅπλον, -ου, τό
army, στρατιά, -ᾶς, ἡ; στράτευμα, στρατεύματος, τό
arrange, τάττω; κατασκευάζω
arrive, ἀφικνέομαι (εἰς)
as, ὡς; just as, ὥσπερ
ask, ἐρωτάω, δέομαι
as many as, τοσοῦτοι . . . ὁπόσοι
assembly, ἐκκλησία, -ας, ἡ
at, ἐν + dat.; of time, dat. alone
Athenian, n., Ἀθηναῖος, ὁ
Athens, αἱ Ἀθῆναι; from Athens, Ἀθήνηθεν
attack, ἐπιτίθεμαι + dative
attend, προσέχειν τὸν νοῦν
attend to, προσέχειν τὸν νοῦν + dat.

B

bad, κακός, -ή, -όν; πονηρός, -ά, -όν
barbarian, βάρβαρος, -ου, ὁ
battle, μάχη, -ης, ἡ; fight a —, μάχην ποιεῖσθαι
be, εἰμί, γίγνομαι
be badly off, κακῶς ἔχω; κακῶς πράττω
be near, πάρειμι
be with, σύνειμι
bear, φέρω
beast, wild, θηρίον, -ου, τό
beautiful, καλός, -ή, -όν
because of, διά + acc.
become, γίγνομαι
befall, τυγχάνω
before, πρίν, adv.; πρό + gen., prep.
beg, δέομαι + gen.
behalf of, in, ὑπέρ + gen.
believe, πιστεύω + dat., νομίζω (suppose)
beneath, ὑπό + gen. or acc.

beseech, αἰτέω
beside, παρά + dat.
best, ἄριστος, -η, -ον
betray, προδίδωμι
better, ἀμείνων, -ον; get the — of, κρατέω + gen.
bitter, πικρός, -ά, -όν
blow, v., πνέω
body, σῶμα, -ατος, τό
bodyguard, φυλακή, -ῆς, ἡ
book, βιβλίον, -ου, τό
both . . . and, καί . . . καί; τε . . . τε; τε . . . καί
boy, παῖς, παιδός, ὁ
brave, ἀγαθός, -ή, -όν; ἀνδρεῖος, -α, -ον
bravely, ἀνδρείως
bread, ἄρτος, -ου, ὁ
bridge, γέφυρα, -ας, ἡ
briefly, βραχέως
bring, φέρω
brother, ἀδελφός, -οῦ, ὁ
but, ἀλλά, δέ
by, ὑπό + gen. (personal agent); dat. alone (means)

C

call, καλέω
calm, to be, ἡσυχίαν ἄγειν
calmness, ἡσυχία, -ας, ἡ
camp, στρατόπεδον, -ου, τό
campaign, make a, στρατεύομαι
can, v., δύναμαι
capture, λαμβάνω; αἱρέω; be captured, ἁλίσκομαι
care for, take care of, τρέφω
carry, φέρω
carry up, ἀναφέρω
cavalry, ἱππεῖς, -έων, οἱ
cease, παύομαι
Cerberus, Κέρβερος, -ου, ὁ
certain, a, τις, τι
character, τρόπος, -ον, ὁ (often used in plural with singular meaning)
characteristic, n., τρόπος, -ου, ὁ
charge (military), v., ἐλαύνω
charge, be in — of, ἐφίστημι in middle + dat.
child, παῖς, παιδός, ὁ (gen. pl. παίδων); παιδίον, -ου, τό

214

choose, αἱρέω in mid.
citizen, πολίτης, -ου, ὁ
city, πόλις, εως, ἡ
Clearchus, Κλέαρχος, -ου, ὁ
clever, δεινός, -ή, -όν
cloak, ἱμάτιον, -ου, τό
collect, συλλέγω
come, ἔρχομαι; ἥκω
come back, ἀπέρχομαι
command (order), v., κελεύω
commander, ἄρχων, -οντος, ὁ
common, κοινός, -ή, -όν
companion, ἑταῖρος, -ου, ὁ
concern, v., μέλει, impersonal, + dat.
conquer, νικάω
consider, νομίζω; ἡγέομαι
consider important, περὶ πολλοῦ ποιεῖσθαι
consult with, συμβουλεύω in mid.
contest, n., ἀγών, ἀγῶνος, ὁ
contest, v., ἀγωνίζομαι
control, v., ἴσχω
corrupt, v., διαφθείρω
counsel, v., βουλεύω; n. βουλή, ῆς, ἡ
country, χώρα, -ας, ἡ; native land, πατρίς, -ίδος, ἡ
cowardly, κακός, -ή, -όν
Croesus, Κροῖσος, -ου, ὁ
cross, v., διαβαίνω
crown, n., στέφανος, -ου, ὁ
Cylon, Κύλων, -ωνος, ὁ
Cyrus, Κῦρος, -ου, ὁ

D

Darius, Δαρεῖος, -ου, ὁ
day, ἡμέρα, -ας, ἡ
death, θάνατος, -ου, ὁ
deathless, ἀθάνατος, -ον
deceive, ψεύδω
declare, φράζω
defeat, v., νικάω
Delos, Δῆλος, -ου, ἡ
Delphi, Δελφοί, οἱ, accusative, Δελφούς
democracy, δημοκρατία, ἡ
deposit, v., κατατίθημι
destroy, λύω, διαφθείρω
die, ἀποθνήσκω
dinner, δεῖπνον, -ου, τό
difficult, χαλεπός, -ή, -όν

disaster, συμφορά, -ᾶς, ἡ
disgraceful, αἰσχρός, -ά, -όν
divide, διαδίδωμι
divinity, δαίμων, -ονος, ὁ
do, πράττω
doctor, ἰατρός, -οῦ, ὁ
dog, κύων, κυνός, ὁ
door, θύρα, -ας, ἡ
down, κατά + acc.
Draco, Δράκων, -οντος, ὁ
draw up, τάττω; συντάττω
drive, v., ἐλαύνω
drug, n., φάρμακον, -ου, τό
dwell, οἰκέω

E

each, ἕκαστος, -η, -ον
each other, ἀλλήλων
eager, be, σπεύδω
eager follower, ἐπιθυμητής, οῦ, ὁ
earth, γῆ, γῆς, ἡ
easy, ῥᾴδιος -α, -ον
eat, ἐσθίω
educate, παιδεύω
education, παιδεία, -ας, ἡ
either . . . or, ἤ . . . ἤ
elder, πρεσβύτερος, -α, -ον
elsewhere, from, ἄλλοθεν
elude, λανθάνω
empire, ἀρχή, -ῆς, ἡ
end, n., τέλος, -ους, τό
end, v., τελευτάω
endure, ἀνέχομαι
enemy (civil), πολέμιος, -ου, ὁ;
    (personal) ἐχθρός, -οῦ, ὁ
enough, ἅλις
equal, ἴσος, -η, -ον
err, ἁμαρτάνω
escape, v., φεύγω; ἀποφεύγω
escape notice, λανθάνω
establish, τίθημι; — peace, εἰρήνην
    ποιεῖσθαι
even, adv., καί; adj. ἴσος, -η, -ον
events, πράγματα, -ων, τά
every, πᾶς, πᾶσα, πᾶν
everything, πάντα, -ων, τά
evident, φανερός, -ά, -όν; δῆλος, -η,
    -ον
evil, κακός, -ή, -όν; do evil, ἀδικέω
examine, ἐξετάζω

excellence, ἀρετή, -ῆς, ἡ
except, πλήν + gen.
exist, εἰμί (ἔστι)
expect, ἀξιόω
experience, πεῖρα, -ας, ἡ

F

fair, καλός, -ή, -όν
fall, πίπτω
fall out, ἐκπίπτω
false, ψευδής, -ές
fame, κλέος, -ους, τό
fare badly, κακῶς πράττω
fare well, καλῶς πράττω
fast, ταχύς, -εῖα, -ύ, faster, θάττων,
    θᾶττον
father, πατήρ, πατρός, ὁ
fatherland, πατρίς, -ίδος, ἡ
favor, n., χάρις, -ιτος, ἡ
fear, n., φόβος, -ου, ὁ
fear, v., φοβέομαι; δείδω
fearful, φοβερός, -ά, -όν
few, ὀλίγοι, -αι, -α
fight, v., πολεμέω; fight a battle,
    μάχην ποιεῖσθαι
finally, τέλος
find, εὑρίσκω
fine, καλός, -ή, -όν
fire, πῦρ, πυρός, -τό
first, πρῶτος, -η, -ον
first, adv., πρῶτον
flee, φεύγω; ἀποφεύγω
foe, πολέμιος, -ου, ὁ
follow, ἕπομαι
folly, μωρία, -ας, ἡ
food, σῖτος, -ου, ὁ
for, conj., γάρ
for, prep., ὑπέρ + gen.
foreigner, ξένος, -ου, ὁ
forgive, ἀφίημι
formerly, πρότερον
fortune, τύχη, -ης, ἡ
four hundred, τετρακόσιοι, -αι, -α
fourteen, τέτταρες καὶ δέκα
four times, τετράκις
freedom, ἐλευθερία, -ας, ἡ
friend, φίλος, -ου, ὁ
friendship, φιλία, -ας, ἡ
from, ἀπό + gen.; ἐκ + gen.; παρά
    + gen.

G

gather, συλλέγω
general, στρατηγός, -οῦ, ὁ
geometry, learn, γεωμετρέω
get, λαμβάνω; αἱρέω
get back, ἀπολαμβάνω
gift, δῶρον, -ου, τό
give, δίδωμι
give back, ἀποδίδωμι
give laws, νόμους τιθέναι
give over, παραδίδωμι
go, ἔρχομαι; εἶμι
go about, περίειμι
go along, συνέρχομαι
go away, ἀπέρχομαι
go back, ἀπέρχομαι
go by (of time), προέρχομαι
go in, go into, εἴσειμι
go on, προέρχομαι
god, θεός, -οῦ, ὁ
good, ἀγαθός, -ή, -όν
good, do, εὐεργετέω
Gorgon, Γοργώ, -όνος, ἡ
government, πολιτεία, -ας, ἡ
grain, σῖτος, -ου, ὁ
great, μέγας, μεγάλη, μέγα
Greece, Ἑλλάς, -άδος, ἡ
Greek, n., Ἕλλην, -ηνος, ὁ
Greek, adj., Ἑλληνικός, -ή, -όν
guard, n., φύλαξ, -ακος, ὁ
guard, v., φυλάττω
guest, ξένος, -ου, ὁ

H

halt, ἵστημι
hand, χείρ, -ός, ἡ
hand over, παραδίδωμι
happen, τυγχάνω
happen along, παρατυγχάνω
happily, ἡδέως
happy, ὄλβιος, -α, -ον; μακάριος, -α, -ον
hard, χαλεπός, -ή, -όν
harm, do harm to, βλάπτω; κακῶς ποιέω
harmful, βλαβερός, -ά, -όν
harsh, χαλεπός, -ή, -όν
have, ἔχω
health, ὑγίεια, -ας, ἡ

216

hear, ἀκούω
heaven, οὐρανός, -οῦ, ὁ
help, βοηθέω + dat.; ὠφελέω
helpful, ὠφέλιμος, -ον
herald, κῆρυξ, -υκος, ὁ
here, ἐνταῦθα
hidden, κρυπτός, -ή, -όν
himself, intensive, αὐτός; reflexive, ἑαυτοῦ
hinder, κωλύω
Hippias, Ἱππίας, -ου, ὁ
his, αὐτοῦ
hold, ἔχω
home, οἶκος, -ου, ὁ
homeward, οἴκαδε
honor, n., τιμή, -ῆς, ἡ
honor, v., τιμάω
hoplite, ὁπλίτης, -ου, ὁ
horse, ἵππος, -ου, ὁ, ἡ
hour, ὥρα, -ας, ἡ
house, οἶκος, -ου, ὁ; οἰκία, -ας, ἡ
how, πῶς; ὅπως; τίνι τρόπῳ
how many, πόσοι, -αι, -α; ὁπόσοι, -αι, -α
how much, πόσος, -η, -ον; ὁπόσος, -η, -ον
hundred, ἑκατόν
hurry, σπεύδω
husband, ἀνήρ, ἀνδρός, ὁ

I

I, ἐγώ, ἐμοῦ
if, εἰ; ἐάν; ἄν; ἤν
ill, be, νοσέω; κακῶς ἔχω
immortal, ἀθάνατος, -ον
important, consider, περὶ πολλοῦ ποιεῖσθαι
in, ἐν + dat; of manner, μετά + gen.
in order that, in order to, ἵνα, ὡς, ὅπως
indeed, δή
inferior, κακίων, κάκιον; ἥττων, ἧττον
inquire, πυνθάνομαι
inscribe, ἐγγράφω + acc. and dat.
insolence, ὕβρις, -εως, ἡ
into, εἰς + acc.
island, νῆσος, -ου, ἡ

J

jealousy, φθόνος, -ου, ὁ
journey, ὁδός, -οῦ, ἡ
judge, v., κρίνω
juryman, δικαστής, -οῦ, ὁ
just, δίκαιος, -α, -ον
justice, δικαιοσύνη, -ης, ἡ
justly, δικαίως
justly, do, δίκαια ποιέω

K

keep in mind, ἐν νῷ ἔχειν
keep silent, σιωπάω
kill, ἀποκτείνω
kindness, do, εὐεργετέω
king, βασιλεύς, -έως, ὁ
kingdom, βασιλεία, -ας, ἡ
know, γιγνώσκω; οἶδα; μανθάνω
know how to, ἐπίσταμαι

L

Lacedemonian, n., Λακεδαιμόνιος,
    -ου, ὁ
land, γῆ, γῆς, ἡ
large, μέγας, μεγάλη, μέγα
latter, the, οὗτος, αὕτη, τοῦτο
law, νόμος, -ου, ὁ
lead, ἄγω
leader, ἄρχων, -οντος, ὁ
learn, μανθάνω
leave, λείπω
leave behind, καταλείπω
Leonidas, Λεωνίδας, -ου, ὁ
letter, ἐπιστολή, -ῆς, ἡ
lie down, κεῖμαι
life, βίος, -ου, ὁ
light, n., φῶς, φωτός, τό
lion, λέων, λέοντος, ὁ
live, ζάω
long, μακρός, -ά, -όν
long ago, πάλαι
long, as long as, ἕως; ἔστε; μέχρι
love, v., φιλέω

M

Machaon, Μαχάων, -ονος, ὁ
make, ποιέω
man, ἄνθρωπος, -ου, ὁ; ἀνήρ, ἀνδρός, ὁ

manner, τρόπος, -ου, ὁ
many, πολλοί, -αί, -ά
many, so, τοσοῦτοι, -αι, -α
Marathon, Μαραθών, -ῶνος, ὁ
march, v., ἐλαύνω
marry, γαμέω
marvelous, θαυμαστός, -ή, -όν
matters, these, ταῦτα
measure, μέτρον, -ου, τό
Melian, n., Μήλιος, -ου, ὁ
Menon, Μένων, -ωνος, ὁ
mercenary, n., ξένος, -ου, ὁ
messenger, ἄγγελος, -ου, ὁ
middle, μέσος, -η, -ον
midst of, μέσος in predicate posi-
    tion
mighty, μέγας, μεγάλη, μέγα
Miletus, Μίλητος, -ου, ἡ
mind, νοῦς, νοῦ, ὁ
misfortune, συμφορά, -ᾶς, ἡ
money, χρήματα, -άτων, τά
more, πλείων, πλέον
most, πλεῖστος, -η, -ον
mother, μήτηρ, μητρός, ἡ
much, πολύς, πολλή, πολύ
much, so, τοσοῦτος, τοσαύτη, το-
    σοῦτο
must, δεῖ; χρή

N

name, ὄνομα, -ματος, τό
native land, πατρίς, -ίδος, ἡ
near, ἐγγύς + gen.; πρός + dat.
near, be, παραγίγνομαι; πάρειμι
necessary, it is, δεῖ; χρή; ἀνάγ-
    κη (ἐστί)
need, v., δέομαι + gen.
neither, οὐδέ
neither . . . nor, οὔτε . . . οὔτε
never, οὔποτε; μήποτε (when μή
    would replace οὐ)
new, νέος, -α, -ον
night, νύξ, νυκτός, ἡ
no one, none, οὐδείς, οὐδεμία, οὐδέν
noble, ἐσθλός, -ή, -όν
nor, see neither . . . nor
not, οὐ, οὐκ, οὐχ; μή
not even, οὐδέ
not only . . . but also, οὐ μόνον . . .
    ἀλλὰ καί

217

O

obey, πείθω in middle
observe, θεωρέω
occasion, on each, ἑκάστοτε
often, πολλάκις
old, παλαιός, -ά, -όν
old friend, ξένος, -ου, ὁ
old man, γέρων, -οντος, ὁ
older, πρεσβύτερος, -α, -ον
on, ἐπί + gen.; (in hostile sense),
 εἰς + acc.
once, ποτέ
once, at, εὐθύς
only, μόνος, -η, -ον
open, v., ἀνοίγνυμι
opinion, γνώμη, -ης, ἡ
or, ἤ
order, v., give orders, κελεύω
order, in order that or to, ἵνα; ὡς;
 ὅπως
ornament, κόσμος, -ου, ὁ
other (of several), ἄλλος, -η, -ο; (of
 two), ἕτερος, -α, -ον
ought, δεῖ
our, ἡμέτερος, -α, -ον
out of, ἐκ + gen.
outside, ἔξω + gen.

P

paradox, παράδοξον, -ου, τό
parent, γονεύς, -έως, ὁ
part, n., μέρος, -ους, τό
pay down, κατατίθημι
pay the penalty, δίκην διδόναι
peace, εἰρήνη, -ης, ἡ
peace, make, εἰρήνην ποιεῖσθαι
pelt, v., βάλλω
perish, ἀπόλλυμι in middle
perplexed, be, ἀπορέω
Persian, n., Πέρσης, -ου, ὁ
persuade, πείθω
Phaedo, Φαίδων, -ωνος, ὁ
philosopher, φιλόσοφος, -ου, ὁ
Pisistratus, Πεισίστρατος, -ου, ὁ
place, n., τόπος, -ου, ὁ
plain, n., πεδίον, -ου, τό
plan, v., βουλεύω
Plato, Πλάτων, -ωνος, ὁ
pleasant, ἡδύς, -εῖα, -ύ

pleasure, ἡδονή, -ῆς, ἡ
pleasure, get or take, ἥδομαι
plot, v., βουλεύω
plot against, ἐπιβουλεύω + dat.
poet, ποιητής, -οῦ, ὁ
point out, δείκνυμι
poison, φάρμακον, -ου, τό
poor man, πένης, -ητος, ὁ
Poseidon, Ποσειδῶν, -ῶνος, ὁ
possess, κτάομαι
possession, κτῆμα, -ματος, τό
possible, it is, ἔξεστι
power, δύναμις, -εως, ἡ
praise, v., ἐπαινέω
present, see gift
present, be, πάρειμι; παραγίγνομαι
pride, ὕβρις, -εως, ἡ
prison, δεσμωτήριον, -ου, τό
prize, ἆθλον, -ου, τό
proceed, πορεύομαι
profit, v., κερδαίνω
promise, v., ὑπισχνέομαι
property, use neuter plural of
 article, e.g. τὰ Πλάτωνος
prove to be, γίγνομαι
province, ἀρχή, -ῆς, ἡ
Proxenus, Πρόξενος, -ου, ὁ
prudent, φρόνιμος, -η, -ον
punish, κολάζω
pursue, διώκω
put up with, ἀνέχομαι

Q

question thoroughly, ἐξετάζω
quickly, ταχέως; as quickly as
 possible, ὡς τάχιστα

R

race, n., γένος, -ους, τό
rather, μᾶλλον
rather than, μᾶλλον ἤ
ready, ἕτοιμος, -η, -ον
rear, v., τρέφω
receive, δέχομαι
remain, μένω
remarkable, θαυμαστός, -ή, -όν
reply, v., φημί
report, n., ἀγγελία, -ας, ἡ
report, v., ἀγγέλλω

reproach, v., ὀνειδίζω
rescue, v., βοηθέω
reveal, φαίνω
revolt, v., ἀφίστημι in middle
rich, πλούσιος, -α, -ον
rich, be, πλουτέω
river, ποταμός, -οῦ, ὁ
road, ὁδός, -οῦ, ἡ
rock, πέτρα, -ας, ἡ
rule, v., ἄρχω
ruler, ἄρχων, -οντος, ὁ
run, τρέχω
rustic, n., ἄγροικος, -ον, ὁ

S

sacrifice, v., θύω
safe, ἀσφαλής, -ές
sail, v., πλέω
same, αὐτός, -ή, -ό
say, λέγω; φημί
scatter, σκεδάννυμι
scorn, v., ὀνειδίζω
sea, θάλαττα, -ης, ἡ
second, δεύτερος, -α, -ον
secure, βέβαιος, -α, -ον
see, ὁράω
seek, ζητέω
seem, δοκέω
seems best, δοκεῖ
seize, αἱρέω
self, intensive, αὐτός, -ή, -ό; reflexive, use reflexive pronouns
send, πέμπω; ἵημι
set up, ἵστημι; ἀνατίθημι
seven, ἑπτά
shamefully, αἰσχρῶς
sherd, ὄστρακον, -ου, τό
shield, n., ἀσπίς, -ίδος, ἡ
ship, ναῦς, νεώς, ἡ
show, v., δείκνυμι
silent, keep, σιωπάω
sin, v., ἁμαρτάνω; n., ἁμαρτία, -ας, ἡ
since, ἐπεί; ἐπειδή
sit, κάθημαι
six hundred, ἑξακόσιοι, -αι, -α
sky, οὐρανός, -οῦ, ὁ
slave, δοῦλος, -ου, ὁ
slay, ἀποκτείνω; for passive, use
ἀποθνήσκω, die
sleep, n., ὕπνος, -ου, ὁ

small, μικρός, -ά, -όν
so, οὕτως
so as to, ὥστε
so that, ὥστε
Socrates, Σωκράτης, -ους, ὁ
soldier, στρατιώτης, -ου, ὁ
Solon, Σόλων, -ωνος, ὁ
someone, something, τις, τι
sometime, ποτέ
son, υἱός, -οῦ, ὁ
sort, of such a, τοιοῦτος, -αύτη,
-οῦτο
sort, of what, relative, οἷος, -α, -ον;
interrogative, ποῖος, -α, -ον
soul, ψυχή, -ῆς, ἡ
Spartan, Σπαρτιάτης, -ου, ὁ
speak, λέγω
stand, ἵστημι
state, n., πολιτεία, -ας, ἡ
state, v., λέγω
steal, κλέπτω
stone, λίθος, -ου, ὁ
strong, ἰσχυρός, -ά, -όν
strongly: as — as possible, ὡς
κράτιστα
struggle, n., ἀγών, ῶνος, ὁ
such, demonstrative, τοιοῦτος, τοιαύτη, τοιοῦτο; relative, οἷος, -α, -ον
suffer, πάσχω
suffering, πάθος, -ους, τό
sun, ἥλιος, -ου, ὁ
surely, δή
surrender, παραδίδωμι
suspect, v., ὑποπτεύω
swift, ταχύς, -εῖα, -ύ

T

take, λαμβάνω; αἱρέω
take away, ἀπολαμβάνω; ἀφαιρέω
talent, τάλαντον, -ου, τό
teach, διδάσκω
teacher, διδάσκαλος, -ου, ὁ
tear down, v., κατασκάπτω
tell, λέγω
temple, ἱερόν, -οῦ, τό
ten, δέκα
ten thousand, μύριοι, -αι, -α; group
of ten thousand, μυριάς, -άδος, ἡ
tent, σκηνή, -ῆς, ἡ
terrible, δεινός, -ή, -όν

219

than, ἤ
that, conjunction, ὅτι
that, demonstrative, ἐκεῖνος, -η, -ο
that, so, ὥστε
the, ὁ, ἡ, τό
their, αὐτῶν, ἑαυτῶν
themselves, intensive, αὐτοί, -αί, -ά;
　　reflexive, ἑαυτῶν, etc.
then, τότε
there, ἐνταῦθα; ἐκεῖ
therefore, οὖν
Thermopylae, Θερμοπύλαι, -ῶν, αἱ
thief, κλώψ, κλωπός, ὁ
thing, χρῆμα, -ματος, τό; or neuter
　　plural of adj.
think, νομίζω
thirty, τριάκοντα
this, οὗτος, αὕτη, τοῦτο
thousand, χίλιοι, -αι, -α
Thracian, Θρᾷξ, Θρακός, ὁ
thrice, τρίς
through, διά + gen. or acc.
throw, βάλλω
Thucydides, Θουκυδίδης, -ου, ὁ
time, χρόνος, -ου, ὁ
time, at some, ποτέ
to, εἰς + acc.; πρός + acc.
today, σήμερον
tomorrow, αὔριον
too, καί
tooth, ὀδούς, ὀδόντος, ὁ
tragedy, τραγῳδία, -ας, ἡ
treasure, θησαυρός, -οῦ, ὁ
treasure house, θησαυρός, -οῦ, ὁ
trial, πεῖρα, -ας, ἡ
trophy, τρόπαιον, -ου, τό
trouble, πράγματα, -ων, τά
trouble, cause, πράγματα παρέχειν
Troy, Τροία, -ας, ἡ
true, ἀληθής, -ές; truly, ἀληθῶς
trumpeter, σαλπιγκτής, -οῦ, ὁ
trust, v., πιστεύω + dat.
trust, n., πίστις, -εως, ἡ
truth, ἀλήθεια, -ας, ἡ
turn away, ἀποτρέπω
twice, δίς
two hundred, διακόσιοι, -αι, -α
tyranny, τυραννίς, -ίδος, ἡ
tyrant, τύραννος, -ου, ὁ

U

unfortunate, δυστυχής, -ές
unjust, ἄδικος, -ον
unjust, be, ἀδικέω
unobserved or unseen, be, λανθάνω
until, ἕως; ἔστε; μέχρι
unwilling, be, οὐκ ἐθέλω
upon, ἐπί + gen., dat., or acc.
us, acc. of ἡμεῖς
used to: use the imperfect of the
　　verb involved

V

very, the, -περ, suffix
victory, win a, νικάω
view, v., θεωρέω
virtue, ἀρετή, -ῆς, ἡ
voice, φωνή, -ῆς, ἡ
vote, v., ψηφίζομαι

W

wall, τεῖχος, -ους, τό
wander, πλανάω
war, πόλεμος, -ου, ὁ
watch out for, φυλάττω
water, ὕδωρ, ὕδατος, τό
way (manner), τρόπος, -ου, ὁ
way, put out of, ἐκποδὼν ποιεῖσθαι
we, ἡμεῖς
weak, ἀσθενής, -ές
wealth, πλοῦτος, -ου, ὁ
weapon, ὅπλον, -ου, τό
well, εὖ
well-born, εὐγενής, -ές
what, τί
what sort of, relative, οἷος, -α, -ον;
　　interrogative, ποῖος, -α, -ον
when, conjunction, ἐπειδή; ἐπειδάν;
　　ἐπεί
when, relative, ὅτε, ὁπότε; interroga-
　　tive, πότε
whenever, ὁπότε; ὁπόταν; ἐπειδή;
　　ἐπειδάν
where, relative, ὅπου; interrogative,
　　ποῦ
whether, πότερον; εἰ
which, relative, ὅς, ἥ, ὅ; ὅστις,
　　ἥτις, ὅ τι
which (of two), relative, ὁπότερος,
　　-α, -ον; interrogative, πότερος,
　　-α, -ον

who, relative; ὅς, ἥ; ὅστις, ἥτις; interrogative, τίς
whoever, whatever, ὅστις, ἥτις, ὅ τι
whole, ὅλος, -η, -ον
wholly, ὅλως; τελείως
why, τί
wicked, πονηρός, -ά, -όν
wife, γυνή, γυναικός, ἡ
wild, ἄγριος, -α, -ον
willing, be, ἐθέλω
wind, ἄνεμος, -ου, ὁ
wise, σοφός, -ή, όν
wish, ἐθέλω; βούλομαι
with, μετά + gen.; σύν + dat.
within, of time: use genitive
woman, γυνή, γυναικός, ἡ
wonderful, θαυμαστός, -ή, -όν
wood, ὕλη, -ης, ἡ
word, λόγος, -ου, ὁ

worse, κακίων, κάκιον
worst, κάκιστος, -η, -ον
worthy, ἄξιος, -α, -ον
write, γράφω
write on, ἐγγράφω
wrong, do, ἀδικέω

X

Xenophon, Ξενοφῶν, -ῶντος, ὁ
Xerxes, Ξέρξης, -ου, ὁ

Y

young, νέος, -α, -ον
young man, νεανίας, -ου, ὁ
your, of singular possessor, σός, σή, σόν; of plural possessor, ὑμέτερος, -α, -ον